Santa Barbara & California's Central Coast

Enjoy your fabulous new
life in Santa Barbara!
We'll miss you all.
Love Bridget, Michael
& Dylan

Santa Barbara
& California's
Central Coast

A Great Destination

Donna Wares

The Countryman Press ✳ Woodstock, Vermont

Interior photographs by the author unless otherwise specified
The California Surf Project photograph by Chris Burkard; it and the book's cover
  were used by permission of Chronicle Books.
Maps by Mapping Specialists, © The Countryman Press
Book design by Joanna Bodenweber
Composition by Eugenie S. Delaney

Santa Barbara & Californias Central Coast: A Great Destination
978-1-58157-110-3

Published by The Countryman Press, P.O. Box 748, Woodstock, VT 05091
Distributed by W. W. Norton & Company, Inc., 500 Fifth Avenue, New York, NY 10110

Printed in the United States by Versa Press, East Peoria, Illinois.

10 9 8 7 6 5 4 3 2 1

To Eben Aloysius Wares, my guide

EXPLORE WITH US!

This book will take you on a Central Coast journey from south to north, through Santa Barbara County, San Luis Obispo County, and the Big Sur Coast, as well as surrounding areas and the nearby Channel Islands. The Santa Barbara area is an especially popular getaway, and many lesser-known destinations along US Highway 101—the region's primary north–south freeway—also are choice spots for a weekend escapes or longer vacations.

Summertime is the peak travel season in beach towns along the Central Coast, once school lets out and the steely Pacific Ocean actually warms up. Many resorts and inns charge their highest prices of the year during July and August. Campgrounds fill up fast then. Beaches, parks and popular attractions such as Hearst Castle can be crowded. But it is possible to beat the prices and full houses while still enjoying the best of the Central Coast: Spring and fall are warm and balmy seasons to visit here, too. High season in the nearby wine-growing areas, away from the coast, generally runs from May through harvest time in October.

The Central Coast is a vast region that covers more area than many states. Throughout this book you'll find a sampling of choice accommodations, restaurants, wineries, wilderness areas and other attractions. Many establishments change their rates from season to season, and some raise and lower prices more often, especially in an unpredictable economy. So this book offers a general range of what you can expect to pay for lodging and dining, rather than specific prices.

HOTELS

Lodging price codes are based on double occupancy during summer months. You'll find that off-season winter rates, particularly along the beach, are much cheaper, sometimes a third less than high season prices. Generally, rates during spring and autumn fall somewhere between the two extremes.

FOOD

Restaurant price ratings in this book are based on the cost of menu entrées, and do not include extras such as appetizers, dessert, wine, cocktails, and tip.

Price Codes

Prices	Lodging	Restaurants
Inexpensive	Under $125	Up to $10
Moderate	$125–200	$10–20
Expensive	$200–300	$20–35
Very expensive	$300 or more	$35 or more

In general, costs for lodging and food along the Central Coast are comparable to or less expensive than Los Angeles and San Francisco. Big Sur is the exception. The area is so remote, and supplies are so limited, that you can expect to pay top dollar on just about everything. It's the land of the $14 burger (fries often are extra) and some of California's highest-priced gasoline, too.

This book includes a range of budget-minded accommodations and camping options, even in Big Sur, and you'll find the best deals if you're willing to travel during winter months. Yes, the Central California coast sees some cooler, rainy days during the off-season, but the weather here still is far more inviting than in most parts of the country. Winter months are an especially good time to savor uncrowded tasting rooms at the Santa Barbara and San Luis Obispo area wineries.

As you plan your trip, be sure to contact attractions to check costs, opening times, and other information. Every effort was made provide current information at press time, but restaurants and other businesses often change prices and hours with no notice.

KEY TO SYMBOLS

☉ **Weddings**. The wedding-ring symbol appears next to properties that specialize in weddings.

🐾 **Pets**. The dog-paw symbol appears next to venues that accept pets (usually with prior notice).

✐ **Child-friendly**. The crayon symbol appears next to lodging, restaurants, activities, and shops of special

♿ **Handicapped access**. The wheelchair symbol appears next to lodgings, restaurants, and attractions that are partially or completely handicapped accessible.

"📶" **Wireless Internet**. The wireless symbol appears next to lodging, restaurants, and attractions that offer wireless Internet access.

✪ **Authors' favorites**. These are the places we think have the best to offer in each region, whether that means great food, outstanding rooms, beautiful scenery, or overall appeal.

Thank you for taking along *Santa Barbara & California's Central Coast: A Great Destination* on your trip. If you find any can't-miss spots not mentioned in this book, I'd love to hear from you. Please send your e-mails to papertigersink @gmail.com.

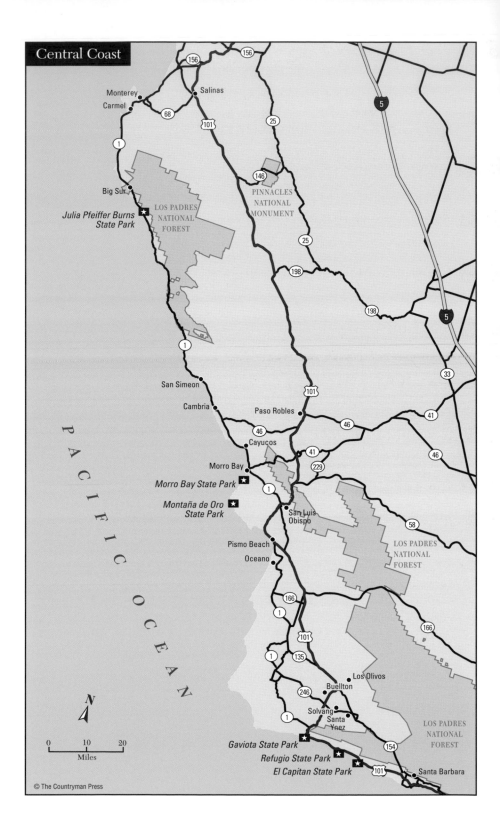

Central Coast

156 156

Monterey Salinas
Carmel
68 101 25

1 146

Big Sur PINNACLES
NATIONAL
Julia Pfeiffer Burns ★ LOS PADRES MONUMENT
State Park NATIONAL
FOREST 25

198

1 198

33
San Simeon

101
Cambria Paso Robles 41
46 46
P A C I F I C Cayucos
46
41
Morro Bay 229
Morro Bay State Park ★
1
Montaña de Oro ★
State Park San Luis
Obispo 58
LOS PADRES
O C E A N Pismo Beach NATIONAL
Oceano FOREST

166
1 166

101
1 135

Los Olivos
N Buellton
246
0 10 20 Solvang LOS PADRES
Miles 1 Santa NATIONAL
Ynez FOREST
Gaviota State Park ★ 154
© The Countryman Press Refugio State Park ★
El Capitan State Park ★ 101 Santa Barbara

5

5

CONTENTS

AN INTRODUCTION
TO THE CENTRAL COAST

From the laid-back beach towns south of Santa Barbara to the rugged beauty of Big Sur, California's Central Coast offers a spectacular triptych of landscapes—surf, forests, and picturesque towns—spread out along a legendary, sweeping, winding coastline that has to be experienced to be believed.

This is California unplugged and remarkably unspoiled.

Tucked between San Francisco to the north and Los Angeles to the south, California's Central Coast straddles more than 200 miles along the western edge of the continent. It's a world of farmers, foodies, cowboys, surfers, college students, and urban refugees. The region's allure is relentless, like the Pacific waves that crash into the windswept cliffs beneath beach-hugging US Highway 1. Enormous stands of oaks, sycamores, and redwoods stand sentry close to shore, just as they did 8,000 years ago when the Chumash Indians first roamed this epic stretch of coastal California. Rocky tide pools dot the shoreline. Pelicans, kestrels, red-tailed hawks, and

PFEIFFER BEACH, BIG SUR

the endangered California condor soar through wide-open skies. Just after daybreak, as the coast's foggy blanket lifts, fishermen sell live crabs and spiny lobsters right off the boats at Santa Barbara's harbor. The beach towns exude a quiet, contented vibe, a mood occasionally shattered by the barking of elephant seals that congregate on the shore like gaggles of know-it-all teenagers.

FISHERMEN SELL SPINY LOBSTER RIGHT OFF THE BOATS AT SANTA BARBARA'S HARBOR.

The choice of destinations is end-less—El Capitan, Shell Beach, Los Olivos, Paso Robles, Morro Bay, and Big Sur, just to name a few idyllic spots. Getting there is a big part of the thrill.

Take the car: The drive along Highway 1, the westernmost thoroughfare in the continental United States, overlooks the rocky coastal cliffs and broad flat beaches, and in the Big Sur region the hairpins and switchbacks offer unforgettable vistas.

Better still, take the train: The oceanfront journey between Santa Barbara and San Luis Obispo is mesmerizing, offering vantage points you simply can't see when traveling by car. Grab a window seat on the ocean side of the train, crank up your iPod, and sit back in big comfy seats as Amtrak's Pacific Surfliner zips along the coast. The ride offers mile after mile of breaking waves and ventures deep into the wild lands of the off-limits Vandenberg Air Force Base before making the briefest of stops at Lompoc's Surf Beach. There you'll see a tiny train station in the middle of nowhere, and you'll be tempted to follow the surfers out to the sand.

Veering inland, the Central Coast's byways offer equally inviting retreats and roadside attractions. You'll find bucolic towns with horse ranches, rolling vineyards, and hangar-sized nurseries bursting with fresh blooms. Growers great and small tend grapes, olives, lavender, avocados, Meyer lemons, heirloom tomatoes, and blueberries on family farms where you can pull over and pick your own if the season is right. In the past decade the wineries of the Santa Ynez Valley and neighboring San Luis Obispo County, particularly in Paso Robles, have expanded to rival the quality of California's famous grape producers up north in Napa and Sonoma.

WATCHING THE TIDE POOLS AT SHELL BEACH

Slow food is a pleasing obsession in these parts—locals talk about it all the time, and by "slow food" they don't mean bad restaurant service. The region is a hot spot for the slow food movement—the philosophical, nutritional, and environmental opposite of fast food. It emphasizes carefully grown and prepared dishes using plants and animals raised locally and sustainably, with farming techniques that preserve rather than destroy ecoregions. The Central Coast is an increasingly sustainable world of fresh and local foods, where the distance between farm and plate is often a few miles, or even just a few feet. It's a place where you can enjoy interesting, unhurried conversations with the family farmers who are making some of California's best Cabs and other red wines right now.

Green living is a way of life here. The nation's modern environmental movement was born on the Central Coast in the late 1960s, in the wake of a massive oil spill off the Santa Barbara coast, and residents have fought long and hard to preserve their wild lands and beaches from development.

THE DISTANCE BETWEEN FARM AND PLATE IS ONLY A FEW MILES

Trendy Santa Barbara and its neighbors went green long before green and local came into fashion. The region is a leading center for the sustainable agriculture movement, and many farmers and wine growers eschew chemicals in favor of eco-friendly, biodynamic growing techniques.

For many, the Central Coast embodies the heart and soul of the California Dream. Its opulent headquarters can be found midway between Los Angeles and San Francisco at a vast mountaintop Mediterranean estate overlooking the Pacific. In 1919 newspaper magnate William Randolph Hearst issued these simple instruc-

FRESH AND LOCAL FOODS CAN BE FOUND AT MANY FARMER'S MARKETS

tions to San Francisco architect Julia Morgan: "Miss Morgan, we are tired of camping out in the open at the ranch in San Simeon and I would like to build a little something." The result was the landmark Hearst Castle, "La Cuesta Encantada," a still-lavish palace with 56 bedrooms, 41 fireplaces, 61 bathrooms, and 127 acres of gardens, terraces, and swimming pools, where Hearst cavorted with actress Marion Davies and hosted Hollywood stars and Bay Area socialites for weekend soirees.

The Hearst Castle remains California's most popular non-theme-park destination, and thousands flock to San Simeon daily with their own dreams of swimming laps in Hearst's Neptune Pool. Through the decades, innumerable other celebrities, from Ronald Reagan to Michael Jackson to Oprah Winfrey, have followed the Hearst example and created Central Coast hideaways, too. After even a brief visit to California's Gold Coast, you'll understand why.

A BIT OF CENTRAL COAST HISTORY For eighty centuries, the Chumash Indians thrived along the Central California coast, living in caves and fishing the waters off what is now Santa Barbara and San Luis Obispo. They left behind their shell and stone implements and, in the case of Painted Cave State Historic State Park near Santa Barbara, their vivid murals. Inland, the Salinan Indians roamed the hills and valleys near Paso Robles, while the Esalan Indians settled farther north along the Big Sur Coast.

In 1542 explorer Juan Cabrillo laid claim to the entire coastline in the name of Spain and sought to establish friendly relations with the Natives. Cabrillo is known as the first European to discover California (his name still graces parks, buildings, and roads up and down the state).

But just a few months after cruising California, Cabrillo was injured and died on Catalina Island, and his Central Coast discoveries went largely unnoticed for many years. Half a century passed before the Spanish sent Sebastian Vizcaíno, a fisherman, to explore the area in 1602. Vizcaíno traveled the coast and gave new names to places Cabrillo previously roamed—among them Santa Barbara and Monterey. By now the Spaniards had come to realize that this vast new land was part of the continent, rather than a separate island.

In the 1770s Spain dispatched a force of missionaries, soldiers, and settlers to California, and they began building a string of Spanish missions along the Central

GREEN LIVING IS A WAY OF LIFE ON THE CENTRAL COAST

A BEAUTIFUL AND TRANQUIL SPOT AT JULIA PFEIFFER BURNS STATE PARK

Coast, a major construction effort aided by the labor of Indian workers who helped the missionaries farm this fertile region and plant California's first vineyards. The Franciscan padres set about converting the indigenous people to Catholicism.

The adobe missions served as vital hubs for the farming communities that grew up around them in San Luis Obispo and elsewhere. These historic missions remain treasured California landmarks. In San Luis Obispo and Santa Barbara, for example, the missions are working parishes and popular tourist attractions that reflect the region's cultural and agricultural roots.

It's remarkable how closely many communities along the Central Coast still hew to the region's agrarian roots. More remarkable still is that huge swaths of California's coastline, from the Santa Barbara area to the wilds of the Big Sur Coast, remain largely pristine and undeveloped, much of it unchanged from the days of Cabrillo's voyage.

That means that you'll find a seemingly endless expanse of wild spaces and wide-open beaches to explore as you cruise California's middle ground. It's a beautiful place to hike, swim, surf, kayak, or camp out right along the shore. Perhaps the best part is that the Central Coast is so vast and so varied that you can return again and again, as I do, and still discover something new, surprising, and delightful with each visit.

WHAT'S WHERE IN SANTA BARBARA AND CALIFORNIA'S CENTRAL COAST

AIR SERVICE The **Santa Barbara Municipal Airport** (805-967-7111; 24-hour info line 805-683-4011; flysba.com), 500 Fowler Rd., Santa Barbara, is located near Goleta, off US 101. The **San Luis Obispo County Regional Airport** (805-781-5205; sloairport.com), 903-5 Airport Dr., San Luis Obispo, is just south of the city of San Luis Obispo. **Monterey Peninsula Airport** (montereyairport.com) is about 30 miles from Big Sur. The **Los Angeles International Airport** (LAX) is about 100 miles south of Santa Barbara at the southern end of this book's region, while the **San Francisco International Airport** is 150 miles from Big Sur on the northern end. Car rentals and shuttle services are available at each facility and are detailed in their respective chapters.

AREA CODE The area code 805 covers most of the Central Coast region. The Big Sur area uses the area code 831.

BEACHES Central California's coastline spans hundreds of miles, and you can happily cruise Hwy. 1 or US 101 and pull over when you see a scenic stretch that calls out to you. The unde-veloped swath of coastline just north of Santa Barbara is a recreational and ecological wonderland that includes **El Capitan** and **Refugio** state beaches, while the dramatic cliffs and pounding surf of the **Big Sur** have kept writers, musicians, and nature lovers waxing poetically for generations. **Rincon Point** and **Jalama Beach** (along coastal Santa Barbara County) and **Pismo Beach** (SLO County) are favorites with surfers (surfline.com). Another choice spot: **Arroyo Burro County Park**, aka Hendry Beach,

MAKING A GOOEY ADDITION TO THE WALL AT BUBBLEGUM ALLEY IN DOWNTOWN SAN LUIS OBISPO

(countyofsb.org/parks), is an out-of-the-way cove 5 miles west of Santa Barbara's city center where you can swim, run along the shore, or sit on the porch of a beachfront restaurant enjoying breakfast and watching the crashing waves.

BICYCLING Central California loves bicycles, and bicyclists love it back. The nonprofit **Santa Barbara Bicycle Coalition** (sbbike.org) has compiled a collection of downloadable bike treks through Santa Barbara County. **Santa Barbara Wine Country Cycling Tours** (805-686-9490; winecountry cycling.com) creates custom treks that wind past the vineyards, lavender fields, and horse ranches of the Santa Ynez Valley with frequent stops for grazing and snapping photos. In San Luis Obispo cycling routes cover more than 25 miles and loop past the cluster of wineries along Hwy. 227. Maps are available from the SLO County Bicycle Coalition (slobikelane.org). On Thursday nights the San Luis Obispo Farmer's Market reserves its premium valet parking for shoppers who arrive by bike.

BIRD-WATCHING Some of California's (and the nation's) richest bird-watching zones are here—from the endangered condors that soar above **Andrew Molero State Park** and the Big Sur coast, to the bald eagles that make their home each winter at Santa Barbara County's **Cachuma Lake**, to the teeming heron sanctuary at Morro Bay, which hosts its annual **Winter Bird Festival** (morrobaybirdfestival .org), a four-day celebration of birds and bird-watching. Also see *Wildlife-Watching*.

BOOKS Take along *Down to a Soundless Sea* by Thomas Steinbeck, a magical collection of short stories set along

SLO'S FARMER'S MARKET FEATURES VALET PARKING FOR BIKES

PELICAN AT PISMO PIER

the California coast from the turn of the century through the 1930s; *Santa Barbara Stories*, an easy-reading fiction sampler featuring work by Wallace Stegner, T. C. Boyle, Ross McDonald, Margaret Millar, John Sayles, and Gayle Lynds; or *A Wild Coast and Lonely*, by Rosalind Sharpe Wall, a personal history of the Big Sur Coast. Horse country lovers will enjoy *Seabiscuit: An American Legend*, the nonfiction bestseller by Laura Hillen-brand about the knobby-kneed horse who became a thoroughbred champ. Better still, listen to the mesmerizing audio CD of *Seabiscuit* (read by actor Campbell Scott) while cruising the Santa Ynez Valley, where some of the *Seabiscuit* movie was filmed.

BUS SERVICE Greyhound Lines (800-965-7551; greyhound.com) has stations throughout the region. **Santa Barbara Airbus** (800-423-1618; santabarbaraairbus.com) offers coach service from LAX to the Santa Barbara area as well as San Luis Obispo, Pismo Beach, Santa Maria, and Buellton. Farther north, the **Monterey-Salinas Transit System** (888-688-2881; mst.org) offers daily bus service between Monterey and the Big Sur Valley from Memorial Day through Labor Day. Once you arrive, Santa Barbara's convenient waterfront shuttle is an easy way to get around; San Luis Obispo and Morro Bay also run visitor-friendly trolleys in town.

CAMPING From Carpinteria to the Big Sur Coast, campgrounds are scattered throughout Central California and offer budget-minded lodging amid natural beauty. Many camping areas accept reservations (reserveamerica .com handles booking for state parks) months in advance, while other sites welcome overnight campers on a first-come, first-served basis. Your favorite state park may have undergone changes since your last visit, due to weather conditions or state budget cuts, so be sure to call ahead for current information.

CHILDREN, ESPECIALLY FOR Throughout the book, the ✦ symbol indicates restaurants, lodgings, and attractions that are especially fun for children and families. The best places

include the **Santa Barbara Zoo** (santabarbarazoo.org), a small but memorable gem with lush natural habitats and a welcoming flock of flamingos, and the **San Luis Obispo Children's Museum** (slocm.org), a hands-on imagination center where kids can dabble in moviemaking, pretend careers, and science experiments. For a special family treat, check into **El Captain Canyon** (elcapitancanyon .com), an upscale eco-resort with cedar cabins complete with kid-pleasing lofts, free beach cruisers to roam the grounds, Saturday-night concerts in summer, and hiking trails that lead to a nearby llama farm.

FARMER'S MARKETS Up and down the Central Coast the region's expanding network of open-air farmer's markets is a revelation almost any day of the week. In the middle of **Santa Barbara's** busy State Street, locals and tourists alike cram open-air stalls heaped with long-legged leeks, rainbow-colored chard, rotund summer peaches, juicy pluots, lemon cucumbers, artichokes the size of softballs, California pistachios, berries in every

SANTA BARBARA FARMER'S MARKET ON STATE STREET

imaginable hue, and lettuce that tastes like crisp bites of sunshine. Neighboring San Luis Obispo County has about 15 farmer's markets (slocountyfarmers .org), including Thursday night's mega-market and street fair in downtown SLO.

FARM VACATIONS You'll cruise past sprawling ranches, family farms, and rolling vineyards throughout the region. Some have farm stands that beckon visitors to taste just-picked apples, blueberries, strawberries, or avocados, while other welcome guests to experience the joys and rigors of farm life overnight. At the **Rinconada Dairy** (rinconadadairy.com) in the hills of San Luis Obispo County, you can check in to a rural dairy ranch and tag along with the owner as she makes fresh-pressed raw sheep's-milk cheese, or rise with the sun to help collect hens' eggs for your family's breakfast. At **Hollyhock Farms** (hollyhock-farm .com) in Templeton, guests have the choice of a cottage or larger two-room bungalow on the 30-acre property and are treated to country breakfasts featuring organic eggs and just-picked produce raised on the farm.

GOLF Courses dot the Central Coast, and golfers will find links in some of the region's most scenic locales. Here are three stunning places to play: The 18-hole **Morro Bay Golf Course** (slocountyparks.com), known as "Poor Man's Pebble Beach," sits in the middle of Morro Bay State Park and an adjacent heron rookery. **Avila Beach Golf Resort** (golfslo.com), a par 71, 6,500-yard championship course, is nestled in the hills between San Luis Obispo and Pismo Beach and on the bay. **Sandpiper Golf Club** (sand-pipergolf.com), an 18-hole public course in Santa Barbara County, offers challenging play and great waterfront

HORSEBACK RIDING AT RANCHO OSO

views. The *Los Angeles Times* included Sandpiper on its list of California's top 15 destinations in 2009.

HORSEBACK RIDING There may be no better way to experience the rugged wildlands of Central California than from the back of a horse, and opportunities for riding abound; see the listings under *To Do* in each chapter. Check out **Circle Bar B Ranch** north of Santa Barbara; the remote **Rancho Oso Guest Ranch** in the Santa Ynez Valley; and **Andrew Molera State Park**, where you'll ride through redwood groves and on to the beach along the Big Sur Coast.

LODGING Most travelers have little trouble finding chain hotels and restaurants on their own, so this book generally spends little time on those—with a few exceptions that fill a particular niche or offer good value. For instance, I had to include Santa Barbara's Motel 6, which opened in 1962 as the very first motel in the no-frills chain. The modest pink-and-aqua motor lodge still is a very good deal and just a block from the sand in pricey Santa Barbara. This book includes a wide range of accommodations—including deluxe resorts, modest beachfront motels, working family farms, yurt encampments, tiny B&Bs, wine-country inns, and backcountry campsites—with an emphasis on one-of-a-kind establishments that offer good hospitality, unique services, or appealing surroundings.

Be sure to check out lodging in various price ranges, even those places you think might be too expensive, when planning a Central Coast trip. The reason is simple: Travel deals abound in all price categories, and they change from week to week. Even the most upscale California hotels now offer discount rates and throw in extra nights free—especially during slow winter months—and that trend shows no sign of ending anytime soon. It helps if you're flexible enough to travel on weekdays.

MISSIONS The 21 missions that make up **California's Historic Mission Trail** (parks.ca.gov) are located on or near US 101, which roughly traces El Camino Real (The Royal Road), named in honor of the Spanish monarchy that launched empire-building expeditions on the West Coast. Founded in 1786, **Mission Santa Barbara** (santabarbaramission.org) is known as "the Queen of the Missions" and was restored to its terra-cotta and carved-wood splendor after being destroyed in a 1925 earthquake. The mission sits on a hilltop overlooking the city and remains both an active parish and one of Santa Barbara's most enduring attractions. You'll find more historic missions scattered throughout the Central Coast (and this book), including **San Luis Obispo de Tolosa** (missionsanluisobispo.org), a red-tiled adobe that remains at the cultural and spiritual center of downtown San Luis Obispo.

PETS, TRAVELING WITH The Central Coast is impressively pet-friendly; even some of the region's swankiest properties, such as **San Ysidro Ranch** (sanysidroranch.com) near Santa Barbara and the **Hotel Cheval** (hotelcheval.com) in downtown Paso Robles, welcome pooches with cozy bedding, doggy treats, and, in the case of San Ysidro Ranch, in-room pet massages. Look for the 🐾 icon throughout this book and be sure to call ahead about pet-related fees and room availability.

RESTAURANTS When dining in Santa Barbara and the Central California coast, you'll have a choice of traditional fine dining, inexpensive but tasty local fare, and an increasing number of restaurants that embrace the farm-to-table movement. Many restaurants feature locally caught seafood and grass-fed beef raised on area farms and ranches. In some eateries you'll be served food by the same folks who grow it. A fresh example: One of Paso Robles's top

ON SHELL BEACH

DUNGENESS CRAB QUESADILLAS (YUM!) AND A FISH COMBO AT GIOVANNI'S FISH MARKET AND RESTAURANT ON THE WATER IN MORRO BAY

Bubblegum Alley, an oddity along Higuera Street downtown (between Garden and Broad) that attracts a constant parade of visitors who deposit wads of chewed gum and gooey messages on a pair of brick walls. Farther south along the 101 in Buellton, you'll find **Ostrich Land** (ostrichlandusa .com), a sprawling property that's more lunar landscape than bucolic farm and teeming with hungry ostriches and emus that visitors can hand-feed. The Ostrich Land gift shop sells ostrich and emu eggs, emu oil and postcards, as well as frozen ostrich meat and ostrich jerky harvested from the herd just outside.

chefs recently opened **Farmstand 46** (farmstand46.com), a delectable roadside deli where many of the ingredients found in the gourmet sandwiches, soups, and wood-fired pizzas are grown just steps away from the restaurant.

ROAD CONDITIONS Be sure to check road and weather conditions along California's Central Coast before setting out, especially if you're traveling near the Big Sur Coast in winter months. CalTrans has a toll-free hotline (888-836-0866) that provides information about traffic and road conditions on Hwy. 1 from Cambria to Carmel.

ROADSIDE CURIOSITIES You can't miss the screaming pink sign on US 101 and you won't want to: San Luis Obispo's landmark **Madonna Inn** (madonnainn.com) is irresistible with its faux Swiss facade, kitschy themed rooms, 8-foot waterfall urinal in the lobby men's room, and signature pink champagne cake. Even if you don't check in, stop by for breakfast at the hotel's ornate Copper Cafe, a local favorite, or swing dancing on Monday nights. SLO also is the home of

SEA KAYAKING Nature lovers will have a blast kayaking here and will find plenty of outfitters on the SLO Coast. Morro Bay is a choice location: Rent equipment right off the Embarcadero at **Rock Kayak** (rockkayak.com) and paddle out toward the towering hulk of Morro Rock. You'll spy shorebirds of all descriptions, cruise past sea lions swimming beside you in the bay, and, if you're lucky, spot a few otters, too. Another great adventure: Visit Santa Cruz Island in the **Channel Islands**

TRY SEA KAYAKING IN MORRO BAY

(nps.gov/chis) and kayak through the sea caves, which actually glow in multicolors. **Aquasports** (islandkayaking.com) offers experienced guides.

SPECIAL EVENTS Each chapter includes a rundown on events that occur year after year (see *Special Events*). These run the gamut from film festivals to marathons and celebrations of wine, food, classic cars, surfing, and ethnic heritage (Spanish, of course, and even Danish in the ersatz Danish outpost of Solvang). There are concerts, cook-offs, and visits from birds, butterflies, and movie idols, too.

SHOPPING Skip the malls and instead bring home a sampling of the Central Coast's bounty. You'll want to buy a bottle of wine or two from tasting rooms you liked best. Also pick up locally pressed olive oil from the **Pasolivo Olive Oil Tasting Room** (pasolivo.com) at Paso's Willow Creek Olive Ranch or the **We Olive** tasting bars (weolive.com) in Paso Robles and San Luis Obispo; lavender soaps, sachets, lotions, and bath scrubs from **Clairmont Farms** (clairmontfarms

.com) in Los Olivos; and gourmet pistachios (santabarbarapistachios.com), honey, and organic jams from **Santa Barbara's Farmer's Market**, which offers a wide selection of goodies.

TRAIN SERVICE Amtrak's **Pacific Surfliner** runs between San Diego and San Luis Obispo, and trains are equipped with bicycle and surfboard racks. The double-decker **Coast Starlight** runs from Los Angeles to Seattle, with stops throughout the Central California region. Check for details and train station locations in each chapter.

WILDLIFE-WATCHING Nearly 30 different types of whales, dolphins, and sea lions can be seen along Central Coast. From mid-May to November, blue whales and humpback whales travel past the coastline here, while Pacific gray whales cruise through on their migration between Alaska and Baja from December to May. Whale-watching opportunities are listed in each chapter under *To Do*.

Andrew Molera State Park along the Big Sur Coast has a new **Discovery Center** (ventanaws.org/discovery_center), where naturalists from the Ventana Wildlife Society explain the group's work with the endangered California condor and offer tours of their songbird-banding lab. And no trip up Hwy. 1 in the Central Coast is complete without a stop at **Piedras Blancas**, home to one of California's largest elephant seal rookeries, where you can see the giant seals up close. The vista point at Piedras Blancas (elephantseal.org) is 4.4 miles north of Hearst Castle on Hwy. 1. Also see *Bird-Watching*.

WINE Commercial winemakers have long recognized this region's grape-friendly microclimates and the lengthy

VIEWING THE SEA LIONS IN MORRO BAY

Image courtesy of Ron Bez photography, www.ronbez.com

VINEYARDS IN PASO ROBLES

growing season of warm days and crisp cool evenings as ideally suited to vineyards and fine wine. Historically overshadowed by the better-known Napa and Sonoma Valleys, Central California has emerged as a world-class wine country. The popular 2004 film *Sideways* did much to pique public interest in the region's grapes.

The **Santa Barbara County** Vintners' Association says that the county now has more than 100 wineries in the Santa Ynez Valley, Santa Maria Valley, and Santa Rita Hills appellations. Poke along the **Foxen Canyon Wine Trail** (foxencanyonwinetrail.com), a route that winds from Los Olivos to Santa Maria. You'll find 16 wineries on and around the trail, and many other premium growers and tasting rooms scattered throughout Santa Barbara County. **San Luis Obispo County** boasts some 200 wineries and is naturally divided by the San Lucia Mountain Range into two distinct wine regions: the SLO vineyards on the county's southern end and the fast-growing Paso Robles area to the north.

Visitors will find excellent wines and inviting family-run vineyards throughout the Central Coast. Winery fees vary, but many tasting rooms charge about $5–10 for a selection of wines, and then refund the fee if you make a purchase.

AT THE QUICKSILVER RANCH, A MINIATURE HORSE FARM IN SOLVANG

Santa Barbara

SANTA BARBARA

"The climate and the atmosphere recall the French Riviera between Marseille and Nice, except that area of France has now become terribly touristy. Very often, being there on the Riviera, where we used to have a little house, I'd look at all the tourists and say, 'Well, I'd just as soon be in Santa Barbara.'"

—Legendary chef and Santa Barbara resident Julia Child, talking about her hometown in a 2002 interview with *National Geographic*

Santa Barbara is often touted as America's Riviera, California's own glittering Gold Coast. The marketing imagery would sound pretentious but for the fact that the locals have it right: Santa Barbara *is* one of California's most beautiful, livable, prosperous, and sophisticated cities. The village of whitewashed walls, red-tiled roofs, and lushly tropical courtyards evokes the richness of a New World Med, cradled between the Santa Ynez Mountains and 2.5 miles of south-facing Pacific beach.

Like the Mediterranean region, the Santa Barbara area offers a wide range of vacation possibilities: from family-friendly getaways to fine dining and wine-country experiences; from car-dependent road trips to car-free eco-journeys; from State Street fine shopping to one of the liveliest farmer's markets around. The Spanish and Mexican influence is strong here, apparent in the historic sites, such as Mission Santa Barbara (a National Historic Landmark), as well as in the local cuisine (no visit to Santa Barbara is complete without a pilgrimage to the humble-appearing, palate-pleasing La Super Rica restaurant, a favorite of chef Julia Child). It is a university city, a beach town, and a cultural center, ringed by more rustic lands devoted to farming, ranching, and grape growing.

One of Santa Barbara's standout features—travelers always take notice of it as Highway 101 delivers them to town—is the architecture, the result the city's famously rigorous design standards and slow growth policies that have preserved the distinctive look and historical ambience. The blend of Spanish, Mediterranean, and Moorish styles come together in carefully orchestrated harmony against a

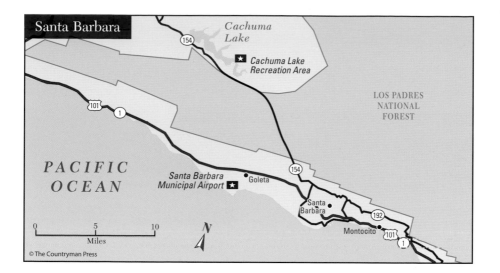

backdrop of towering palms and vivid purple acacia trees on State Street, the city's main boulevard.

The city's famous building standards date back to the 1925 earthquake that destroyed much of downtown Santa Barbara. Residents mobilized after the disaster to restore their city's Spanish Revival treasures, then established an enduring tradition of painstaking building and design review. Local preservationist Pearl Chase steered the effort, and she would eventually be nicknamed the First Lady of Santa Barbara for her role in shaping the city's look from 1927 to the 1970s. Her legacy is visible today, from the downtown's cohesive shops and cafés to the city's signature landmarks, such as the Santa Barbara County Courthouse on Anacapa Street. Flanked by a sunken garden, the Spanish-Moorish-style courthouse has been called the most beautiful government building in America for its elaborate California murals, hand-stenciled ceilings, and tiled, circular staircase leading up to a clock tower that overlooks the city and the coastline. Because of Santa Barbara's strict height limits, only two buildings stand taller than four stories—the spire-topped Arlington Theatre built in 1931 on State Street and, just up the block, the Granada Theater, a Roaring Twenties–era palace that underwent a complete renovation in 2008. The city's taste police have outlawed neon and billboards in Santa Barbara. In 2009 local voters wrestled with the question of whether to lower building height

ON THE BEACH IN SANTA BARBARA

limits further, the latest front in the ongoing battle to preserve Santa Barbara's ambience in an era when the community's population has grown to more than 90,000.

This civic vigilance and sensibility has in recent decades expanded and led Santa Barbara to embrace a strong, bipartisan ecological ethic. The city boasts an environmentally friendly public transportation system fairly unique in car-centric California. Santa Barbara *loves* people who leave their cars behind, and the local government, businesses, and institutions have gone out of their way to make it easy and economical to visit this part of Central California car-free—or to leave your car parked once you arrive.

SPRING IN MONTECITO!

Downtown Santa Barbara is a compact, inviting district easily navigated on foot or by hopping aboard the open-air electric shuttle buses that cruise the business district and the adjacent beachfront. A good place to begin your exploration is State Street, a lively promenade that starts at the beach near Stearns Wharf, then ambles along brick sidewalks past the conveniently located Amtrak station and a mix of shops, restaurants, clubs, and coffeehouses. Farther along State you'll find the city's upscale El Paseo shopping zone and an arts district with galleries, theaters, bookstores, and the stately Santa Barbara Museum of Art. Santa Barbara is a creative community that likes to celebrate in the sunshine, and nearly every weekend brings another outdoor fiesta, food festival, art show, or craft fair. Just follow the music and the crowds.

On Saturday mornings and Tuesday afternoons farmers descend on downtown with a bounty of produce, flowers, and specialty foods from across Santa Barbara County and as far away as Fresno. The farmer's market has been a Santa Barbara staple since the 1970s, and the outdoor market is as much a social gathering as an opportunity to graze the Central Coast's freshest offerings. Residents and Santa Barbara's top chefs arrive with rolling shopping carts to browse stalls crammed with fresh fruit and produce. Visitors will find fragrant lavender, olives, olive oil, pistachios, and honey to bring home, and slabs of just-baked fruit pie to gobble up on the spot. At the Tuesday-afternoon farmer's market in the middle of State Street musicians mingle with the crowd, which swells until the street and nearby sidewalks are nearly

THE HILLS ABOVE SANTA BARBARA

impassable, especially in summer months when the growing season and tourist season peak at the same time.

Anytime of year, nature lovers and families also will want to roam the Santa Barbara Zoo, an enchanting wild kingdom overlooking the Pacific Ocean, and the Andree Clark Bird Refuge just a few minutes from downtown. Strolling the zoo's 30 acres of habitats is as much a pleasant nature trek as anything else, and the walk-through aviaries, where you can mix it up with pheasants, blue-crowned pigeons, and other rare birds, are not to be missed.

Summer is Santa Barbara's high season, though the area has so much to offer visitors that the town is a choice destination anytime of year, as long as you don't mind brisk beach days and the occasional winter storm. From May through November giant blue and humpback whales cruise along the coast here, while winter and spring months bring the California gray whales on their annual migration treks. All year long early risers will savor the quiet delights of the Santa Barbara Harbor, where an army of shorebirds patrol an impressive fleet of vessels great and small as local fisherman set out giant tubs of live rock crab and spiny lobster on the docks—a marine bounty as fresh and tempting as the produce at the farmer's market.

Of course, Santa Barbara's bountiful resources, mild climate, gentle rains, and natural beauty have attracted visitors and settlers since prehistoric times. The Chumash Indians settled in villages along the coast here more than 13,000 years ago, sustaining themselves with seafood from the fish-rich waters of the Pacific Ocean and game from the nearby Santa Ynez Mountains. Spain first claimed the region in 1542, and half a century later, in 1602, explorer Sebastian Vizcaíno sought refuge in the channel here during a violent storm that finally passed on Saint Barbara's feast day. When the crew was spared, a grateful vicar named the coastal enclave in

FRESH FLOWERS AT THE SANTA BARBARA FARMER'S MARKET

honor of Saint Barbara, the patron saint of artillerymen, who was traditionally invoked for protection against lightning, thunder, and gunpowder accidents.

Spanish missionaries arrived in the mid-1700s and coerced the Natives into helping build the Santa Barbara Mission, the 10th of California's historic missions. The California Gold Rush brought an influx of newcomers during the next century, and the first wave of rich and famous tourists arrived in the late 1880s. The Flying A Studio and California's fledgling movie industry set up shop in Santa Barbara in 1910 and produced more than 1,000 movies starring Lon Chaney Sr. and other big names of the era. In 1919 the filmmakers left the Central Coast and relocated 89 miles to the south to found modern Hollywood. Overnight Santa Barbara lost its status as a movie capital, but it soon found a new role as hideaway to stars such as Charlie Chaplin, who built the Montecito Inn as a retreat for his Hollywood friends.

Santa Barbara and the neighboring hamlet of Montecito have been a celebrity haven ever since. Oprah Winfrey, Ellen DeGeneres, Rob Lowe, Kirk Douglas, Jeff Bridges, John Cleese, and many others have homes here. The city draws a celebrity crowd each winter for the Santa Barbara International Film Festival. The gracious Four Seasons Santa Barbara resort has long boasted a Hollywood-studded guest registry and, in 2007, a $240 million makeover by Beanie Baby founder Ty Warner, who also bought up the exclusive San Ysidro Ranch.

Just a two-hour drive from Los Angeles when traffic is rolling (and up to twice as long when gridlock turns the 101 into a parking lot), Santa Barbara is a favorite escape for Southern Californians of all backgrounds, as well as visitors from across the country and the world. The community attracts artists, outdoorsy types, foodies, well-to-do retirees, and vacationing families to its beach inns and resorts, college students to the sprawling University of California–Santa Barbara campus near Goleta, and, in recent years, wine lovers to the lush vineyards and tasting rooms in the Santa Ynez Valley in eastern Santa Barbara County.

SANDY CLIFFS TOWER OVER THE BEACH IN SANTA BARBARA

CAR-FREE SANTA BARBARA

Santa Barbara is an ideal destination for a car-free escape. The Amtrak station is conveniently located on State Street; the city's downtown is compact and easily navigated on foot and by riding the open-air shuttle bus that cruises the waterfront and State Street at regular intervals.

The incentives go beyond simply avoiding the freeway gridlock: Santa Barbara's Car-Free Project offers discounts to visitors who leave their cars at home. Travelers can get 20 percent off on Amtrak train fares and find deals on hotel rooms (more than 20 local hotels participate) and attractions, such as whale-watching cruises and wine-country

GOING CAR-FREE ALONG CABRILLO BOULEVARD

tours in the comfort of a biodiesel-powered Mercedes van. A collaboration between the local pollution control agency and a coalition of business owners, the Car-Free Project is an attempt to ease freeway congestion and cleanse the air in a community that juggles competing personas as playground for the wealthy and birthplace of the modern environmental movement. Santa Barbara, after all, inspired the first national Earth Day in 1970, begun in the wake of the massive Central Coast oil spill, and a collective environmental consciousness runs deep here.

Contact the **Santa Barbara Car Free Project** (805-696-1100; santa barbaracarfree.org, P.O. Box 60436, Santa Barbara 93160) to request a free map and information about current discounts. Or keep up via Twitter: twitter.com/sbcarfree.

GUIDANCE Santa Barbara Car Free Project (santabarbaracarfree.org). Check online for the latest deals and discounts. Or keep up via Twitter: twitter.com/sb carfree.

Santa Barbara Chamber of Commerce (805-965-3021, 805-568-1811; sb chamber.org). Stop by the Santa Barbara Visitor Center, at 1 Garden St., across from the beach, to pick up a visitors map with coupons.

Santa Barbara Conference & Visitors Bureau and Film Commission (805-966-9222; santabarbaraca.com), 1601 Anacapa St. Travel info and bookings for Santa Barbara County.

SANTA BARBARA MUNICIPAL AIRPORT

The airport (805-967-7111; 24-hour info line 805-683-4011; flysba.com), 500 Fowler Rd., is located near Goleta, off the 101 freeway. It offers nonstop flights from Denver, Los Angeles, Phoenix, Sacramento, Salt Lake City, San Francisco, San Jose, and Seattle. The terminal has free WiFi.

SANTA BARBARA–BASED CARRIERS

Alaska Airlines: 800-252-7522; alaskaair.com
American Airlines/American Eagle: 800-433-7300; aa.com
Delta Air Lines: 800-221-1212; delta.com
Horizon Air: 800-547-9308; horizonair.com
United Airlines: 800-241-6522; united.com
US Airways: 800-428-4322; 2.usairways.com

CAR RENTALS AT AIRPORT TERMINAL

Budget: reservations 800-527-0700; terminal 805-964-6792; budget.com
Enterprise: reservations 800-261-7331; terminal 805-683-3012; enterprise.com
Hertz: reservations 800-654-3131; terminal 805-967-0411; hertz.com
National: reservations 800-227-7368; terminal 805-967-1202; nationalcar.com

OFF-SITE CAR RENTALS

Avis: 805-683-4715; avis.com
Thrifty: 805-681-1222; thrifty.com

DOOR-TO-DOOR SHUTTLES

Central Coast Shuttle: 805-928-1977
Road Runner: 800-247-7919

TAXICAB COMPANIES

American Taxi: 805-689-0683
Crown Cab: 805-689-0234
Fly By Night Taxi: 805-886-8617
Roadways Cab: 805-564-2600
Santa Barbara Airport Taxi: 805-895-2422
Santa Barbara City Cab: 805-968-6868
Santa Barbara Checker Cab: 805-560-8284
Santa Barbara Yellow Cab: 805-965-5111

AIRPORT BUS SERVICE

Santa Barbara Metropolitan Transit District (sbmtd.gov) has a public bus stop on Moffett Rd. across from the airline terminal. Bus schedules are available in the terminal's south lobby and online.
Santa Barbara Airbus (800-423-1618; santabarbaraairbus.com) offers coach service from Los Angeles International Airport to Santa Barbara, as well as to Carpinteria, Goleta, Santa Ynez, and several Central Coast locations farther north. *Note:* Discounts are available when you travel with a companion.

Santa Barbara Independent (independent.com). Pick up a copy of this free newspaper or browse online to find events in town.

Green Santa Barbara (greensantabarbara.com). Take a walk on the city's eco-friendly side.

GETTING THERE Santa Barbara is 92 miles north of Los Angeles, 228 miles north of San Diego, and 332 miles south of San Francisco. It is the largest city in Santa Barbara County, which includes the inland Santa Ynez wine country as well as beach communities to the north and south. Santa Barbara is accessible by car, train, plane, and bus, and offers an inexpensive shuttle bus service for getting around downtown.

By car:

From Southern California: Head north on US Hwy. 101 until you reach the Santa Barbara exits.

From Northern California: Head south on the 101.

From the east: Traveling from inland Santa Barbara County and the Santa Ynez Valley, take Hwy. 154 to the 101. Then follow the signs.

By air: You can fly into Santa Barbara Municipal Airport (SBA) or Los Angeles International Airport (LAX), which is 107 miles to the south.

By train: **Amtrak** (800-872-7245; amtrak.com) runs its Pacific Surfliner service between San Diego and San Luis Obispo with daily stops in Santa Barbara and nearby towns. Most Pacific Surfliners are equipped with bicycle and surfboard racks. Amtrak's Coast Starlight service runs between Los Angeles and Seattle.

The Santa Barbara Amtrak station is at 209 State St., in the heart of downtown, two blocks from the beach. The location makes it convenient to take the train to Santa Barbara and simply roll your suitcase to a nearby hotel. Here's another incentive: The Santa Barbara Car-Free Project (805-696-1100; santabarbara carfree.org) offers discounts to visitors who leave their cars at home. Travelers get deals on Amtrak fares, hotel rooms, and attractions such as whale-watching cruises and wine-country tours.

By bus: **Greyhound Lines** (805-965-7551, 800-965-7551; greyhound.com) has a station at 34 W. Carrillo St., Santa Barbara, open daily 6:30 AM–8 PM.

GETTING AROUND Santa Barbara Metropolitan Transit District (805-963-3364; sbmtd.gov) provides daily bus service, including the convenient Downtown–Waterfront Shuttle. Visitors can cruise up and down State St. and along the shoreline in an open-air, electric shuttle for just 25 cents. Shuttles run until 6 PM year-round, and until 9 PM on Fri. and Sat. Apr.–Oct.

Other local bus service includes Rt. 22, which offers daily service to attractions such as the Santa Barbara Mission, Santa Barbara Courthouse, the Museum of Art, the Museum of Natural History, and weekend service to the Botanic Garden.

✳ To See

Santa Barbara is a relatively small community, but its affluent benefactors have a history of supporting local arts and cultural venues. From museums to galleries to live performances, local offerings generally are high quality and compare favorably with those in larger metropolitan areas. Many arts venues open their doors to host free special events during First Thursday nights (santabarbaradowntown.com/go .asp) held monthly across downtown.

HISTORIC BUILDINGS AND SITES Here's an easy way to explore Santa Barbara's history: Download the **Santa Barbara Red Tile Walking Tour** on your iPod (available at santabarbaraca.com) and follow a route to the city's historic buildings narrated by the booming voice of John O'Hurley (the actor who played J. Peterman on *Seinfeld*). If you prefer a live tour, the **Architectural Foundation of Santa Barbara** (805-965-6307; afsb.org) leads two-hour treks every Sat. and Sun. starting at 10 AM. Saturday tours meet at the steps of City Hall at De La Guerra Plaza, just off State St., and include some of the city's original adobe landmarks, courtyards, and fountains. The Sunday tour leaves from the Santa Barbara Public Library, at 40 E. Anapamu St., and focuses on Santa Barbara art and architecture, including stops at the Granada and the Arlington Theatre. A $10 donation is requested.

Santa Barbara County Courthouse (805-962-6464; sbcourts.org/general_info /cthouse_info.htm), 1100 Anacapa St. Free docent-led tours at 2 PM daily, except Sun. Additional tours are 10:30 AM Mon., Tue., and Fri. Designed by William Mooser III, this ornate 1929 Spanish-Moorish-style building occupies a square block downtown. It's both a working courthouse and a cherished Santa Barbara landmark. Visitors will want to check out the El Mirador clock tower for scenic views of the city and coastline. Other highlights include the Mural Room, *Spirit of the Ocean* fountain, ornate tilework throughout the building, and the sunken garden outside.

✿ **Santa Barbara Mission** (805-682-4713; santabarbaramission.org), 2201 Laguna St. Open daily 9 AM–5 PM. Tours cost $5 adults, $4 seniors, $1 ages 6–15; children under 6 are free. The 10th of the California missions, the Santa Barbara Mission was founded on the Feast of Saint Barbara on December 4, 1786. Padre Junipero Serra, who founded the first nine missions, had died two years earlier, so his successor, Padre Fermin Francisco de Lasuen, raised the cross and made the first converts at Santa Barbara. More than two centuries later this picturesque adobe mission remains a cultural landmark and a Catholic parish. The mission grounds include a museum, gift shop, and 10 acres of gardens set amid the Santa Barbara hillsides and just a short distance from another local treasure, the Santa Barbara Museum of Natural History.

MUSEUMS *✿* **Santa Barbara Museum of Art** (805-963-4364; sbmuseart.org), 1130 State St. Open Tue.–Sun. 11 AM–5 PM. $9 adults, $6 children; free for children under 6 and on Sun. Since its founding in 1941, the museum has developed a focus on ancient art, Asian art (Chinese, Japanese, Indian, and Tibetan), French and English 19th- and early-20th-century art, American art, International Modernism, photography, and contemporary art. It features an interactive children's gallery, café, and museum store.

✿ **Santa Barbara Museum of Natural History** (805-682-4711; sbnature.org), 2559 Puesta del Sol. Open daily 10 AM–5 PM. $10 adults, $7 seniors and ages 13–17, $6 ages 3–12; children under 3 are free. Set on 11 oak-shaded acres in Mission Canyon, this museum is a folksy cluster of low Spanish-style buildings with 11

exhibit halls that explore the region's birds, insects, mammals, marine life, paleontology, and Native tribes. Adults and children alike will enjoy wandering the maze of exhibits, which include a life-sized blue whale skeleton and the largest collection of Chumash Indian artifacts outside the Smithsonian. The museum often hosts community events and guest speakers, so be sure to check the current calendar online.

🐟 **Ty Warner Sea Center** (805-962-2526; sbnature.org), 211 Stearns Wharf. Open Daily 10 AM–5 PM. $8 adults, $7 seniors and ages 13–17, $5 ages 2–12; children under 2 are free. Located on touristy Stearns Wharf at the foot of State Street, the Ty Warner Sea Center is operated by the Santa Barbara Museum of Natural History and offers marine exhibits and a window on the Santa Barbara Channel. There's a live shark touch pool, opportunities for children to work like scientists, and a crawl-through tunnel inside a giant tank where visitors can observe sea stars, urchins, limpets, and other sea creatures.

✳ To Do

BEACHES Santa Barbara has more than 2 miles of waterfront where visitors can swim, fish, bike, jog, picnic, or play volleyball. Most of the city's beaches face south and are easily accessible. **East Beach** and **West Beach** are part of an inviting expanse of sandy shoreline separated by **Stearns Wharf** (stearnswharf.org) at Cabrillo Blvd. and State St. downtown. Stearns Wharf is California's oldest wharf, a tourist magnet with shops, restaurants, and the Ty Warner Sea Center. The **Santa Barbara Harbor** is just west of the wharf along Cabrillo Boulevard.

Another choice spot for sun worshipping and people-watching is **Butterfly Beach**, a scenic stretch east of East Beach in Montecito. Butterfly Beach faces west, so it's a good place to enjoy a sunset. **Arroyo Burro County Park** (county

SANTA BARBARA'S HARBOR

ON BUTTERFLY BEACH

ofsb.org/parks), 2981 Cliff Dr., is an out-of-the-way beach 5 miles west of Santa Barbara's city center on Cliff Drive near Hope Ranch. Also called Hendry's Beach by locals, the park is a magical cove where you can surf, run along the shore, or sit on the porch of the Boathouse Restaurant enjoying breakfast and watching the crashing waves.

BICYCLING The nonprofit **Santa Barbara Bicycle Coalition** (sbbike.org) has compiled a collection of downloadable bike treks through Santa Barbara County, including three rides that begin downtown at Stearns Wharf. Rent a mountain bike, beach cruiser, tandem, or four-wheel surrey downtown at **Wheel Fun Rentals** (805-966-2282; wheelfunrentalssb.com), 22 State St. and also at 23 E. Cabrillo Blvd. For serious cyclists, **Santa Barbara Bikes to Go** (805-617-3364; sbbikestogo.com) rents high-performance bikes and hybrids and delivers them throughout the area.

Another way to cruise the waterfront on two wheels: Rent a Segway at **Segway of Santa Barbara** (805-963-7672; segayofsb.com), 16 Helena Ave., #A.

GARDENS AND WILDLIFE **Andree Clark Bird Refuge** (santabarbaraca.gov/parks), 1400 E. Cabrillo Blvd. Open sunrise–10 PM. Located across the East Beach, this wetlands area provides a haven for a diverse bird population including ducks, geese, egrets, and black-crowned night herons. The park has a bikeway, walking path, and interpretive self-guided tours for visitors.

Santa Barbara Botanic Garden (805-682-4726; sbbg.org), 1212 Mission Canyon Rd. Open daily 9 AM–6 PM, Mar.–Oct.; 9 AM–5 PM, Nov.–Feb. $8 adults; $6 seniors, ages 13–17, college students, and military; $4 ages 2–12; children under 2 are free. Founded in 1926, the garden spans 65 acres in Mission Canyon and features more than 1,000 species of native California plants. Visitors can stroll miles of walking paths, which are lush with vegetation and offer ocean and mountain vistas. Guided tours are at 2 PM weekdays and at 11 AM and 2 PM on weekends.

Lotusland (805-969-9990; lotusland.org; reservation@lotusland.org). Open mid-Feb.–mid-Nov. Tours at 10 AM and 1 PM. $35 adults, $10 children; under 5, free. Madame Ganna Walska bought this 37-acre estate in 1941 and began collecting the most exotic and rare plants she could find to create a botanical wonderland in the foothills of Montecito. The socialite named her home Lotusland in honor of the sacred Indian lotus growing in one of the ponds on the property. She died in 1984 and left her garden and her fortune to the Ganna Walska Lotusland Foundation. Lotusland in located in a private residential neighborhood, and visitors must make advance reservations for two-hour walking tours of the estate. Family-friendly tours are available.

VISITORS CAN FEED GIRAFFES BISCUITS
AT THE ZOO

⊙ ✎ **Santa Barbara Zoo** (805-962-5339; santabarbarazoo.com), 800 Ninos Dr., Santa Barbara. Open daily 10 AM–5 PM. Gift shop, café, and carousel. Admission: $12 adults, $10 children and seniors; children under 2, free. The Santa Barbara Zoo is a small but memorable gem. Located close to downtown, the zoo features more than 500 mammals, reptiles, and birds on 30 well-tended acres of animal habitats and natural landscaping. Visitors are welcomed by a troupe of pink Chilean flamingos near the entrance and there's a new condor exhibit. Younger children will especially enjoy the zoo's small train, which is a fun introduction to the park. (See sidebar next page).

GOLF The Santa Barbara area has several public 18-hole golf courses, including the **Sandpiper Golf Club** (805-968-1541; sandpipergolf.com), 7925 Hollister Ave., which offers a challenging play and ocean views. "On several holes, retrieving wayward shots might require a snorkel and fins," notes the *Los Angeles Times*, which ranked Sandpiper as one of California's top 15 destinations in 2009.

MONKEYS AT THE ZOO

INSIDE THE ZOO

The **Santa Barbara Zoo** is an idyllic place to spend two or three hours in the late morning or early afternoon, when you can hand-feed biscuits to towering Baringo giraffes, stare deeply into the eyes of rare silverback gorillas, listen to the weirdly evocative whoops and ululations emanating from Gibbon Island, and meander though the dark bug-, snake-, and lizard-filled confines of an exhibit appropriately entitled "Eeeww!" With its emphasis on habitats and natural landscaping, strolling through the zoo's 30 acres is as much a pleasant nature hike as anything else, and the walk-through aviaries, where you can mix it up with pheasants, blue-crowned pigeons, and other rare birds, are not to be missed.

Be sure to check out the new Condor Country exhibit, which opened in 2009 with four juvenile

THE NEW CONDOR COUNTRY EXHIBIT IS A MUST SEE AT THE ZOO

condors in a 6,000-square-foot habitat designed in cooperation with the California **Condor Recovery Program** (cacondorconservation.org). A young adult condor joined the flock in 2010. Santa Barbara is one of only four zoos in the world to display the endangered condor (the others are the San Diego Wild Animal Park, San Diego Zoo, and the Chapultepec Zoo in Mexico City).

Younger visitors will especially enjoy the zoo's small train, which makes a complete sweep of the park and offers an excellent vantage point for spotting wildlife. Favorite moment: The African lioness will occasionally climb onto a platform just on the other side of the glass window separating her habitat from human visitors, and she will stare intently with her golden predator's eyes before she lunges. Parents jump and kids squeal with delight and fear, and everyone knows, for just a moment, what it's like to be a lion's prey. Info: Santa Barbara Zoo (805-962-5339; www.sbzoo.org), 500 Ninos Dr., Santa Barbara.

Condor photos by Sheri Horiszny

David Orias

CATALINA FOX

More choices: **Rancho San Marcos** (805-683-6334; rsm1804.com), 4600 Hwy. 154, is a 6,800-yard, par 71 course in the heart of the Santa Ynez River Valley, about 12 miles from downtown along scenic Hwy. 154. Owner (and Beanie Baby founder) Ty Warner renovated the course. The city-run **Santa Barbara Golf Club** (805-687-7087; santabarbaraca.gov/Resident/Recreation_and_Sports/Golf), 3500 McCaw Ave., is a par 70 course open from dawn until dusk seven days a week. For more golf offerings, visit santabarbaraca.com.

WHALE-WATCHING Nearly 30 different types of whales, dolphins, and sea lions can been seen along Central Coast. From mid-May to November, you can take a whale-watching cruise to see blue whales and humpback whales off the Santa Barbara coast. From December to May, Pacific gray whales cruise through Santa Barbara Harbor on their migration between Alaska and Baja. **Condor Cruises** (805-965-0942; condorcruises.com), 301 W. Cabrillo Blvd., offers whale-watching expeditions.

✳ Lodging

The Santa Barbara area offers a range of options, from no-frills digs at the nation's very first Motel 6 (good news: Those 1962-era $6 rooms were renovated in 2009), to beach and boutique inns, to deluxe sanctuaries catering to guests seeking pampering and privacy. Santa Barbara room rates typically spike during summer months, particularly on Friday and Saturday nights. Rates, however, fluctuated in all price categories during 2009 and 2010, so it pays to shop around for deals year-round. More than 20 local establishments now offer discounted room rates (as much as 20 percent off) to visitors who arrive by public transportation (details at santabarbaracarfree.org).

&. "1" **Bath Street Inn** (805-682-9680, 800-549-2284; bathstreetinn.com; innkeepers@bathstreetinn.com), 1720 Bath St., Santa Barbara 93101. Moderate–expensive. Credit cards are accepted. One room has handicapped-accessible features: "Guests with mobility issues should call first and we'll be happy to discuss the room and our facility and see how we might be a suitable fit." This bed & breakfast is a hospitable Queen Anne Victorian with 12 comfortable rooms. "The home was built in the 1890s, so Victorian was the obvious choice," says co-owner Deborah Gentry, who co-owns it with Marie Christensen. "We don't like fussy rooms, so although the inn is furnished with antiques and period wallpapers, we don't have lots of clutter or teddy bears or china collections." Some rooms have fireplace, whirlpool tub. Guests enjoy a bountiful breakfast in the dining room or wisteria-covered patio outside, and tea and wine during the afternoon. As *Los Angeles Times* travel editor Catharine Hamm observes, "Staying at this B&B feels more like coming home to visit your Aunt Alice—if her taste and culinary skills were excellent and her only desire were to help you relax."

&. "1" **Canary Hotel** (877-468-3515; canarysantabarbara.com), 31 W. Carillo St., Santa Barbara 93101. Expensive–very expensive. Credit cards are accepted. Casablanca meets SoCal at the Canary, a chic new hot spot downtown with a tropical vibe. The owners of Santa Monica's well-regarded Shutters Hotel took over the property (formerly the Hotel Andalucia) and pulled off an extreme makeover in 2008: The 97 guest rooms and suites feature Majorcan-style four-poster beds, dark wood floors, bold prints, and sea grass matting instead of wall-to-wall carpets. Located close to State Street's arts and shopping hub, the Canary also boasts a rooftop swimming pool with outdoor fireplaces and panoramic views of the city. Restaurant, bar, pool.

ⓓ 🐾 ⅋ "🍴" **Fess Parker's Double-tree Resort** (805-564-4333, 800-879-2929; fessparkersantabarbarahotel.com), 633 E. Cabrillo Blvd., Santa Barbara 93103. Very expensive. Credit cards are accepted. Actor Fess Parker traded in his Daniel Boone coonskin cap and turned developer in the 1980s, opening this sprawling coral stucco resort on 24 acres across the street from the beach. The 360-room Doubletree offers spacious rooms, multiple restaurants, nicely landscaped grounds, and a host of amenities, though the property is so large it lacks the warmth

of some of the Central Coast's smaller inns. The hotel is a popular destination for weddings and corporate gatherings. Guests traveling with pets will enjoy walks on the scenic waterfront path that runs along the resort on Cabrillo Boulevard. Pool, spa, tennis, on-site dining.

ⓓ ⅋ "🍴" **Four Seasons Santa Barbara** (805-969-2261, reservations 805-565-8299, 800-819-5053; fourseasons.com/santabarbara), A1260 Channel Dr., Santa Barbara 93108. Very expensive. Credit cards are accepted. Check into the Four Seasons to engage your inner Gatsby. Built in the 1920s as a private mansion, the Spanish-Colonial-style resort is a venerable oasis with 207 rooms and suites, along with 12 luxurious cottages tucked amid winding paths on the hotel's beautifully landscaped grounds. The resort is sequestered along Butterfly Beach and serves up a vacation

IN THE GARDENS AT THE DELUXE FOUR SEASONS HOTEL

experience that blends Old World elegance with modern amenities such as rainfall showers and flat-screen plasma TVs. Owner Ty Warner completed a no-expense-spared remodel of the Four Seasons in 2007, updating the entire property and adding hand-painted tile, rare marble, and antique furnishings. The hotel is ideal for a romantic getaway (waiters pedal the grounds on bicycles delivering meals, champagne, and chocolate-covered strawberries) or an upscale family vacation (rates include the hotel's Kids For All Seasons program and use of beach cruisers). Guests enjoy access to the oceanfront Coral Casino Beach and Cabana Club, the perfect spot to work on your tan or sip an icy margarita while lapping up views of the breaking waves. Spa, pool, tennis courts.

 ♿ "ᵀ" **Hotel Santa Barbara** (800-549-9869; hotelsantabarbara.com; info@hotelsantabarbara.com), 533 State St., Santa Barbara 93101. Located in the heart of Santa Barbara's State St. Expensive. Credit cards are accepted.This 75-room Mediterranean boutique hotel is quintessential Santa Barbara: cool, quirky, and sprinkled with tasteful extras throughout. A vintage elevator with a sliding metal cage door ferries guests upstairs to modern rooms bathed in warm tones, light woods, and Provence fabrics. Standard rooms are compact, but airy and quite comfortable. In the morning, staff set out a spread of pastries, bagels, croissants, waffles, and coffee in the hotel's spacious Moroccan-style lobby. The location is a major reason to stay here: The Hotel Santa Barbara sits in the heart of the State Street action, just a short stroll from shopping, restaurants, shows, and the train station. On Tuesday afternoon the downtown farmer's market assembles right outside the hotel's front door. Rates start at $209 a night during summer.

♿ "ᵀ" **Inn of the Spanish Garden** (866-564-4700; spanishgardeninn.com; info@innofthespanishgarden), 915 Garden St., Santa Barbara 93101. Expensive–very expensive. Credit cards are accepted. With just 23 rooms, the Inn of the Spanish Garden is an upscale boutique property that traffics in quiet luxury. The inn, which opened in 2001, is walking distance to upper State Street, but far enough away (two blocks) on a nondescript street so that the property exudes a private, relaxed ambience. The decor is vintage Santa Barbara (white adobe walls, red tile roof, ornate ironwork) complemented by a sunny courtyard and amenities such as a deep tub and gas fireplace in every room. Rates include a continental breakfast buffet with cappuccino and espresso. Heated pool, wine bar.

🐶 ♿ "ᵀ" **Hotel Mar Monte** (800-643-1994, 805-963-0744; hotelmarmonte.com; reservations@hotelmarmonte.com), 1111 E. Cabrillo Blvd., Santa Barbara 93103. Expensive–very expensive. Credit cards are accepted. Built in 1931, the Mar Monte is a full-service Spanish-style hotel by the beach. The 173-room property may not be up-to-the-minute trendy, but it offers spacious rooms and often-discounted rates (prices dip to as low as $129 a night in winter); room renovations were planned as this book went to press. Beach lovers will like the location—oceanfront rooms with patios that open out to the Pacific along Cabrillo Boulevard. Pet lovers will be pleased that dogs are welcome to stay. The Airbus from LAX makes its daily stop in Santa Barbara here. On-site restaurant, lounge, spa, pool.

♿ "ᵀ" **Montecito Inn** (800-843-2017; montecitoinn.com; info@montecitoinn.com), 1295 Coast Village Rd., Santa Barbara 93108. Expensive. Credit cards are accepted. Actor Charlie Chaplin built this historic inn in 1928 as a getaway for his Hollywood friends. Standard rooms are compact, decked out in a courtly, old-fashioned style with the feel of a bygone era. Located 4 miles east of Santa Barbara on Montecito's quaint main drag, the inn offers a less costly alternative to the suburban community's über resorts and is two blocks from Butterfly Beach. Rates jump here in summertime, and the hotel is by far a better value (and a more reasonable fit) at its lower, off-season prices. A complimentary conti nental breakfast is served in the downstairs lobby; the inn's lively café bar opens for lunch and dinner. Pool.

☀ 🐾 ᵗ⒯ **Motel 6 Santa Barbara— Beach** (805-564-1392; motel6.com), 443 Corona Del Mar, Santa Barbara 93103. Inexpensive–moderate. Credit cards are accepted. In 1962 Motel 6 co-founders William Becker and Paul Greene launched their empire in Santa Barbara, charging $6 a night for a basic room by the beach. The duo's first pale-pink-and-aqua motor lodge is still going strong. Just a block away from the sand at East Beach, the maiden Motel 6 offers the chain's trademark no-frills lodging—bed, TV, small pool outside—and remains one of the best deals in this pricey beach town. Rooms dip as low as $66 a night on weekdays during the winter off-season. A remodel was completed in spring 2009. Pool, microwaves.

ᵗ⒯ **Presidio Motel** (805-963-1355; thepresidiomotel.com), 1620 State St., Santa Barbara 93101. Moderate–expensive. Credit cards are accepted. This basic box of a 1960s-era motel has been renovated and remade into a cool, funky comfortable, no-frills boutique lodge in the midst of the State Street scene. Each room has been decorated with custom vinyl decals creat-

ed by local artists in bold colors and eclectic designs: parachuting elephants and giraffes in one room, purple clouds and dangling vines in others. A large sundeck features retro lounge chairs, beach cruiser bikes are available for guests to use, and there's a complimentary continental breakfast of muffins and coffee each morning. Off-season rates dip below $100 a night. One room is wheelchair accessible. Pool, free bicycles.

∞ 🐾 ᵗ⒯ **San Ysidro Ranch** (805-565-1700; sanysidroranch.com; sanysidro@rosewoodhotels.com), 900 San Ysidro Lane, Santa Barbara 93108. Very expensive. Credit cards are accepted. The San Ysidro Ranch is a legendary California retreat where John and Jackie Kennedy famously spent their honeymoon and Laurence Olivier and Vivien Leigh exchanged vows in the hotel garden. This old-money resort has 41 private bungalows and suites along creek- and tree-lined paths that wind through the Montecito foothills. Cottages are fully loaded with

THE NATION'S FIRST MOTEL 6 IS BY THE BEACH IN SANTA BARBARA

antique furnishings, a hot tub on a private outdoor patio, stone fireplace, flat-screen TV, and radiant-heated bathroom floor. Pets are not only invited to stay, but pampered with massages as well. The hotel's Stonehouse Restaurant is an elegant woodsy dining room with a crackling fireplace. Chef John Trotta focuses on regional cuisine prepared with herbs and vegetables from the on-site chef's garden. Heated pool, spa, 17 miles of hiking trails.

& "T" **West Beach Inn** (805-963-4277, 800-716-6199; coasthotels.com), 306 W. Cabrillo Blvd., Santa Barbara 93101. Moderate–expensive. Credit cards are accepted. This is a sweet 46-room motel located across the way from Santa Barbara Harbor. It's an older Mediterranean-style property, but guest rooms have been freshly refurnished, and some have patios with harbor views. The *Los Angeles Times* calls the West Beach Inn "five-star furnishings at a three-star price." Rates include a continental breakfast and afternoon wine-and-cheese reception. The inn also is walking distance to State Street and the beach. Heated pool, hot tub.

MORE LODGING Even more Santa Barbara–area options—including wine county inns, nature retreats, and campgrounds—are just a few miles up the coast (chapter 4) or inland in the Santa Ynez Valley (chapter 3).

✳ Where to Eat

Santa Barbara offers an array of restaurants and cuisines: traditional fine dining, inexpensive but tasty local fare, and an increasing number of restaurants that embrace the farm-to-table local foods movement.

Bouchon (805-730-1160; bouchon santabarbara.com), 9 W. Victoria St., Santa Barbara 93101. Open daily for dinner at 5:30 PM. Expensive. Credit cards are accepted. Reservations suggested. Hidden behind a shrubbery wall just off State Street, Bouchon offers a French-inspired menu that changes with the season and delights carnivores and vegetarians alike. Owner Mitchell Sjerven puts a premium on serving local ingredients—fish caught in the Santa Barbara Channel, produce from the farmer's market, meats and poultry from local micro-ranches, and wines from Santa Barbara County. One specialty dish—the popular bourbon and maple-glazed duck—remains on the menu year-round. Foodies regularly mention Bouchon as one of Santa Barbara's best. Sjerven also owns the nearby Seagrass Restaurant (at 30 E. Ortega St., just off State St.), which opened in 2008 with a focus on sustainable seafood.

Brophy Brothers (805-966-4418; brophybros.com), 119 Harbor Way, Santa Barbara 93109. Open Sun.–Thu. 11 AM–10 PM, Fri.–Sat. 11 AM–11 PM. Moderate. Credit cards are accepted, but not reservations. The fish is fresh and the cocktails flow like water, but the main reason to come to this busy seafood house is the location. Brophy Brothers is perched atop the Santa Barbara Harbor with a second-story outdoor patio offering sweeping views of the mountains, the boats and fishermen below, and the coastline beyond. Try the garlic baked clams, a local favorite. Note that this is an older second-story restaurant with stairs; there's no elevator for patrons in wheelchairs who want to dine upstairs.

The Boathouse (805-898-2628; sbfish house.com), 2981 Cliff Dr., Santa Barbara 93109. Open daily 7:30 AM–9 PM. Moderate–expensive. Credit cards are accepted. Perched on the sand at Hendry's Beach, one of Santa Barbara's prettiest beaches, the Boathouse is a

FLAMINGOS GREET VISITORS AT SANTA BARBARA'S ZOO

good choice for a relaxing breakfast or weekend brunch away from town. Sit on the outdoor patio with your morning java and soak up the scene as surfers work the swell and dogs run along the shore with their owners. The Boathouse opened in 2009 (at the site of the old Brown Pelican restaurant) and serves sandwiches, salads, seafood entrées, and cocktails on its lunch and dinner menus. The cove here is a favorite beach among residents, though finding a parking spot inside Arroyo Burro County Park can be challenging during summer. Full bar, great off-the-beaten-path location.

Elements Restaurant and Bar (805-884-9218; elementsrestaurantand bar.com), 129 E. Anapamu St., Santa Barbara 93121. Open Mon.–Sat. 11:30 AM–2 PM, Sun. 11:30 AM–2 PM; Sun.–Wed. 4:30–9 PM, Thu.–Sat. 4:30–10 PM. Expensive. Credit cards are accepted. Elements opened downtown in 2004 and is known for its imaginative world-fusion cuisine and martini menu. Diners can enjoy lunch, dinner, or Sunday brunch on the restaurant's outdoor patio, which overlooks the Santa Barbara Courthouse and sunken garden. House specialties include a lemongrass-and-panko-crusted local sea bass with Thai green coconut curry sauce. Elements is a choice spot for a special occasion. Extensive martini and wine list.

Restaurant Julienne (805-845-6488; restaurantjulienne.com), 138 E. Canon Perdido St., Santa Barbara 93101. Open daily for lunch and dinner. Expensive. Credit cards are accepted. Julienne is a newcomer to the Santa Barbara dining scene, a small, innovative restaurant that embraces the locavore movement with gusto. Owners Emma and Justin West change the menu constantly, so you can sample new tasting menus (three, five, or seven courses) each time you visit. Entrées include such offerings as local abalone served with cauliflower, capers, chili, almonds, and a sea broth or a crispy pork belly with potato-corn hash, thyme, and porky jus. One of

Julienne's nice touches: cheese plates with selections from nearby C'est Cheese.

Pierre LaFond Wine Bistro (805-962-1455; pierrelafond.com), 516 State St., Santa Barbara 93101. Open daily 9 AM–9 PM. Moderate–expensive. Credit cards are accepted. This is a tasty spot to grab breakfast or lunch while strolling downtown Santa Barbara. Diners have a choice of fresh pastries and a gourmet selection of sandwiches and salads. The bistro has a daily happy hour (4:30–6:30 PM) featuring local wines and an appetizers; there's a full dinner menu, too. Good selection of wine by the glass. Find a table under one of the green umbrellas outside to soak up the Santa Barbara sunshine and the State Street scene. Santa Barbara winemaker Pierre LaFond also has second local eatery: the Montecito Deli and Market (805-565-1502; 516 San Ysidro Rd., Montecito; open 7 AM–8 PM), which is good for breakfast and lunchtime goodies on the go.

✪ **La Super Rica** (805-963-4940); 622 N. Milpas St., Santa Barbara 93103. Open Sun., Mon., and Thu. 11 AM–9 PM, Fri.–Sat. 11 AM–9:30 PM; closed Wed. Inexpensive. Bring cash—credit cards are not accepted here, nor are reservations. The line often winds down the block outside this modest aqua taco stand with white plastic patio tables and a daily menu scrawled on a blackboard. Offerings include handmade tortillas stuffed with tri-tip steak, grilled marinated pork, chorizo and melted cheese, and grilled chicken breast, along with mouthwatering daily *especials*. Beer is served. The food is so reasonably priced (dishes range from about $1.50 to $7) that you'll want to order several small plates to sample as many flavors as possible. This humble taqueria is a local favorite that counted renowned chef Julia Child among its

fans. Be patient. La Super Rica is worth the wait.

✔ **Natural Café** (805-962-9494; the naturalcafe.com), 508 State St., Santa Barbara 93101. Open daily 11 AM–9 PM. Inexpensive. Credit cards are accepted. A casual spot for simple vegetarian fare, quesadillas, turkey burgers, and freshly made soup. The shakes and fruit smoothies are very good. And the Natural Café is a good deal, too: Menu items are less than $10. Beer and wine available; children's menu.

Palace Grill (805-963-5000; palace grill.com), 8 E. Cota St., Santa Barbara 93101. Open daily 11:30 AM–3 PM; Sun.–Thu., dinner is 5:30–10 PM; Fri.–Sat., 5:30–11 PM. Moderate–expensive. Credit cards are accepted. Reservations available for the early seating only. This popular Cajun-Caribbean hot spot opens for dinner at 5:30, but there's often a line outside long before then. The Palace Grill is a winning mix of good, spicy food and good fun in a lively, often boisterous dining room where the icy margaritas arrive in mason jars and the crawfish is flown from the Gulf Coast. On Friday and Saturday nights the restaurant only accepts reservations for the 5:30 seating; after that diners are seated on a first-come, first-served basis. To ease the wait, the staff serve up live music and complimentary appetizers to patrons waiting outside. Save room for the dark chocolate soufflé.

✪ **Tupelo Junction Cafe** (805-899-3100; tupelojunction.com), 1218 State St., Santa Barbara 93101. Open daily for breakfast and lunch, 8 AM–2 PM; dinner Tue.–Sun. 5:30–9 PM. Moderate–expensive. Credit cards are accepted. Tupelo Café serves comfort food with flair. The restaurant puts a California spin on southern staples, such as the fried chicken salad, a healthier version of its artery-clogging namesake

MARKET FORAYS

For a taste of the Santa Barbara lifestyle, spend Saturday touring local markets with Laurence Hauben, a French-born chef and the leader of Slow Food Santa Barbara (slowfoodsantabarbara.org). With Laurence as your expert guide, you'll join a small group at Santa Barbara Harbor at 8 am to select live spiny lobsters or crabs or rockfish right off the boats from local fisher-

PRODUCE AT THE SANTA BARBARA FARMER'S MARKET

men. Next stop: the downtown Farmer's Market, where you sample the season's bounty and shop for produce, locally raised meat or poultry, and just-baked bread. Then it's off to the C'est Cheese shop (805-965-0318; 825 Santa Barbara St.) before heading to Laurence's Santa Barbara home to help prepare a five-course feast, complemented by selections of local wines. This is one of the most delicious days you'll ever spend—and you return home with some great recipes, too. Cost: $135 (805-259-7229; market forays.com).

that comes with corn bread, dried cranberries, and a lemony herb-buttermilk dressing. Some menu items, like the Maine lobster, potato and sweet corn chowder, and flavor-packed red beans and rice with roasted shallots, tomatoes, corn, and sautéed greens, are positively addictive. Every bite here is delicious. Live music and happy-hour menu on Thu.

FOOD PURVEYORS & SPECIALTY SHOPS C'est Cheese (805-965-0318; cestcheese.com), 825 Santa Barbara St. This small, family-run cheese shop is gourmet heaven, offering 120 different cheese selections, cured meats, wine, and picnic items.

McConnell's (805-569-2323; mcconnellsonmission.com), 201 W.

Mission. Stop by Santa Barbara's hometown ice cream emporium for simple, rich flavors, such as Island Coconut, Brazilian Coffee Chip, and Chocolate Burnt Almond, made from natural ingredients. Delicious.

Mayo's Carniceria and Market (805-569-1591), 2708 De La Vina St. A tasty little taco joint with a market where you can find Mexican delicacies.

Renaud's Patisserie (805-569-2400; renaudsbakery.com), 3315 State St. This sweet bakery specializes in French pastries and French-style cakes; it's great for croissants and breakfast, too.

Santa Barbara Roasting Co. Get a java fix close to the train station downtown (805-962-0320; sbcoffee.com;

321 Motor Way) or several blocks up along State St. at the Paseo Nuevo outpost (805-962-2070; 607 Paseo Nuevo).

Tuttini Bake Shop & Café (805-963-8404), 10 E. Carrillo St. Make a detour at this petit side street café for fresh muffins, chocolate croissants, and Tuttini's Chai Charger, a tasty chai latte with a blast of espresso to jump-start the day.

✳ Entertainment

THEATERS AND VENUES Arlington Theatre (805-963-4408; the arlingtontheatre.com), 1317 State St. Located downtown, the Arlington Theatre features live performances, including symphonies, plays, ballets, and rock-and-roll concerts. Built in 1931, it hosts the annual Santa Barbara Film Festival and still shows first-run Hollywood films.

The Granada (805-899-3000; granada sb.org), 1214 State St. Originally opened in 1924 and reopened in 2008 after extensive renovations, the landmark Granada is Santa Barbara's only eight-story building, the tallest in town. The Spanish-Moorish-style theater hosts the Santa Barbara Symphony, State Street Ballet, Opera Santa Barbara, CAMA concerts, Music Academy of the West, the UC Santa Barbara's Arts & Lectures Series, a Broadway Series, and many community events.

Lobero Theatre (805-966-4946; lobero.com), 33 E. Canyon Perdido. Founded in 1873, the Lobero is one of California's oldest continuously operating theaters. With a seating capacity of 680, the theater features classical concerts, lectures, dance, films, and special events.

NIGHTLIFE During summer months the **Santa Barbara Bowl** (805-962-7411; sbbowl.com), 1122 N. Milpas St., is a good bet for concerts. It's a rela-tively small outdoor amphitheater (4,562 seats), but the Bowl has a history of attracting big names, such as Stevie Wonder, Paul Simon, Gwen Stefani, Pearl Jam, the Eagles, Norah Jones, and Radiohead. The amphitheater is set in a gorge; parking is at nearby Santa Barbara High School. The venue advises concertgoers to arrive about 90 minutes before showtime to allow time for parking and making your way inside.

Downtown Santa Barbara and State Street jump after dark with lively cafés, bars, and clubs. You can stroll the boulevard and look for a place that calls to you. Or head to these popular spots:

Blue Agave (805-899-4694; blue agavesb.com), 20 E. Cota St., has an upstairs bar for enjoying happy hour, mojitos, and mingling, and serves a wide selection of tequilas and mescals. There's a nice tapas menu, too.

Santa Barbara Brewing Co. (805-730-1040), 501 State St., is a boisterous outpost serving up an excellent selection of specialty brews and sporting events on big screens. There is a children's menu, but people generally come here for the beer.

Soho Restaurant and Music Club (805-962-7776; sohosb.com), 1221 State St., Suite 205, is an intimate venue offering live music and dancing seven nights a week; live jazz every Mon. The menu emphasizes steaks, chops, and bistro fare, but the selections also include braised wild boar shanks and a full bar.

✳ Selective Shopping

Shoppers will enjoy browsing Mediterranean-style courtyards overflowing with upscale shops at **Paseo Nuevo** (805-965-7147; paseonuevoshopping .com), the city's open-air mall in the heart of State St. at De La Guerra.

MY PERFECT DAY IN SANTA BARBARA, BY LAURENCE HAUBEN

"A perfect day for me might start early in the morning at the harbor, shopping for fresh seafood and watching the morning sun spray the hills with gold. Lobster and ridgeback shrimp are in season during fall and winter, colorful rockfish most of the year, rock crab—a favorite of mine—all year round. Sometimes we even score live spot prawns or sea urchins. Then a tour of the farmer's market, running into friends, admiring the colorful stalls tumbling over with gorgeous foods to take home and play with in the kitchen. A stop for breakfast at Renaud's Patisserie (best croissants in town) is always fun, a detour by C'est Cheese (a Frenchwoman must have a supply of artisan cheeses on hand at all times), browsing at a local bookshop (my favorite bookstore is Chaucer's, but Thrasher Books, the used-book store next to C'est Cheese, is fun, too), then playing in my garden for a couple of hours. Maybe bike down the hill for lunch at Mayo's Carniceria—great burritos, tacos, tortas, and shopping for fresh crema, queso fresco, little quail, and other Mexican delicacies—then cooking for a couple of hours, perhaps making a batch of preserves from farmer's market fruit.

LAURENCE HAUBEN, THE HEAD OF SLOW FOOD SANTA BARBARA, AT THE FARMER'S MARKET

"A late-afternoon walk on Hendry's Beach (off leash with my dog), then getting together with friends for a visit to an art gallery and dinner, whether we cook together at home or enjoy one of Santa Barbara's many good restaurants. I have had excellent dinners lately at Elements, Julienne, San Ysidro Ranch.

"Throughout the day, there are two things that really stand out and make Santa Barbara a special place to live. First, everywhere you look there is something pretty: a garden in bloom, the graceful arches of a tree's canopy, shadows on an old wall, the silhouette of the hills behind the city. Second, every time I step out of the house, it is practically impossible not to run into someone I know and love. This is a very tight-knit community."

—Hauben is a French chef and leader of Slow Food Santa Barbara. She also is the founder of Market Forays (marketforays.com) and hosts springtime jam-making sessions at area farms such as Shepherd's Farm (shepherdfarmscsa.com) in Carpinteria.

Paseo Nuevo is anchored by two department stores, Nordstrom and Macy's, and has more than 60 boutiques, name-brand retailers, eateries, and coffee shops. Most businesses are open Mon.–Fri. 10 AM–9 PM, Sat. 10 AM–8 PM, and Sun. 11 AM–6 PM. Also close by: three movie screens at the **Metropolitan Paseo Nuevo Cinemas** (877-789-6684; 8 W. De La Guerra Place).

BOOKSTORES Downtown Santa Barbara has a number of appealing indie bookstores. **Chaucers** (805-682-6787; chaucersbooks.com), 3221 State St., is a small shop with helpful staff. The **Book Den** (805-962-3321; book den.com), 15 E. Anapamu St., is right across the street from the excellent **Santa Barbara Public Library** (sbplibrary.org) and sells new, used, and out-of-print books. Karen Thrasher's **Thrasher Books** (805-568-1936), 827 Santa Barbara St., specializes in used books. Downtown also has a **Borders Books, Music and Café** (805-899-3668; 900 State St.).

ALONG STATE STREET, A SIGN GUIDES PEDESTRIANS TO THE PASEO NUEVO SHOPPING AREA

FARMER'S MARKETS On Sat., the downtown farmer's market (805-962-5354; sbfarmersmarket.org) materializes at Cota and Santa Barbara Sts., 8:30 AM–12:30 PM. On Tue., the market takes over the 500 and 600 blocks of State St., 4–7:30 PM in summer, 3–6:30 PM in winter. On Fri., Montecito holds its farmer's market at 1100 Coast Village Rd., 8–11:15 AM.

✳ Special Events

January–February: **Santa Barbara International Film Festival** (sbfilm festival.org)—always a celeb-studded affair.

April: **Earth Day Festival** (communi tyenvironmentalcouncil.org) at the Santa Barbara County Courthouse's Sunken Garden.

May: **Santa Barbara Historic Homes Tour** (pearlchasesociety.org). **I Madonnari Festival** (imadonnari festival.com) is an Italian street painting celebration at Old Mission Santa Barbara.

June: **Summer Solstice Celebration** (solsticeparade.com).

July–August: **Old Spanish Days Fiesta** (oldspanishdays-fiesta.org) downtown.

THE PASEO NUEVO SHOPPING DISTRICT

Santa Ynez
Valley

2

SANTA YNEZ VALLEY

"The beauty of driving through the mountains behind Santa Barbara is that it's a perfect place and way for getting lost. And whatever you stumble into will have the feeling of a rare discovery that not so many people know about."

—Travel author and Santa Barbara resident Pico Iyer

The winding, hilly route from the city of Santa Barbara to the Santa Ynez Valley is one of Southern California's prettiest drives. Every gentle curve of Highway 154 seems to reveal something new: a sprawling forest, idyllic pastures, foothills carpeted with gold and purple wildflowers. Horses and cows graze on ranches seemingly untouched by time, hawks and bald eagles soaring overhead. Twenty miles from the city a massive shimmering topaz lake appears out of nowhere, peeking through thick stands of trees and heralding the string of bucolic country towns just up ahead.

This is back-road Santa Barbara—the county, not the city—where you can find a few peaceful hours of nature and rustic charm or, if you choose, a few glorious days of relaxing escape in a valley of family farms, ranches, and rolling vineyards. It's a sheltered area with a gentle climate and fertile land, cradled by the Santa Ynez and San Rafael mountain ranges and bordered north and south by the sprawling Los Padres National Forest.

You don't have to drive very far through the valley to see that it's horse country. Just about anywhere you look as you drive the country roads you'll see horses grazing and foraging and nudging their foals. *Seabiscuit*, the 2005 Academy Award–nominated film about a famous racehorse, was filmed

ON THE SHORE AT CACHUMA LAKE

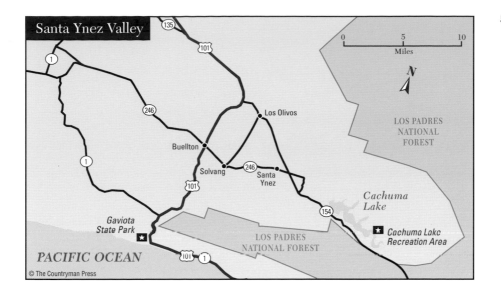

Santa Ynez Valley

in the valley, and Monty Roberts, the queen of England's "horse whisperer," has his ranch here. From Kentucky Derby winners to dainty miniature show horses that can sell for $15,000 apiece, more than 30 equine breeds thrive on the valley's horse farms.

The Santa Ynez Valley is even better known as wine country. Another popular film, *Sideways*, piqued public interest in the region's grapes in 2004 and put the valley's wineries on the map after many years in the shadow of Napa and Sonoma. In the movie two friends, Miles (Paul Giamatti) and Jack (Thomas Hayden Church), careen through the Central Coast on a wine-country binge, chasing women and swilling Pinot Noir. As Miles explains to Maya the waitress (Virginia Madsen) in the film: "It's a hard grape to grow . . . And, in fact, it can only grow in these really specific, little tucked-away corners of the world. And only the most patient and nurturing of growers can do it, really."

The Santa Barbara County Vintners' Association says that the county now has more than 100 wineries, located primarily in the Santa Ynez Valley, Santa Maria Valley, and Santa Rita Hills appellations. The region has become especially well known for its Pinot, Chardonnay, and Syrah.

When you visit, you'll want to spend time poking along the Foxen Canyon Wine Trail, a gorgeous route that winds past many of the valley's premium wineries, including Foxen, Firestone, and Fess Parker. Begin the

HORSES AT RANCHO OSO

STROLLING IN LOS OLIVOS: CHARMING BOUTIQUES, RESTAURANTS, AND TASTING ROOMS

canyon trek in Los Olivos, a farm town with a grocery store unlike any other. It has a gourmet café and outdoor patio where you pick up farm-fresh provisions before launching your own version of the *Sideways* tour.

Los Olivos is an upscale hamlet originally established in 1887 as a stagecoach stop at Mattei's Tavern, now a popular restaurant and historical landmark. The town flourished with the founding of Rancho Los Olivos, where a new rancher from New York planted 5,000 of the namesake olive trees. The completion of railroad service to the area turned the sleepy valley into hub of farming and commerce. In recent years Los Olivos has become known for its restaurants and art galleries, as well as for being the site of the late pop singer Michael Jackson's Neverland Ranch.

Nearby Santa Ynez, which sits astride Highway 154, was founded as a western town in 1882. The quaint downtown still retains its original Old West character. The town is adjacent to the Santa Ynez Indian Reservation and the boxy Chumash Casino and Resort, the valley's biggest employer, which brought Vegas-style gambling to the area.

Solvang, a replica of a Danish village, looks like a suburb of Disneyland with its distinctive, rococo architectural style. The theme runs deep and includes a Hans Christian Andersen Park, a Hans Christian Andersen Museum, and the annual Danish Days every September, a town celebration that even drew the king and

SOLVANG STREET SCENE

THE TOWN OF SOLVANG (DANISH FOR "SUNNY FIELD") RETAINS A DISTINCTIVE DANISH CHARACTER.

queen of Denmark back in the 1930s. *Solvang* means "sunny fields," and the community's European flavor dates back to the Danish American corporation that established a colony and folk school in the valley in 1911. Solvang is well known for its baked goods—authentic Danish pastries, what else?

Buellton is a horsey blue-collar town, home of the highly recommended Hitching Post restaurant and funky, fun Ostrich Land, two of the local attractions featured in *Sideways*. Technically the newest city in the valley—Buellton was officially established in 1920—the community's true beginning was in 1875, when the old land grant that encompassed the area was bought by a former gold miner named R. T. Buell. He built a sprawling dairy, cattle, and horse ranch that became a veritable town in itself. As the 20th century approached, the Buell family began selling off land, and the community began to take its current shape. The transformation was completed when Buellton became the final link in the newly constructed US Highway 101 in 1922; it remains a major crossroads to the rest of the valley.

OSTRICH LAND IN BUELLTON WAS BRIEFLY FEATURED IN THE MOVIE *SIDEWAYS*

These wine-country towns are clustered close together, and you can easily reach them by traveling the pair of country roads—Highways 154 and 246—that amble through the valley and crisscross in Santa Ynez. Along Highway 154 you'll spy beautiful

Cachuma Lake, which does double duty as a wildlife haven and reservoir for Santa Barbara County's drinking water. The lake is a popular recreation area, fishing spot, and campsite.

As you drive across the Santa Ynez Valley and meander its dusty side roads, you'll find a wealth of small farms, excellent wineries, and roadside curiosities such as miniature horses, llamas, emus, and, of course, ostriches. The valley is only a 45-minute drive or so from downtown Santa Barbara—an easy day trip. But the area is such a

BOATS AT CACHUMA LAKE

tranquil, remote sanctuary that it truly feels like another universe entirely.

GUIDANCE **Buellton Visitors Bureau and Chamber of Commerce** (805-684-5479; buellton.org).

Los Olivos Business Association (losolivosca.com).

Santa Barbara Vintners' Association (805-688-0881; sbcountywines.com), 3669 Sagunto St., Santa Ynez 93460-1558.

Solvang Visitors Bureau (800-468-6765; solvangusa.com), 1511-A Mission Dr., Solvang 93464.

Santa Ynez Valley Visitors Association (800-742-2843; syvva.com), P.O. Box 1918, Santa Ynez 93460.

Santa Ynez Valley Wine Country Association (800-563-3183; santaynezwine country.com).

BOATING AT CACHUMA LAKE

SUNSET ON CACHUMA LAKE

GETTING THERE The Santa Ynez Valley is about 30 miles northeast and inland of Santa Barbara at its nearest edge. The oval-shaped valley is flanked by two mountain ranges, the San Rafael and Santa Ynez, and a vast wilderness, Los Padres National Forest. Highways 154 and 246 are the main routes in and around the valley. The longest Central Coast river is the Santa Ynez, which flows by the towns of Solvang, Buellton, and Santa Ynez, and on to Cachuma Lake.

By car:

From Santa Barbara: You'll start your road trip in town by taking Hwy. 101 north to Hwy. 154 west (also called San Marco Pass Rd.) until you reach the Santa Ynez Valley. The closest town is Santa Ynez, 30 miles from Santa Barbara. If you continue on Hwy. 154 past Santa Ynez, you'll reach Los Olivos and the Foxen Canyon Wine Trail. If you turn left at the intersection of Hwys. 154 and 246, you'll pass through Santa Ynez, then Solvang and Buellton. (You can complete the full loop from Buellton by continuing on Hwy. 246 to Hwy. 101 south, which passes by Gaviota State Park on its way back to the ocean, then hugs the coast back to Santa Barbara.)

A LOCAL VINEYARD OFFERS WINE TASTINGS

From Los Angeles: Take Hwy. 101 north to Santa Barbara. Follow the signs to Hwy. 154 and the Santa Ynez Valley. About 125 miles.

From San Francisco: Take Hwy. 101 south until you reach the Santa Ynez Valley. Exit at Hwy. 154 (toward Los Olivos) or Hwy. 246 (toward Buellton and Solvang). It's nearly 300 miles.

By bus: **Santa Barbara Airbus** (800-423-1618; santabarbaraairbus.com) offers coach service from Los Angeles International Airport (LAX) to the Santa Barbara area and has expanded its offerings to include stops in Buellton and Santa Maria.

Central Coast Shuttle (805-928-1977; http://cclax.com) offers one-way and round-trip transportation from LAX to Santa Maria and Buellton. Wine-country shuttle bus service also is available.

SUNSET APPROACHES AT CACHUMA LAKE

By air: **Santa Barbara Municipal Airport** (805-967-7111, 805-683-4011; flysba .com), 500 Fowler Rd., Santa Barbara, offers nonstop flights from Denver, Los Angeles, Phoenix, Sacramento, Salt Lake City, San Francisco, San Jose, and Seattle. (See "Santa Barbara" for more airport information.)

By train: **Amtrak** (800-872-7245; amtrak.com) stops on State St. in downtown Santa Barbara; there's daily train service along the West Coast between Seattle and Los Angeles.

✳ To See

MUSEUMS AND HISTORIC SITES Hans Christian Anderson Museum (805-688-2052; bookloftsolvang.com), 1680 Mission Dr., Solvang. Located at the Book Loft, a local bookstore, this small museum is devoted to the father of the modern fairy tale.

Old Mission Santa Ines (805-688-4815; missionsantaines.org), 1760 Mission Dr., Solvang. The 19th of the 21 California missions established by Franciscan priests from 1769 to 1823, the Old Mission Santa Ines is known as the "hidden gem of the missions." It was founded in Solvang on September 17, 1804, and named in honor of Saint Agnes, an early Christian martyr. This picturesque adobe landmark remains an active parish church that serves about 1,000 families. It's also a popular tourist draw and a mecca for California fourth graders doing school mission projects. Interesting fact: The mission has the largest and most valuable collection of early California church vestments, dating from the 15th century to 1718. Want to know more? The mission is open to the public daily, and visitors can take taped audio tours (between 9 AM and 4:30 PM) of the museum and grounds. $5 adults; ages 11 and under are free.

✎ **Wildling Art Museum** (805-688-1082; wildlingmuseum.org), 2928 San Marcos Ave., Los Olivos. The Wildling is a small museum dedicated to the art of America's wilderness. It hosts four exhibits each year, featuring artists and photographers such as Ansel Adams, John James Audubon, Bob Kuhn, Josef Muench, and Diane C. Orr, and offers programs for families throughout the year.

✳ To Do

BICYCLING Once you reach the valley, you actually don't have to drive. Instead, hop on a high-performance, 24-speed bike in Santa Ynez and pedal your way through the back roads with an expert guide. **Santa Barbara Wine Country**

BIKING IS POPULAR IN SOLVANG

Cycling Tours (805-686-9490; wine countrycycling.com), 3630 Sagunto St, Santa Ynez, creates custom treks for two or more cyclists. There are frequent stops for browsing, wine tasting, and snacking as you cruise past vineyards, lavender fields, and horse ranches, perhaps catching a glimpse of Michael Jackson's Neverland Ranch or the thoroughbred farm where *Seabiscuit* was filmed. The half-day rides cover 8 to 40 miles, depending on the riders' interests and abilities. "We stop along the way, we take cameras," says co-owner Tim Gorham, a retired geologist. "It's not a race or anything." Half-day tours with picnic lunch and vineyard wine tasting are $135; full-day rides are $160.

✂ **HORSEBACK RIDING Rancho Oso Guest Ranch** (805-683-5110; rancho-oso.com), 3750 Paradise Rd., Santa Barbara. This is a rural stable down Paradise Rd., one of the side roads that veers off Hwy. 154 near Cachuma Lake. Getting to the stables is a bit of an adventure; you'll traverse a twisting, often-pencil-thin route that runs through the Los Padres National Forest. Once you arrive at Rancho Oso, you'll find a friendly stable, where you can enjoy trail rides ($40 for a one-hour ride) through a scenic wilderness area.

HORSEBACK RIDING AT RANCHO OSO

EMUS AT OSTRICH LAND

A FOAL NIBBLES GRASS AT QUICKSILVER
MINIATURE HORSE RANCH

MORE ANIMAL ATTRACTIONS

Ostrich Land (805-686-9696), 610 E. Hwy. 246, Buellton. Open Mon.–Fri. 10–4, Sat.–Sun. 10–6. $4 adults, $1 children.

Quicksilver Miniature Horse Ranch (805-686-4002), 1555 Alamo Pintado Rd., Solvang. Open daily 10–3. Free.

Flag Is Up Farms (805-688–6288, montyroberts.com/flag_intro.html), 901 E. Hwy. 246, Solvang. Visitors are welcome daily 9 AM–5 PM, with no fee or reservation required, at the farm founded by Monty Roberts, horse whisperer and author of *The Man Who Listens to Horses*. Roberts created a nonprofit company to help spread the world about his humane, nonviolent method of training horses, which emphasizes instruction on equine psychology rather than riding skills. He offers courses and clinics.

✳ Wineries

Santa Barbara County has more than 20,000 acres of vineyards and over 100 wineries. Wine grapes are the county's number two agricultural product, exceeded only by strawberries, according to the Santa Barbara County Vintners' Association. Nearly 70 varieties of grapes are planted here, though 75 percent of the vineyards produce the region's Big Three—Chardonnay, Pinot Noir, and Syrah.

Some of the valley's best wineries are located along the Foxen Canyon Wine Trail (foxencanyonwinetrail.com), a route that winds along Foxen Canyon Road, from Los Olivos to Santa Maria. You'll find 16 wineries on and around the trail, and many other premium growers and tasting rooms throughout the valley and elsewhere in Santa Barbara County.

Here's a sampler of the region's wineries and tasting rooms.

Beckmen Vineyards (805-688-8664; beckmenvineyards.com), 2670 Ontiveros, Los Olivos 93441. Open daily 11–5. The Beckman winery is a small, family-run operation tucked along a dirt road, past a neighborhood llama farm, far enough from the highway that the wine-country tour buses don't find their way here. Owners Tom and Steve Beckmen are among the valley growers who have switched to biodynamic cultivation methods, a form of organic farming. They specialize in Rhône varietals, such as Syrah and Grenache, and their tasting room is housed in a sunny red barn. Outside, a gazebo overlooks a small duck pond where you can eat a picnic lunch or just enjoy the peaceful setting.

VINEYARDS ABOUND IN THE SANTA YNEZ VALLEY

Carina Cellars (805-688-2459; carinacellars.com), 2900 Grand Ave., Los Olivos 93441. Tasting room open 11 AM–5 PM daily. Carina Cellars is among the handful of winemakers with tasting rooms in downtown Los Olivos, and Carina's outpost on the town's charming main drag is a choice spot for sampling Syrahs and other Rhône varietals crafted in small, handcrafted lots. (Check the winemaker's website for coupons offering two-for-one tastings.) In 2009 Carina Cellars expanded its growing operation beyond the Santa Ynez Valley, moving north to open the new Rancho del Cielo, or "Ranch of the Sky," winery and vineyards, a 76-acre spread on the west side of Paso Robles.

Firestone (805-688-3940; firestonewine.com), 5000 Zaca Station Rd., Los Olivos 93441. Tasting room open 10 AM–5 PM daily. Firestone is a big winery in a visually beautiful setting, consisting of 500 acres of Chardonnay, Cabernet Sauvignon, Merlot, Sauvignon Blanc, and Syrah vineyards. It was part of the *Sideways* tour— this is the winery where Miles, Jack, and their two female friends wander back through the barrel room. You, too, can go behind the scenes at the winery's daily tours at 11:15 AM, 1:15 PM, and 3:15 PM. Firestone is a popular winery and can get crowded on weekends.

Foxen Winery & Vineyard (805-937-4251; foxenvineyard.com), 7200 Foxen Canyon Rd., Santa Maria 93454. Open daily 11 AM–4 PM. Long considered one of Santa Barbara's premium winemakers, Foxen received a makeover in 2009 with the completion of its new solar-powered winery and tasting room at the 2,000-acre Rancho Tinaquaic. Visitors to the new winery can taste Foxen's Burgundian and Rhône varietals, then head down to the property's modest wine shack to try the Cal-Ital and Bordeaux wines. Foxen owners Bill Wathen and Dick Doré have been making wine together here since 1985. Their winery is named in memory of William Benjamin Foxen, an English sea captain and Doré's great-great-grandfather, who came to Santa Barbara in the early 1800s. In 1837 the captain purchased Rancho Tinaquaic, a Mexican land grant that originally totaled nearly 9,000 acres and made up most of what is now known as Foxen Canyon.

Gainey Vineyard (805-688-0558; gaineyvineyard.com), 3950 E. Hwy. 246, Santa Ynez 93460. Open daily 10 AM–5 PM. Gainey is a stylish hacienda-style winery with Mission furnishings and handcrafted tilework throughout its inviting tasting center. The winery is set amid 1,000 acres of rangeland that the Gainey family has devoted to cat-

THIS RANCH HAS A MAGNIFICENT VIEW

tle, Arabian horses, and rolling vineyards on the east end of the Santa Ynez Valley. The focus is on Bordeaux varieties, Pinot Noir, Chardonnay, and Syrah. Free winery tours allow visitors a glimpse inside the winemaking process; the tours are held at 11 AM, 1 PM, 2 PM, and 3 PM.

Rancho Sisquoc (805-934-4332; ranchosisquoc.com), 6600 Foxen Canyon Rd., Santa Maria. Open Mon.–Thu. 10 AM–4 PM, Fri.–Sat. 10 AM–5 PM. The Rancho Sisquoc Winery is part of a 37,000-acre cattle ranch, a spectacular expanse of wide-open spaces, hills, and pastures along the Foxen Canyon Wine Trail. The vineyards produce Bordeaux, Burgundy, and Tuscan varietals grown on 300 acres of south-facing slopes along the Sisquoc River. Every fall winemakers from across Santa Barbara County gather here for the Vintners' Association's annual Harvest Celebration.

Roblar Winery and Cooking School (805-686-2603; http://roblarwinery.com), 3010 Roblar Ave., Santa Ynez 93460. Wine-paired lunches Mon.–Sat. 11 AM–3 PM; Sun. wine-paired brunch 11–3. Roblar produces a range of reds and whites, including Merlot, Syrah, Riesling, Cabernet Sauvignon, and Sauvignon Blanc. But the winery is about much more than grapes. Along with vineyards, the owners sowed fruit trees, a vegetable garden, and a chicken coop, and they built a demonstration kitchen where visitors could not only taste fine wine and food pairings, but also learn to create farm-to-table dishes themselves. Roblar offers a Saturday-evening cooking school and brings in guest chefs such as Leonardo Curti, the owner of Trattoria Grappolo in Santa Ynez, and Laurence Hauben, the French chef who heads Slow Food Santa Barbara. On Sunday the winery hosts a wine-tasting brunch where diners can graze an omelet station (with eggs from the farm's Rhode Island Red hens), a wine-paired buffet, and dessert bar.

MANY VALLEY VINEYARDS GROW THE BIG THREE: CHARDONNAY, PINOT NOIR, AND SYRAH GRAPES

WINE COUNTRY TIP
Instead of driving, let **Sustainable Vine Wine Tours** (sustainablevine .com) chauffer you around in a biodiesel Mercedes Benz Sprinter van to visit area wineries that are producing premium wines while engaging in sustainable agricul-

ture. Tours are $125 a person and include tastings at three locations, a gourmet organic picnic lunch, and door-to-door transportation from the Santa Barbara or Santa Ynez Valley areas.

Sanford Winery (805-688-3300; sanfordwinery.com), 7250 Santa Rosa Rd., Buellton 93427. Tasting room hours: 11 AM–4 PM daily. Sanford is located midway between Buellton and Lompoc in the Santa Rita Hills, another *Sideways* setting where Miles ostentatiously lectured his pal about the finer points of wine tasting. Sanford, known for its Pinot Noir, was the first winery in the area to plant Pinot Noir grapes. Owned by the Terlato family, Sanford strives to be a sustainable winery using energy-efficient and natural growing techniques, with 127 acres of the vineyard placed in a conservation easement to protect habitats and species on the property.

Sunstone Winery (805-688-9463; sunstonewinery.com), 125 N. Refugio Rd., Santa Ynez 93460-9303. Tasting room hours: 10 AM–4 PM daily. Sunstone is a sun-drenched vineyard with winery, gardens, courtyard, tasting room, and views that evoke Tuscany or Provence—a beautiful setting for picnics with a glass of red in hand, this winery's specialty. Sunstone's Syrahs and Eros wine, a blend of Bordeaux, have received numerous awards. The winery has been organic and pesticide-free for 20 years.

For more info: the **Santa Barbara County Vinters' Association** (805-688-0881; sbcountywines.com), 3669 Sagunto St., Santa Ynez 93460-1558, is a nonprofit group founded in 1983 to support the county's growing wine industry. Visit the association's website to request a wine-country guide.

✳ Lodging

You'll find a range of experiences in the valley, from camping and a fun, no-frills stays in a lakefront yurt, to the creature comforts and roaring fireplaces of small inns and an upscale dude ranch. Wherever you stay, you'll likely find a common ingredient: the quiet.

⊙ ❡ ⅃ ⁗Τ⁗ **Alisal Guest Ranch and Resort** (805-688-6411; alisal.com), 1054 Alisal Rd., Solvang 93463. Very expensive. Credit cards are accepted. Just outside the faux Danish hamlet of Solvang, this deluxe dude ranch has been welcoming families since 1946. The resort offers a lovely, if rather expensive, pastoral setting where guests can ride horses across a 10,000-acre working cattle ranch and savor western-style cottages with high-beamed ceilings and wood-burning fireplaces. There's no roughing it involved in staying at the Alisal, unless you consider the absence of in-room televisions and telephones a hardship. The ranch offers an impressive lineup of amenities and activities, including a 100-acre spring-fed lake for fishing and two 18-hole championship courses for golfers. Room rates include a breakfast buffet and dinner in the Ranch Room; guests are asked to dress for dinner. Spa, pool, and fitness center.

FISHING AT CACHUMA LAKE

& **Chumash Casino and Resort** (800-248-6274; chumashcasino.com), 3400 E. Hwy. 246, Santa Ynez 93460. Moderate–expensive. Credit cards are accepted. The Santa Ynez Band of Chumash Indians brought gaming to the valley in 2004 with the opening of the tribe's sprawling casino complex, which dwarfs everything else in the surrounding community. The casino offers a modern 106-room hotel with a swimming pool and spa. The property also boasts three restaurants, a show-room featuring such retro fare as Earth, Wind and Fire, and nonstop action at the slot machines and poker tables. The hotel is geared toward adults, so families traveling with children might want to consider other options; reservation clerks pointedly mention that children should not be left unattended in rooms and are not permitted to linger near gambling areas. Every day there's shuttle service between the casino and nearby communities including Santa Barbara, Lompoc, Santa Maria, and Goleta. The Chumash Casino isn't Vegas, but it is open 24/7. Located about 30 miles from Santa Barbara. Internet access $9.95 a night.

& **"ŋ" Fess Parker Wine Country Inn & Spa** (805-688-1942, 800-446-2455; fessparker.com; reservations @fessparker.com), 2860 Grand Ave., Los Olivos 93441. Expensive. Credit cards are accepted. Actor Fess Parker and his wife, Marcy, opened a nearby winery and this companion wine-country B&B, one of the valley's upscale inns. It's located on Los Olivos's highly strollable main drag, close to galleries, eateries, and tasting rooms. The inn's decor has a proper French country feel; rooms offer such cozy touches as down comforters and fireplaces. Rates include breakfast at the inn's Petros restaurant, and there's a two-night minimum stay on weekends. Spa.

& **Hadsten House Inn** (800-457-5373; hadstenhouse.com; info @HadstenHouse.com), 1450 Mission Dr., Solvang 93463. Moderate–expensive. Credit cards are accepted. This former motor lodge has been reborn as a stylish boutique inn in downtown Solvang, and it's one of the valley's more affordable and stylish lodgings. The 71 rooms have French modern furnishings with hardwood floors, fireplace, and flat-screen TV.

Nightly rates include a full breakfast. Guests are welcomed with a wine-and-cheese happy hour from 3 to 5 PM daily. Spa, heated pool, on-site restaurant.

 ♿ "↑" **Santa Ynez Inn** (805-688-5588; santaynezinn.com; info@santaynezinn.com), 3627 Sagunto St., Santa Ynez 93460. Expensive. Credit cards are accepted. This 20-room inn is an elegant Victorian-style B&B in the middle of town, walking distance to Santa Ynez's shops and restaurants. The property is nicely appointed with antique furnishings, flat-screen TVs, and the requisite wine-country fireplace in every room. Nightly rates include happy-hour wine and a full breakfast in the inn's dining room. There's a two-night minimum stay on weekends. Spa, whirlpool tubs.

Santa Ynez Vacation Rentals (805-245-9667; santaynezvacationrentals.com; info@santaynezvacationrentals), P.O. Box 704, Santa Ynez 93460.

Instead of staying in a hotel, consider renting a private home, ranch, cottage, or guesthouse in the Santa Ynez Valley. This might be a good option for extended family gatherings in wine country.

CAMPING Cachuma Lake Recreation Area (805-686-5054; sbparks.org), HC 59/Hwy. 154, Santa Barbara. Inexpensive. This large and well-maintained county park has three lakefront yurts (see the sidebar) with a two-night minimum on weekends; campsites and cabins also are available. A small general store on site carries necessities such as matches, firewood, and s'mores fixings, and there's a food stand open on the lake on weekends. Swimming is not permitted in the lake, but the swimming pool opens Memorial Day weekend for the summer season. Located about 5 miles east of Santa Ynez and a 25-mile drive from Santa Barbara. Flush toilets, showers, fire pits, picnic tables.

CACHUMA LAKE

YURT ADVENTURES AT CACHUMA LAKE

Cachuma Lake is just a few miles from Los Olivos and the other bucolic towns of the Santa Ynez Valley, so it makes for a great base of operations for touring the wine country, with the added bonus of having hiking, fishing, wildlife cruises, and glorious sunsets literally at your doorstep. If you're looking to go rustic, inexpensive, outdoorsy, and fun, Lake Cachuma is a good choice.

The lake is a bird lover's dream. It's a favorite haunt of the bald eagle during winter months and a great place to find unusual and beautiful birds all year long.

There are ample campsites and some cabins available at the park, but the lodging to try for is one of the lakeside yurts—they have the park's most primo location and come equipped with bunk beds, electricity, portable electric heaters (the wind can blow strong and cold off the chilly lake waters), and wraparound decks for sitting in the sun, gazing at the lake, and sipping that bottle of wine you picked up at one of the nearby wineries.

The park has just three yurts, so book your reservations well ahead of time, especially in summer. The yurts are sturdy wood-framed and canvas structures with locking front doors, rather than a tent-like flap opening—and they sit atop a tree-lined bluff overlooking the water. They have wood flooring, double-decker beds (queen-sized mattresses on the bottom, singles on top), and a cold-water faucet outside, along with a fire pit and picnic table. There are campground bathrooms with coin-operated showers, and strategically

YOU CAN RENT A WATERFRONT YURT AT CACHUMA LAKE

placed (and scrupulously clean) portable restrooms. All in all, a no-frills, spotless, lovely location.

The park offers a boat dock for renting small watercraft and fishing equipment. The trout fishing is good, with fishing lessons available for kids. There is no swimming in the lake, which serves as a reservoir for Santa Barbara, but the park has a swimming pool open from Memorial Day to Labor Day.

There are guided nature hikes and cruises, a general store, and a snack stand open on weekends. A charming Nature Center provides a wealth of local history and kid-pleasing, hands-on exhibits inside. The center's back room opens out to a wondrous bird-feeding station with a mirrored picture window where you can see hummingbirds, hooded orioles, band-tailed pigeons, bright blue scrub jays, blackbirds, acorn woodpeckers, tiny finches, mourning doves, and many other wild birds up close: Bird TV.

THE CACHUMA LAKE NATURE CENTER IS A MODEST WHITE BUILDING THAT HOSTS A WEALTH OF LOCAL HISTORY AND KID-PLEASING, HANDS-ON EXHIBITS.

DETAILS

Cachuma Lake Recreation Area (805-686-5054; sbparks.org), Hwy. 154, Santa Barbara. Lakefront yurts cost $60–70 a night and have a two-night minimum on weekends; a three-night minimum on holiday weekends. Campsites and cabins also are available. Day visit parking is $8.

BRING ALONG

Flashlights, toilet paper, sleeping bags, warm clothes, bug spray, food if you plan to cook, fishing gear if you plan to fish. Bicycles are a great addition, too—there are plenty of places to ride in the park.

CACHUMA LAKE

* Where to Eat

You'll eat well in the valley, where local farms supply restaurants with fresh fruits and vegetables. Here are a few choice spots to check out.

Brothers' Restaurant at Mattei's Tavern (805-688-482; matteistavern .com), 2350 Railway Ave., Los Olivos 93441. Open daily for dinner at 4 PM; last dinner seating at 9 PM. Expensive. Credit cards are accepted; you can make reservations online. First built in 1886 as a stagecoach stop, Los Olivos's famous tavern passed from generation after generation of the Mattei family. In 2002 new owners—brothers Matt and Jeff Nichols—finished renovating the familiar white landmark on the edge of town and created a new incarnation of their Brothers' restaurant. Their menu is a mix of the familiar (steak, lamb, a smattering of seafood and roast chicken breast stuffed with goat cheese) infused with local ingredients and served with Old West ambience. Said *Los Angeles Times* food critic S. Irene Virbila: "These are the kinds of unfussy dishes anybody would be happy to eat over and over (something that locals particularly appreciate)."

Cold Springs Tavern (805-967-0066; coldspringtavern.com), 5995 Stagecoach Rd, Santa Barbara 93105. Open daily, lunch 11 AM–3 PM, dinner at 5 PM; Sat.–Sun. breakfast 8–11 AM. Moderate–expensive. Credit cards are accepted. Time moves slowly—some say backward—at this Old California pub in the woods with its woodsy interior and red-checked curtains. Cold Springs Tavern has been a way station for travelers trekking through the mountains since 1865. It still attracts a loyal clientele. Don't miss the chance to stop by this funky old stagecoach stop covered with vines and hidden in the hills, about 15 minutes outside

Santa Barbara along Hwy. 154. Watch for the STAGECOACH ROAD sign—the turn comes up fast and can be easy to miss. The menu includes hearty offerings like pork chops and wild game black bean chili—a blend of venison, rabbit, and buffalo simmered with black beans and chiles. Cold Springs Tavern opens for breakfast on weekends, and there's usually live music on Friday, Saturday, and Sunday.

Hitching Post (805-688-0676; hitchingpost2.com), 406 E. Hwy. 246, Buellton 93427. Open daily 5–9:30 PM. Expensive. Credit cards are accepted. Reservations suggested. This western steak house and barbecue restaurant is known for its wonderful cuts of meat served with three kinds of potatoes and simple salads. Ostrich is also on the menu if you're feeling adventurous. The Hitching Post is a local treasure that became wildly popular with tourists after the movie *Sideways* debuted in 2004. In the film, Miles's romantic interest, Maya, worked as a waitress at the Hitching Post. The movie inspired tipplers to stop by the Hitching Post for drinks or dinner so they could bellow lines from the film, including Miles's explosion, "If anyone orders Merlot, I'm leaving . . ."

Los Olivos Café (805-688-7265; los olivoscafe.com), 2879 Grand Ave., Los Olivos 93441. Open daily 11:30 AM–10 PM. Moderate–expensive. Credit cards are accepted. This sunny bistro with a California-Mediterranean menu is always a delectable choice for lunch or dinner. The menu features fresh seasonal fare from local farms and dishes like the Caprese salad of organic tomatoes, fresh mozzarella, shaved red onion, basil, extra-virgin olive oil, balsamic reduction, and pine nuts. The café (which also had a cameo in *Sideways*) serves rustic pizzas, salads, and pastas for lunch; dinner offerings are

A TASTY SPOT FOR LUNCH OR PICNIC FARE: LOS OLIVOS GROCERY

more extensive, and there's always a tasting menu with a good selection of Central Coast wines.

⚫ **Los Olivos Grocery and Café** (805-688-5115; losolivosgrocery.com), 2621 W. Hwy. 154, Los Olivos 93460. Open daily 7 AM–9 PM. Moderate–expensive. Credit cards are accepted. The Los Olivos Grocery and Café is a well-stocked outpost that showcases the bounty of the Santa Ynez Valley. Stop here for breakfast or lunch on the patio, or to pick up picnic ingredients before you hit the local wine trail. The downside: The selection of salads, artisan cheeses, sandwiches, side dishes, fresh baked breads, and sweets is so vast and mouthwatering that it's always hard to make a choice as you're standing before the display counters. From homemade soups to curried chicken salad to Kobe steak burgers, this is a deli to die for.

Paula's Pancake House (805-688-2867), 1531 Mission Dr., Solvang 93463. Open daily 6 AM–3 PM. Price: Inexpensive. Credit cards are accepted. Come to this hometown favorite for light, fluffy Danish pancakes, served plain or heaped with fresh strawberries, blueberries, or cinnamon spiced apples. Breakfast is served all day at Paula's, and you'll want to follow the locals to this popular eatery on Solvang's main street. As one reviewer on Yelp put it: "Kind of reminded me of a Danish-themed IHOP."

⚫ **Trattoria Grappolo** (805-688-6899; trattoriagrappolo.com), 3687 Sagunto St., Santa Ynez 93460. Open Tue.–Sun. for lunch, 11 AM–2:30 PM; daily for dinner, 5–10 PM. Moderate–expensive. Credit cards are accepted. Reservations suggested on weekends. Located next to a cowboy bar in downtown Santa Ynez, Grappolo is a gem of an Italian trattoria with a wood-fired oven and exceptional pizza. (The eggplant pizza, for instance, is a simple menu item packed with unforgettable flavor.) The restaurant makes its own pasta, and chef Leonardi Curti specializes in rustic dishes such as veal scaloppine, homemade tortellini, and cioppino. Grappolo has a dedicated following, and after just one visit you'll see why people rave about the place.

(Curti and his team share their secrets in their cookbook *Trattoria Grappolo: Simple Recipes for Traditional Italian Cuisine.*)

BAKERIES Solvang is known for its authentic Danish pastries and other baked goods: the butter ring, a very buttery coffee cake filed with almond paste; the kringle, a traditional coffee cake shaped like a pretzel and stuffed with custard, raisins, and marzipan; and varieties of cookies, strudels, bear claws, and fruit-stuffed pastries. Real Danish baking employs generous amounts of real butter, almonds, and almond paste, and tastes rather different than the packaged, supermarket pastries most Americans know as "Danish." Here are few choice bakeries in town:

Mortensen's Danish Bakery (805-688-8373; greenhousesolvang.com /Bakery/Home.html), 1588 Mission Dr., has been family owned for 30 years; the kringle is very popular here.

Solvang Bakery (805-688-4939; solvangbakery.com), 460 Alisal Rd., offers a full complement of Danish

treats with a few twists: The jalapeño onion cheese bread is a crowd-pleaser, and even the *Live with Regis and Kelly* TV show took note of the bakery's personalized holiday gingerbread houses.

Danish Mill Bakery & Coffee Shop (805-688-5805; danishmillbakery.com), 1682 Copenhagen Dr., serves authentic Danish-style pastries. Another favorite on the breakfast menu is the "French Waffle," a crinkly torpedo pastry stuffed with raspberry and buttercream.

✳ Entertainment

NIGHTLIFE Maverick Saloon (805-686-4785; mavericksaloon.org), 3687 Sagunto St., Santa Ynez. Lively cowboy bar with live music in downtown Santa Ynez. Eat dinner at Trattoria Grappolo and then stroll next door to Maverick's.

Chumash Casino (800-CHUMASH; chumashcasino.com), 3400 E. Hwy. 246, Santa Ynez. It's big, new, and rather generic—plenty of slots, gaming tables. Visitors' biggest gripe: No free alcoholic drinks (or costly ones, for that matter) are served at the gaming tables or slots.

✳ Selective Shopping

Solvang Antique Center (805-688-6222; solvangantiques.com), 486 1st St., Solvang. If you're a collector or just a serious shopper, you'll want to browse the Solvang Antique Center. Anything you ever want to know about antiques, clocks, and watches can be discovered there. The center showcases 65 antiques dealers from around the world. Each week brings new arrivals of 18th- and 19th-century American and European antique furniture, antique clocks, decorative accessories, antique pocket watches and wristwatches, antique music boxes, lighting, pianos, rugs, paintings, prints, sculp-

THE BOOK LOFT IN SOLVANG

ture, porcelain, silver, estate jewelry, and other hard-to-find collector's items. Ron and Julie Palladino have been restoring and selling antiques for three decades.

The Book Loft (805-688-6010; bookloftsolvang.com), 1680 Mission Dr., Solvang. A well-stocked bookstore that features work by local and California writers, along with a collection of antiquarian books upstairs, the **Bulldog Coffee Shop** next door, and a small museum that celebrates Denmark's most famous writer.

FARMS Apple, blueberry, and produce growers sell fresh fruit and vegetables at roadside stands throughout the valley. The offerings change with the season, and often you can pull over to pick your own. Here's a taste:

Apple Lane Farm (805-688-5481, applelanesolvang.com), 1200 Alamo Pintado Rd., Solvang. Grows Gala, Golden and Red Delicious, Fuji, and Granny Smith apples; check for fruit from August through fall.

Los Olivos Homegrown, 2950 Grand Ave., Los Olivos. A farm stand featuring 60 types of garlic grown locally.

Greenhaven Orchard/Dittmar Farms (805-264-7100), 2275 Alamo Pintado Rd., Solvang. Doug Dittmar sells apples of all kinds each season from a table under a big oak tree.

Morrell Nut & Berry Farm (805-688-8969), 1980 Alamo Pintado Rd., Solvang. Pick raspberries and blackberries June–Sept.; sun-dried walnuts are ready in Oct. and Nov.

Restoration Oaks Ranch (805-686-5718; restorationoaksranch.com), 1980 Hwy. 101, Gaviota). This is a sprawling retreat with U-pick blueberry fields; sign up online and the owners will send you an e-mail alert when berries are ready to pick and ship.

Clairmont Farms (805-688-7505; clairmontfarms.com), 2480 Roblar St., Los Olivos. Five-acre lavender farm is open to the public and sells assorted scented products and potions.

Solvang Farmers Market (805-962-5354; sbfarmersmarket.org). Every Wed. growers bring fresh produce, flowers, and baked goods to downtown Solvang, at Copenhagen Dr. and 1st St., 2–6 PM.

✳ Special Events

March: **Solvang Century & Half-Century Bike Ride** (bikescor.com /solvang) attracts more than 5,000 cyclists. **Taste of Solvang** (800-468-6765; solvangusa.com) is an annual food and wine festival.

April: **Vintners Festival** (805-688-0881; sbcountywines.com), Lompoc.

June: **Old Santa Ynez Day** (santa ynezvalleyvisit.com)—parade, arts and crafts, live music. **Jazz and Olive Festival** (losolivosrotary.com), Los Olivos.

TAKE A TRAIL RIDE AT RANCHO OSO

August: **Old Mission Santa Inez Fiesta** (805-688-4815; missionsanta ines.org), Solvang. **Wheels 'n Windmills Car Show** (805-688-6144; wheelsnwindmills.com), Solvang.

September: **Danish Days** (805-688-6144; solvangusa.com)—a celebration of Solvang's heritage.

October: **Harvest Celebration** (805-688-0881; sbcountywines.com), hosted by the Santa Barbara County Vintners' Association.

Coastal Santa Barbara County

3

COASTAL SANTA BARBARA COUNTY

"The Gaviota Coast is a miracle of modern conservation . . . It's best in the winter when it's all lit up and green, the surf is pumping the and the offshores are blowing, but year round it's nice to see a stretch of coast that's been mostly untouched."

—Surfer Magazine's Guide to Southern California Surf Spots

The Gaviota Coast is a 40-mile national treasure, a magical blend of mountains, cliffs, beaches, and unspoiled views arcing across the western edge of Santa Barbara County, where the coastal highway twists and dangles above a vast edge of Pacific blue. The area encompasses half of Southern California's remaining undeveloped coastline.

You can gaze in any direction from the bluffs at El Capitan and soak up California at its untamed best, basking in an endless expanse of foaming surf and ribbons of silvery sand. You'll marvel at distant wind-sculpted ridges untouched except for the occasional hiker or flock of seagulls. You can't help but feel small as you're tromping through the ancient forest that hugs the shore, the same woods that the Central Coast's earliest settlers, the Chumash people, roamed more than 8,000 years ago. On clear days, after the morning's foggy blanket has lifted, you can peer across the waves and see the Channel Islands.

ALONG THE GAVIOTA COAST: BEAUTIFUL AND UNSPOILED

Thirty miles up the coast from Santa Barbara past Goleta, the long and slender beach at El Capitan is a rugged state park where you can kayak, picnic, hike, and pitch tents close to the sand. In summer months the

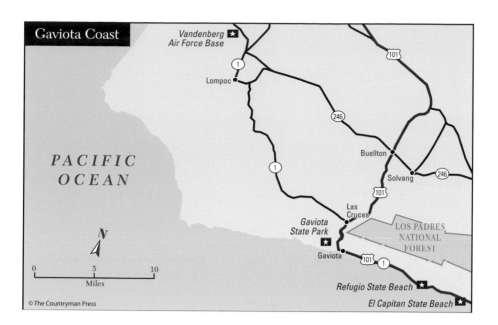

Gaviota Coast

Vandenberg
Air Force Base

Lompoc

PACIFIC
OCEAN

Buellton

Solvang

N

Las
Cruces

Gaviota
State Park

LOS PADRES
NATIONAL
FOREST

Gaviota

0   5   10
Miles

© The Countryman Press

Refugio State Beach

El Capitan State Beach

shoreline teems with families playing in the surf and tiny crabs scurrying for cover in the rocks and tide pools. Red-tailed hawks soar high above the winding bike trail that meanders along the bluffs for several miles to Refugio State Beach, another coastal campground.

You'll find mile after mile of wide-open beachfront, pastoral ranchlands, and wooded arroyos along this rocky edge of Santa Barbara County. And you'll especially savor what isn't here: There are no oceanfront villas or condos or cookie-cutter motels. No Starbucks or strip malls or much of anything else, even remotely close.

Environmentalists, surfers, and area residents have tried hard to keep it that way, fighting to block development near El Capitan and along the entire Gaviota Coast, which extends from Coal Oil Point in Goleta to Point Sal near Lompoc. *Gaviota* is Spanish for "seagull" and it's a fitting name for this biologically rich zone, where the Pacific meets the Santa Ynez Mountains and California's northern and southern ecosystems merge. Dozens of rare animal and plant species thrive along the shore and in the nearby coastal canyon. The region's archaeological sites date back to the Chumash Indians' first encampment here at Ajuilashmu (*ah-wah-whi-lac-mu*), the dancing place of celebration by the sea.

The local community's sustained commitment to preservation has kept this coastal corridor wild and accessible to all who want to enjoy its charms.

You'll find a handful of beachfront campgrounds along the Gaviota Coast, including the state parks at El Capitan, El Refugio, and Gaviota, and the county park at Jalama Beach, a remote surf spot near Lompoc, about an hour north of Santa Barbara. If you like nature but don't care much for sleeping bags, you can check into a cool eco-lodge tucked away in a canyon near El Capitan or book a cottage at a secluded dude ranch in the nearby hillsides.

The Gaviota Coast is a good base of operations for exploring the Santa Barbara

EL CAPITAN

region. You can savor a range of experiences: El Capitan is just short drive—less than half an hour or so—along Highway 101 from the city of Santa Barbara, and the inland Santa Ynez Valley wine country is an easy day trek in the opposite direction.

As you drive along the Gaviota Coast, you'll be tempted to pull over at the various overlook spots and stand atop the bluffs watching the waves crash and the surfers working the swell. Another way to enjoy this beautiful area: Take the train. Both Highway 1 and the 101 freeway veer inland near Gaviota State Park. But the train tracks run right along the shoreline between Santa Barbara and San Luis Obispo, through the vast Vandenberg Air Force Base, where the California coastline juts out into the Pacific. It's an unforgettable ride.

Summer months are the busiest time of year along the Santa Barbara coast, so you'll want to book campgrounds and cottages here as early as possible.

GUIDANCE Gaviota Coast Conservancy (gaviotacoastconservancy.org).

Goleta Valley Chamber of Commerce (800-646-5382; goletavalleychamber .com), 271 N. Fairview, Ste. 104, P.O. Box 781, Goleta 93116.

Green Santa Barbara (greensantabarbara.com). The area's eco-friendly side.

Santa Barbara Conference & Visitors Bureau (805-966-9222; santabarbaraca .com), 1601 Anacapa St., Santa Barbara 93101. Travel info and bookings for Santa Barbara County.

Santa Barbara Surfrider (surfrider.org/santabarbara).

Tixity (tixity.com). Check local events here.

Ventura Visitors and Convention Center (805-648-2075, 800-483-6214; ventura-usa.com), 101 S. California St., Ventura 93001. Travel info and events.

GETTING THERE

By car:

From San Francisco: Take Hwy. 101 south until you reach Santa Barbara County. You'll see exits for El Capitan, Refugio, and Gaviota State Beach campgrounds right off the highway.

From Los Angeles: Take Hwy. 101 north past Santa Barbara and Goleta until you reach the Gaviota Coast. The first coastal campground area you'll reach is El Capitan State Beach.

From the east: Traveling from inland Santa Barbara County and the Santa Ynez Valley, take scenic Hwy. 154 or 246 to the 101 freeway and head toward the coast.

By air: You can fly into **Santa Barbara Municipal Airport** (SBA), just north of the city, or Los Angeles International (LAX), which is about 100 miles to the south. See the Santa Barbara chapter for airline information and ground transportation.

By train: **Amtrak** (800-872-7245; amtrak.com) offers daily service along the Central Coast. The closest stations to the Gaviota Coast are in Santa Barbara and Goleta. Trains also stop at the remote Surf Beach outpost near Lompoc. It's a tiny station right on the sand, adjacent to Vandenberg Air Force Base.

Amtrak's Pacific Surfliner runs between San Diego and San Luis Obispo, and trains are equipped with bicycle and surfboard racks. Amtrak's double-decker Coast Starlight runs from Los Angeles to Seattle. Santa Barbara's Amtrak station is downtown at 209 State St., two blocks from the beach. The Goleta train station is at 25 S. La Patera Lane, but there are no ticket sales in Goleta, so you have to pay on the train.

TIDE POOL

✳ To See

Vandenberg Air Force Base (805-606-3595; vandenberg.af.mil) is the government's vast space and ballistic missile test facility along the northern end of the Santa Barbara County coast that spans 98,400 acres. The base covers more ground than the nearby cities of Lompoc, Santa Maria, and Guadalupe combined. Much of the base is rugged, mountainous, and undeveloped, and the wild lands here are home to numerous endangered and threatened species, including the western snowy plover, a shorebird. The area has three civilian access beaches, including Surf Beach, which has a tiny train station served daily by Amtrak. Although Vandenberg Air Force Base is a closed facility, public tours are offered on the second Wednesday of each month. Reservations are required at least two weeks in advance. Children must be at least 10 years old to attend a tour. Visitors should arrive at the Main Gate Visitor Control Center by 9:45 AM for check-in; tours conclude around 12:30 PM. The base is 9 miles south of Lompoc, and the VAFB website offers detailed directions and maps for getting there.

University of California–Santa Barbara (805-893-8000; ucsb.edu). Located near Goleta in the Isla Vista area, the UC Santa Barbara campus covers more than 1,000 acres near the coast and is a community of more than 20,000 students and staff. Check the university website for the latest events.

✳ To Do

BIKING Try the coastal bike trail from El Capitan State Beach to Refugio State Beach, a 3-mile trek. Refugio Beach, at the mouth of Refugio Canyon, is a rocky beach with tide pools. Turn around here, or continue pedaling up-coast (it's 10 more miles to Gaviota State Beach). You also can hike along this trail.

FARM VISITS Stop by the **Restoration Oaks Ranch** (805-686-5718; restorationoaksranch.com), 1980 Hwy. 101, Gaviota, and pick your own blueberries during spring and summer. The farm offers several different varieties. Call first or check online to make sure the ranch is open. Or visit **Fairview Gardens** (805-967-7369; fairviewgardens.org), 598 N. Fairview Ave., Goleta), a 12-acre farm that produces a vast variety of fruits and vegetables. There's a self-guided tour with 23 different stations, and a produce stand out front with the daily bounty. The farm is open seven days a week, 10 AM–sunset.

HORSEBACK RIDING Saddle up and explore this gorgeous terrain. The **Circle Bar B Ranch** (805-968-1113; circlebarb.com), 1800 Refugio Rd, Goleta, welcomes day visitors for horseback treks through the hills. The cost: $37 for a 1½-hour ride; $75 for a half-day outing; call ahead for reservations.

✳ Lodging

The Gaviota Coast has few lodgings, but there's no shortage of rugged campsites in wilderness areas right along the beach. You'll want to bring supplies for any activities you have planned because there are few places to shop or eat once you get past Goleta. Don't forget: bug spray, fire starters, firewood, flashlights, bottled water, and ingredients for campfire s'mores. Bring provisions if you plan to cook.

EL CAPITAN CANYON IS AN ECO-FRIENDLY RESORT WITH CEDAR CABINS AND LUXURY TENT CAMPING

Beach Rd. exit, and a 10-minute walk from the state beach, this eco-friendly resort offers stays in airy cedar cabins surrounded and shaded by leafy stands of giant sycamores and oaks. A fresh-water creek winds through the trees and across the 300-acre property, providing sanctuary to a host of woodland creatures. The cabins are compact but very comfortable, with hardwood floors, kitchenette, full bathroom, and buttery soft bed linens that feel like they belong at a fancy hotel instead of a coastal campout. Some primo cabins have hot tubs; many come with lofts accessible by climbing ladders, one of many kid-pleasing touches at El Capitan Canyon. Each cabin has a picnic table and fire pit, which comes in handy if you want to grill steaks or sit outside by a roaring fire sipping some of the locally grown Pinot Noir. If all this sounds kind of wimpy, you can always skip the cushy cabins and book a cushy tent instead—canvas safari tents are built on raised wooden decks and outfitted with queen bed, willow chest of drawers, and reading lights, so you can rough it in comfort. El Capi-

🐾 ♿ **El Capitan Canyon Resort**
(866-352-2729; elcapitancanyon.com; terri@elcapitancanyon.com), 11560 Calle Real, Santa Barbara 93117. Moderate–expensive. Credit cards are accepted. El Capitan Canyon is a haven for travelers who enjoy nature—but crave luxury, too. Just off Hwy. 101, next to the El Capitan State

A CABIN AT EL CAPITAN CANYON

tan Canyon offers a fleet of beach cruisers for guests to ride; there are miles of hilly trails for hiking and docent-led treks to a nearby llama farm. Bird lovers will savor the joy of seeing red-splashed woodpeckers and other unusual birds perched in the trees all around. Solar-heated swimming pool; canyon market for dining.

 **Circle Bar B Guest Ranch** (805-968-1113; circlebarb.com; circle barb.info@gmail.com), 800 Refugio Rd., Goleta 93117. Expensive–very expensive. Credit cards are accepted. Hidden away in Refugio Canyon near former president Reagan's mountain ranch, the Circle Bar B guest ranch is a friendly and fun getaway for families, though it's pricey, especially if you're traveling with a group. The hillside cottages are cozy with a rustic charm, and you'll find it easy to unplug here because there are no phones or TVs in the rooms. Instead families can play pool and other games in the ranch house and enjoy nature hikes in the area. Meals are tasty and generous (breakfast, lunch, and dinner are included in nightly rates). One of the best parts of staying at the Circle Bar B is saddling up to go horseback riding and making your way up through the hillsides to ridges that offer sweeping views of the coast and the canyon. Even if you don't stay at the ranch, you can make reservations at Circle Bar B to go horseback riding. The ranch has a dinner theater show on weekends in the old barn. Swimming pool, hot tub.

CAMPING The region's state and county campgrounds are right along the shore, and parks are open for day use as well as overnight stays.

El Capitan State Beach (info 805-968-1033, reservations 800-444-7275; parks.ca.gov or reserveamerica.com), El Capitan Beach State Park (just off Hwy. 101 at the El Capitan exit), Goleta 93117. Inexpensive. El Capitan State Beach has a sandy beach, rocky tide pools, and stands of towering sycamore and oak trees along El Capitan Creek. A stairway provides access from the bluffs to the beach area. Visitors can swim, fish, surf, picnic, and stay overnight at campsites. The park has more than 100 campsites with fire

EL CAPITAN BEACH

WALKING BACK FROM THE BEACH TO EL CAPITAN CANYON

rings, picnic tables, pay showers, restrooms, and a small park store. Pets are allowed in the campground, but not on the beach. No hookups are available. Be sure to make reservations. Group campsites are available. Nature trek: There's a 3-mile hiking or biking trail to Refugio State Beach to the north.

Gaviota State Beach (info 805-968-1033, reservations 800-444-7275; parks.ca.gov or reserveamerica.com), Gaviota Beach Rd. (33 miles from Santa Barbara on Hwy. 101), Gaviota 93117. Inexpensive. Marked by a tall railroad trestle that crosses Gaviota Creek high above the beach parking lot, this park is a popular spot for swimming, picnicking, surf fishing, and camping. Rangers, however, caution that visitors should be prepared for high winds along the coast here. Gaviota State Beach has 39 campsites, and reservations are available Memorial Day–Labor Day. Anglers and divers use the pier on the west end of the beach, and there's a boat hoist, too. Visitors can hike the rugged upland portions of the park from a trailhead in the parking area; ambitious hikers can climb to Gaviota Peak for great views

of the coast and the Channel Islands. Campsite amenities include showers, restrooms, and a convenience store. The campground is closed Oct.–Mar.

Jalama Beach County Park (805-736-3504, 805-736-6316; countyofsb.org/parks), 9999 Jalama Rd., Lompoc 93436. Inexpensive. Located north of Santa Barbara and south of Vandenberg Air Force Base, this isolated 23-acre county park is a favorite with families and especially surfers. Surf line.com offers this take on Jalama: "Considerably bigger and much more exposed than the county's relatively tame south coast, Jalama packs a mean punch, summer or winter, so you can expect truckloads of juice out here if the swell's pumping." Jalama has 98 campsites with fire pits, picnic tables, bathrooms, and showers. Single campsites and RV sites with hookups are available. The park is also the home of Jalama Beach Cafe, a full-service eatery where you can have breakfast, lunch, or dinner and pick up supplies, too.

Refugio State Beach (805-968-1033; reservations 800-444-7275; parks.ca .gov or reserveamerica.com), 10 Refugio Beach Rd. (on Hwy. 101 at the

BEACHES

Beaches are the reason to come here, and as you cruise Highway 101 north of Santa Barbara, you can take your pick of beautiful ones. There's **El Capitan State Beach**, **Refugio State Beach**, and **Gaviota State Beach**, as well as the county's **Jalama Beach**, a surf spot accessi-

ble by the winding road through the Santa Ynez Mountains. Another sweet spot: **Surf Beach**, a 0.5-mile stretch of beachfront adjacent to Vandenberg Air Force Base (vandenberg.af.mil). Surf Beach has its own train station right on the sand near Lompoc; Amtrak's Surfliner stops here daily. Surf Beach also is one of three base beaches that is home to the endangered western snowy plover. The US Fish and Wildlife Service posts signs limiting public access during the bird's nesting season, Mar.–Sept. For a rundown on Central Coast beaches, and current surf conditions, visit Surfline.com.

Refugio exit), Goleta 93117. Inexpensive. Flanked by palm trees, Refugio State Beach is a lovely spot for swimming, fishing, hiking, or enjoying a picnic on the sand. The campground has fire rings, picnic tables, restrooms, pay showers, and a small convenience store, but no RV hookups. Campsites are open year-round, though Refugio sometimes shuts down due to winter flooding. The hiking and biking trail here runs 3 miles to nearby El Capitan State Park.

⁽ᵀ⁾ **Ocean Mesa** (866-410-5783; oceanmesa.com), 100 El Capitan Terrace Lane (next to El Capitan Canyon, just off Hwy. 101), Santa Barbara 93117. Inexpensive. This is a separate campground run by the El Capitan Canyon Resort. Tent and RV camping are available, along with a heated swimming pool and WiFi. Other

amenities include laundry facilities, an ATM, and a convenience store.

✳ South Along the Coast

The towns south of Santa Barbara have much to offer visitors, from great beaches to inland adventures in the region's rich, rolling farming belt. Here's a few highlights of what you'll find as you head south from Santa Barbara along the 101 Highway toward Los Angeles.

The tiny hamlet of Summerland, population 1,500, is the easy-to-miss stop on Highway 101 just south of the Santa Barbara city limits. A funky little beach town, it has a great beach overlook, a namesake winery boutique, several antiques stores, a good breakfast spot, and a quirky history as a haven for spiritualists and mystics. It's certainly easy to navigate: The restaurants and businesses are mostly arrayed along the main drag, Lillie Avenue, which parallels the highway, with the houses rising up the adjacent hillside in a pleasant hodgepodge of styles and winding, narrow streets. The ocean can be seen and reached from **Lookout Park**, set on the cliffs overlooking Summerland's sandy beach. Walkways and trails connect the overlook park area to the beach in a mile-long loop, and there are tide pools in the vicinity. The **Summerland Beach Café** (805-565-9463; summerlandbeachcafe.com), 2294 Lillie Ave., offers a hearty breakfast and lunch menu and a pleasant outdoor patio, and while the vineyards are inland, **Summerland Winery** (805-565-9463, summerlandwine.com), 2330 Lillie Ave., has its tasting room and boutique here. The town was founded in 1883 by H. L. Williams as a community of spiritualists; the community center was known as the séance room for many years until it was razed

in the 1950s during the construction of Highway 101. The founder's home, known as the Big Yellow House, was for many years a popular restaurant stop for travelers, and though it has been closed since 2007, it remains the best-known landmark in town, and most easily spotted Summerland feature from the highway.

Carpinteria. This town of about 14,000 at the southern coastal edge of Santa Barbara County offers several beautiful beaches, including a world-class surfing spot, Rincon Point, and a quaint downtown shopping district. It sits astride Highway 101 about 12 miles south of Santa Barbara, and has an Amtrak station downtown for car-free visits. There are two main drags: Carpinteria Avenue parallels the 101 and is the road into and out of town; the primary cross street is Linden Avenue, which leads to the beach. Linden is the town's major restaurant and shopping avenue (lindenavenue.com),

THE FAIRWAYS AT THE OJAI VALLEY INN & SPA IN OJAI

THE CHANNEL ISLANDS

Channel Islands National Park (nps.gov/chis/index.htm) is a group of five protected islands just off the Central California coast: Anacapa, Santa Cruz, Santa Rosa, San Miguel, and Santa Barbara.

The closest island is Anacapa, 12 miles from the mainland, and it's an easy day trip. The largest and most diverse island is Santa Cruz, the site of Painted Cave, one of the largest known sea caves in the world.

Traveling from Ventura Harbor to east Santa Cruz Island's Scorpion Anchorage takes about an hour. If you're feeling adventurous, plan an overnight camping trip to Santa Cruz Island. Scorpion campground is the largest on any of the islands, and you have to pack in/pack out everything you bring, including trash. At night on the island, the ocean is so wild and dark blue that the sky just seems to melt into the Pacific. The stargazing is great. You'll feel like you're in another universe, not a mere 20 miles off the California coast.

SEA LIONS

During daylight hours, Santa Cruz Island is a nature playground where you can swim, hike, snorkel, and dive. The sea kayaking is particularly awesome here, though you'll want to make sure that you go with a guide if you are venturing into the island's caves, which actually glow in multicolors, including emerald green. **Aquasports** (805-968-7231; islandkayaking.com), 111 Verona Ave., Goleta, offers experienced guides who can help you explore the island's sea caves, truly a one-of-a-kind experience. Another choice for cave treks: **Paddle Sports** (805-899-4925; www.kayaksb.com), 117 B Harbor Way, Santa Barbara. The park website (nps.gov/chis/park mgmt/visitor-services-list.htm) offers additional resources.

In 2009 the island's new Scorpion Ranch Visitor Center opened, and you'll get an interesting overview there of the island's natural and cultural history. **Island Packers** (805-642-1393; islandpackers.com), the concessionaire boat company for the Channel Islands, can help you plan your trip.

In addition to being the largest Channel Island, Santa Cruz also is the most diverse, with two mountain ranges, at least 600 plant species, and more than 120 species of land birds including the endemic island scrub jay, which is found nowhere else in the world. Island Packers also offers excursions to other islands, as well as whale-watching treks during the year into waters where dolphins, seals, and sea lions also abound.

as well as the location of the annual **California Avocado Festival** (avofest.com), a three-day, guacamole-drenched street fair every October featuring multiple live band stages, arts-and-crafts sales, and various contests revolving around the namesake fruit.

Carpinteria State Beach and its popular full-service campground (reservations 800-444-7275; parks.ca.gov) feature a mile-long broad stretch of sand and bluffs with gentle surf (residents call it the "safest beach in the world" because of the lack of undertow), tide pools, hiking, bird-watching, fishing, and clamming. There is a small visitors center with exhibits about marine life and Chumash history (the Spanish named the area Carpinteria after seeing the Chumash "carpenter shop" for building canoes). A short hike down coast from the state beach leads to a harbor seal rookery preserve (one of four in the state). The rookery is "seals-only" May through December, but visitors still can observe the colony from an observation area on the bluffs above the beach. **City Bluffs Park** (at the Ballard exit from Hwy. 101) offers breathtaking views of a nature preserve that Carpinteria residents established after a long battle to save it from development. Bring a picnic lunch and enjoy the view, or take a look in the bluffs' parking lot, where you can find most days a local institution, the "Surf Dog" hot dog truck (silcom.com/~ricky/surfdog.htm). Farther south, straddling the county line at the Bates Rd. exit on Hwy. 101, is the renowned surfer's beach at **Rincon Beach County Park** (countyofsb.org/parks).

Ojai. When film director Frank Capra was making the 1937 classic *Lost Horizon*, he chose Ojai for his scene-setting shots of the mythic, utopian Shangri-la, and the area is still prized for its natural beauty as well as for the town's artistic sensibilities. Ojai is a place to retreat and relax, home to spas and hot springs, nature hikes and art walks. There are 24 different hiking paths in the valley to experience Ojai out-of-doors, from simple nature strolls on the edge of town to the ambitious 6-mile "Last Chance Trail" through Santa Paula Canyon. **The Lavender Inn** (805-646-6635; lavenderinn.com), 210 E. Matilija St., a historic schoolhouse converted to a B&B, offers spa treatments, aromatherapy, and serves as headquarters for the Ojai Culinary School, which offers classes to guests and visitors. Ojai also boasts the stand-alone **Ojai Culinary Studio** (805-646-1124; ojaiculinary.com), 315 N. Montgomery St., run by chef Nancy Michali. The ultimate pamper treatment is available in town, too, at the pricey but lovely **Ojai Valley Inn and Spa** (800-422-6524; ojairesort.com), 905 Country Club Rd.

The shopping arcade in the center

AT THE OJAI VALLEY INN & SPA

of town has an array of galleries and shops, including a unique outdoor bookstore, **Bart's** (bartsbooks.com) and the **Rainbow Bridge** (805-646-4017), 211 E. Matilija St., a well-stocked health food market and café. Another choice spot: **Suzanne's Cuisine** (805-640-1961; suzannescuisine.com), 502 W. Ojai Ave., an upscale eatery featuring locally grown organic fare. Ojai hosts a number of annual events, including these, all in June: the **Ojai Music Festival** (ojaifestival.org); the **Ojai Wine Festival** (ojaiwinefestival.com); and the **Ojai Lavender Festival** (ojaivalleylavenderfestival.org), celebrating an abundant and aromatic local crop.

Ventura. Thirty miles south of Santa Barbara, Ventura is a beach city of 107,000 with fine beaches for swimming, surfing, and fishing(ventura.com/activities/beaches) and a vibrant Main Street district, home of the charming San Buenaventura Mission (805-643-4318; sanbuenaventuramission.org), at 225 E. Main St. San Buenaventura was the ninth and final California mission founded by Father Junipero Serra; it remains a working Catholic parish and museum just three blocks from the ocean.

For a unique AG adventure, check out Ventura County's largest and oldest grower, **Limoneira**, which has 7,000 acres of lemons, avocados, and other fruits and produce. Located 12 miles east of the city of Ventura on Hwy. 126, **Limoneira Ranch** (866-321-9995; limoneiratours.com), 1141 Cummings Rd., Santa Paula, offers tours of the orchards and historic packing-house, hot-air balloon rides, and a learning center/general store.

In Ventura you'll find the **Deckers Factory Outlet Store** (805-676-3571; deckers.com), 4880 Colt St. It's a small, out-of-the-way shop, but this is where you'll find a closeout outlet for Simple, Teva, and Ugg Australia shoes and boots. As at all outlets, the selection is hit or miss, but sometimes there are good bargains. Fifteen miles south of Ventura on Hwy. 101, you'll find a far bigger selection of shops at the **Camarillo Premium Outlets** (805-445-8520; premiumoutlets.com), 740 E. Ventura Blvd., Camarillo. There are 160 stores, including Banana Republic Factory Store, Barneys New York, Coach, Cole Haan, Gap Factory Store, J. Crew, Kenneth Cole, Lucky Brand, Neiman Marcus Last Call, Nike, Polo Ralph Lauren, and Saks Fifth Avenue Off 5th.

✳ Where to Eat

Dining options (and development in general) are limited as you get past Goleta on Hwy. 101 to the Gaviota Coast. But here are a few choices.

"1" **Beachside Bar-Cafe** (805-964-7881), 905 Sandspit Rd., Goleta 93117. Open Sun.–Thu. 11:30 AM–9:30 PM, Fri. 11:30 AM–10 PM, Sat. 11 AM–10 PM, Sun. 11 AM–9:30 PM. Moderate–expensive. Credit cards are accepted. This pleasant café is right on the pier in Goleta, about a mile from the UCSB campus. It's a quiet spot with good food, good cocktails, and very nice views of the waves breaking just outside. It makes a convenient pit stop or meeting place on your way up the coast. WiFi is available, too.

Canyon Market and Deli at El Capitan Canyon (866-353-2729; elcapitancanyon.com), 11560 Calle Real, Santa Barbara 93117. Open daily 11:30 AM–closing (hours vary through the year). Moderate. Credit cards are accepted. The market serves simple, mostly organic fare and doubles as an upscale convenience store with a selection of Santa Ynez Valley wines. Guests can nosh on deli sandwiches, pesto pizza, salads, chocolate ice cream bars,

THE MARKET AT EL CAPITAN CANYON

and espresso drinks; the food is freshly made and delectable. It's the only restaurant for miles around. The market serves barbecue dinners on Saturday evenings. Or you can pick up a ready-made BBQ Kit (with hamburgers, tri-tip, chicken, or fish, plus all the fixings) to cook up your own feast any night of the week. The market also sells handy s'mores kits—a brown-bag sack filled with four roasting sticks, graham crackers, Hershey bars, and a big bag of marshmallows. El Capitan Canyon has live concerts on Saturday nights during summer months: free for resort guests, $10 for visitors.

Jalama Beach Cafe (805-735-8205; jalamabeach.com), 400 E. Ocean Ave., Lompoc 93436. Open daily from 6 AM to "sometimes 9 PM and sometimes 9:30." Moderate. Credit cards are accepted. This local diner is a favorite with the surfers and campers who come to Jalama County Beach. Try the burritos and the house specialty—the Jalama Burger, a ⅓-pounder heaped with lettuce, tomatoes, red onion, and secret sauce. The café also is a local store where you can pick up camping supplies.

✳ Special Events

October: **California Lemon Festival** (800-646-5382; lemonfestival.com). For the past two decades the festival has been a community favorite, with pie-eating contests, entertainment, arts-and-crafts vendors, and the Goleta Fall Classic Car Show.

San Luis Obispo 4

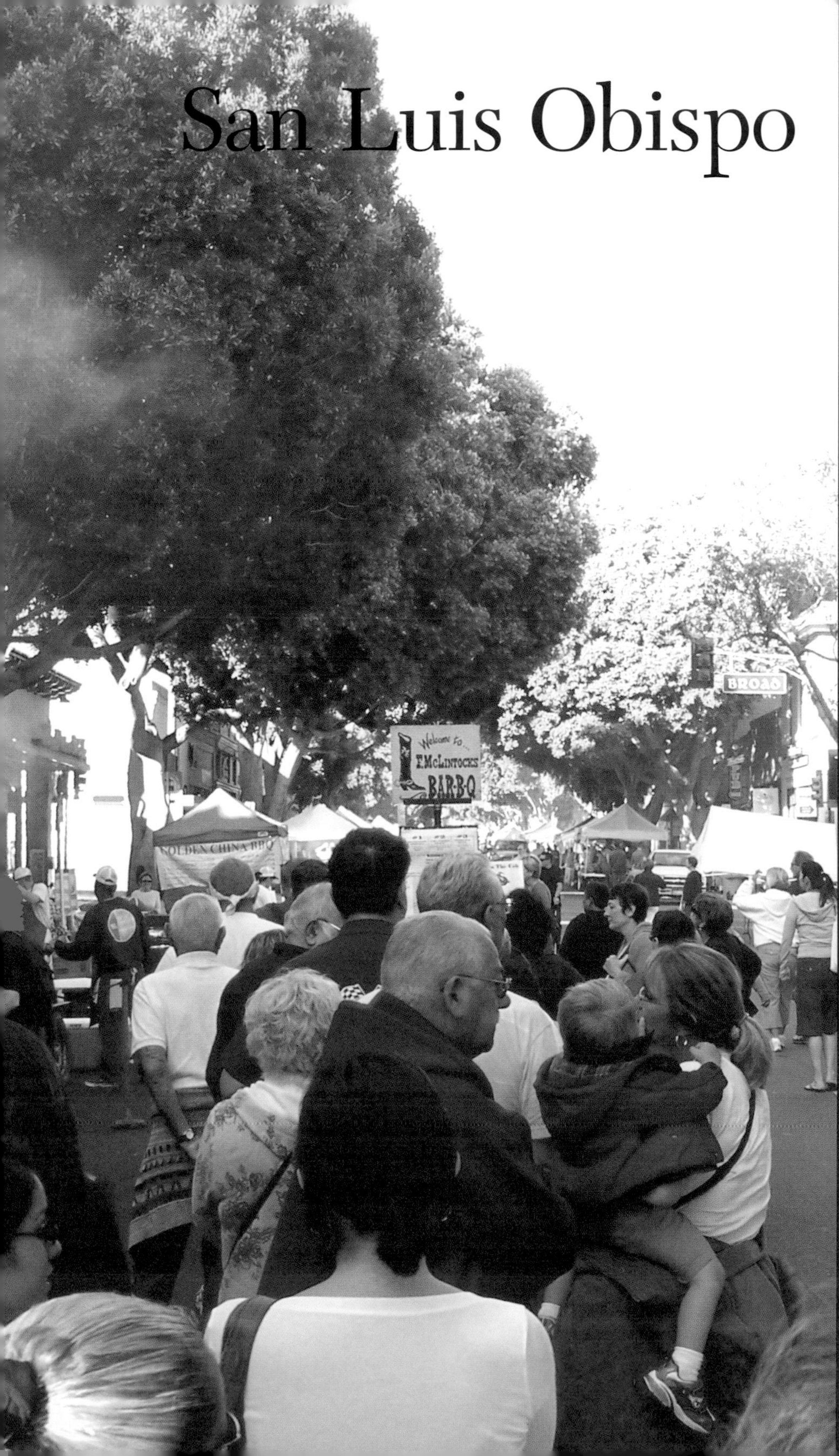

SAN LUIS OBISPO

"What we have is a highly educated country town, almost a beach town, trying very hard not to become someplace else."

—Mike Steere, *Outside* magazine

Father Junipero Serra founded this bucolic Central Coast town in September 1772 when he established the Mission San Luis Obispo de Tulsa beside a gurgling creek in a lush valley. Serra liked the mild climate, the friendly Chumash Natives, and the abundance of bear meat to feed the faithful up and down the coast. His padres, then the settlers who followed them, raised crops, livestock, and wine grapes, gradually transforming California's fifth mission into a thriving community.

San Luis Obispo is now a city of 44,000 and home to the sprawling California State Polytechnic University campus, yet it has not strayed far from the roots Serra planted three centuries ago. After all those years, fertile soil, bountiful farms, a deep appreciation for the region's natural beauty, and a friendly, homey atmosphere still are San Luis Obispo's defining qualities and greatest attractions.

DRIVING THROUGH SAN LUIS OBISPO'S GREEN ACRES

The Franciscan mission's red-tiled adobe remains the cultural and spiritual epicenter of San Luis Obispo's unpretentious downtown. The picturesque mission serves a local parish of about 2,000 families. It's also downtown's signature destination. Visitors come to browse the historical museum and wander the grounds, where a brick path winds past the mission's rose garden, grapevines spill over the arbors, and some of the area's oldest olive

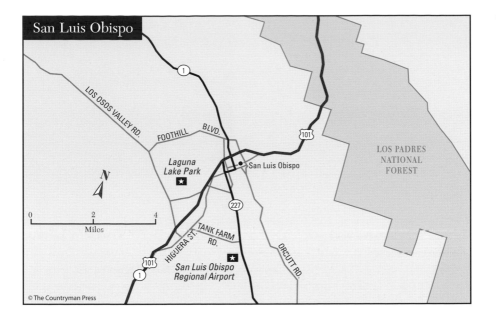

San Luis Obispo

LOS OSOS VALLEY RD.

FOOTHILL   BLVD.

Laguna
Lake Park ★

San Luis Obispo

LOS PADRES
NATIONAL
FOREST

N

0   2   4
Miles

TANK FARM
RD.

HIGUERA ST.

ORCUTT RD.

San Luis Obispo
Regional Airport ★

© The Countryman Press

trees thrive. Residents and tourists come together at the fountains and benches of Mission Plaza, where Friday-night concerts are staged during summer and community events fill the two-block area throughout the year. As always, the adjacent San Luis Creek flows through the heart of town and past the cafés, shops, and pedestrian walkways that have sprouted along its banks over the years.

The little creek also shadows Higuera Street, the city's lively main drag, where a pleasing mix of locally owned boutiques, vintage shops, and farm-to-table eateries mingle more or less in harmony with more sophisticated newcomers such as Victoria's Secret and the Apple Store. One of the first things you'll notice is the town's genial vibe and unhurried pace. At the same time, San Luis Obispo exudes the energy of a college town, with a youthful workforce of students from nearby Cal Poly staffing (and patronizing) many local establishments. Unlike the studiously regulated Mediterranean design of trendy Santa Barbara to the south, San Luis Obispo's downtown is a comfortable jumble of styles old and new. Architectural influences bounce block by block and building by building from art deco to adobe, Victorian to Queen Anne, and California Craftsman to the

DOWNTOWN SLO: STROLLING ON HIGUERA STREET

Romanesque granite and sandstone facade of the Old Carnegie Library on Monterey Street, converted half a century ago to the country's historical museum.

DOWNTOWN TROLLEY

Four days a week an open-air green trolley pokes along Higuera Street as it makes a loop around town, providing an easy, inexpensive way to explore San Luis Obispo. The fare is just 25 cents.

The San Luis Obispo region (the city and the surrounding county bear the same name) is a vibrant part of the Central Coast's booming wine country, with more than 200 wineries between the SLO area and Paso Robles to the north. Downtown you'll find the Taste Center on Osos Street, where local growers have created a high-tech wine center that allows visitors to sample a choice of 72 selections from area wineries—in automated 1-ounce pours activated by a credit card swipe.

Downtown also is the home of the decidedly no-tech Bubblegum Alley, a bizarre nook along Higuera Street, between Garden and Broad, where brick walls are covered with thousands of pieces of used chewing gum—some of it just wads and blobs, other pieces pulled and massaged into designs or messages. People constantly drop by to gawk or make their own gooey additions, and Bubblegum Alley is worth a peek if you happen to be passing. (If you're traveling with kids, they'll most likely insist on a detour to add their own gummy contributions.)

DOWNTOWN FARMER'S MARKET

Outdoor activities—surfing, kayaking, hiking, camping, whale-watching, and bird-watching—abound in the string of nearby beach towns, which include Shell Beach, Morro Bay, Avila Beach, Cambria, and Pismo Beach (see chapter 6). The entire area is ringed with pastoral farms and rolling vineyards. That makes San Luis Obispo a choice spot for serious grazing, from the open-air street markets to eateries featuring locally produced cheeses, olives, organic produce, craft beers, and, of course, the Central Coast wines.

Weekends officially start in San Luis Obispo on Thursday night. That's when the city shuts down five blocks of Higuera Street to car traffic for downtown's famous, not-to-be-missed farmer's market, a rollicking street fair that serves up a lavish spread of fresh produce and a curbside buffet from local restaurants. The local veggies, baked goods, and other fresh products for sale are worth the trip, and the street food is terrific, too. Even the controlled chaos of turning a busy main drag into an incredible street bazaar every Thursday afternoon is something to behold, traffic giving way to the assembly of stands and displays, grills being set ablaze, and plumes of smoke rising from sizzling meat while teams of chefs slice and dice mounds of fresh onions, lettuce, and tomatoes, their knives beating out a chopping-board drumbeat. Premium valet parking is available at the farmer's market, but it's reserved for bicyclists, not gas guzzlers.

The downtown bike valet service is typical of the eco-minded attitudes of San Luis Obispo. This is a community that banned new drive-through restaurants in 1982 and, in recent years, expanded local cycling routes to cover more than 25 miles across the region, including bike routes that loop past the cluster of wineries along Highway 227. The SLO area is regularly mentioned in surveys that laud America's greenest and most livable communities. *Sunset* magazine calls San Luis Obispo the "most Californian place in all of California" and included the city in its listing of Ten Dream Towns in the West.

Yet many travelers overlook San Luis Obispo as they gravitate toward California's more glitzy destinations. Located midway between San Francisco and Los Angeles, this college town is often a green blur (and sudden flash of pink at the landmark Madonna Inn) for motorists racing along US 101. That's a shame, because the San Luis Obispo area has much to offer a wide range of tastes, appetites, and budgets, and definitely is worth visiting on its own or as a base for exploring the region's varied attractions. The landmark Hearst Castle is just 40 miles away in San Simeon, while Paso Robles is even closer, about 25 miles up the 101.

Then again, the lack of crushing crowds and high demand make SLO all the more enjoyable for those who choose to visit.

SLO'S FARMER'S MARKET FEATURES VALET PARKING FOR BIKES

SAN LUIS OBISPO COUNTY'S TOP 10 CROPS, 2007

1. Wine grapes: $141.7 million
2. Broccoli: $78.0 million
3. Strawberries: $55.5 million
4. Cattle and calves: $55.3 million
5. Vegetable transplants: $34.7 million
6. Head lettuce: $31.9 million
7. Cut flowers: $28.6 million
8. Indoor decoratives: $24.3 million
9. Carrots: $22.5 million
10. Cauliflower: $17.4 million

Source: San Luis Obispo County Department of Agriculture (slocounty.ca.gov/agcomm.htm)

GUIDANCE Car-Free San Luis Obispo (slocarfree.org). Like Santa Barbara, SLO launched a communitywide effort in 2009 to encourage use of public transportation. Many hotels, restaurants, and attractions are offering discounts to visitors who leave their cars at home.

San Luis Obispo Chamber of Commerce Visitor Center (805-781-2777; slochamber.org), 1039 Chorro St., San Luis Obispo 93401. Open seven days a week: Sun.–Wed. 10 AM–5 PM, Thu.–Sat. 10 AM–7 PM.

San Luis Obispo County Visitors & Conference Bureau (805-541-8000; 800-634-1414; sanluisobispocounty.com), 811 El Capitan Way, Suite 200, San Luis Obispo 93401. A good resource for information and events throughout San Luis Obispo County.

The Tribune (sanluisobispo.com). Pick up the local newspaper or browse online.

GETTING THERE San Luis Obispo (population 44,000) is the largest city in Santa Luis Obispo County. SLO is bordered by Santa Barbara County to the south, Monterey County to the north, and Kern County to the east.

By car: San Luis Obispo is about 200 miles north of Los Angeles and 220 miles south of San Francisco on US Hwy. 101, which is the most direct route from both Southern and Northern California. The city is located 8 miles from the Pacific Ocean, at the junction of US 101 and scenic Hwy. 1.

From Southern California: Head north on the 101 until you reach San Luis Obispo, about an hour's drive north from Santa Barbara.

From the Bay Area: Head south on the 101. Travelers also can opt for the more leisurely and picturesque route along Hwy. 1, by way of Big Sur. The two-lane route, however, is slow and winding—with many hairpin turns—and can add two hours or more to the trip, especially in bad weather.

From inland California, including Fresno and Bakersfield: Routes from the east include state highways 41, 46, 58 and 166.

BY AIR

SAN LUIS OBISPO COUNTY REGIONAL AIRPORT

(805-781-5205; sloairport.com), 903-5 Airport Dr., San Luis Obispo 93401, is located just south of the city of San Luis Obispo, off US 101. The terminal has free WiFi. Two regional carriers are based at the airport and affiliated with major airlines with connections to Los Angeles, San Francisco, Phoenix, and other cities.

US Airways: 800-428-4322; usairways.com

United Express: 800-241-6522; united.com

CAR RENTALS

Avis: Local office 805-544-0630; 800-331-1212; avis.com

Budget: Local office 805-541-2722; 800-527-0700; budget.com

Enterprise: Local office 805-595-5455; 800-736-8222; enterprise.com

Hertz: Local office 805-781-3380; 800-654-3131; hertz.com

GROUND TRANSPORTATION

Ride-On Transportation (805-541-8747; ride-on.org), a nonprofit, community-based cooperative, provides shuttle service from the airport and Amtrak station. The airport website (sloairport.com) also lists taxis and limousine operators currently serving the airport.

By train: **Amtrak** (local station 805-541-0505; nationwide reservations 800-872-724; amtrak.com), 1011 Railroad Ave., San Luis Obispo 93401, runs its Pacific Surfliner service daily between San Diego and San Luis Obispo. Most Pacific Surfliners are equipped with bicycle and surfboard racks, allowing passengers to bring bikes aboard. Amtrak's two-story Coast Starlight service runs from Los Angeles to Seattle, with stops in San Luis Obispo. The San Luis Obispo's train depot is on Railroad Ave., near Santa Barbara St., about 3 miles northwest of the airport.

TAKE THE TRAIN TO SAN LUIS OBISPO

By bus: **Greyhound** (800-231-2222; greyhound.com), 1011 Railroad Ave., San Luis Obispo 93401, relocated its terminal to the local Amtrak station during 2009.

Santa Barbara Airbus (800-423-1618; santabarbaraairbus.com) offers coach service from Los Angeles International Airport to the Santa Barbara area and has expanded its daily offerings to include San Luis Obispo, Pismo Beach, Santa Maria, and Buellton.

GETTING AROUND SLO Transit (805-541-2877; ci.san-luis-obispo.ca.us) provides daily bus service within city limits, including routes to Cal Poly State University. SLO Transit also runs the downtown trolley shuttle service, which makes a loop from N. Monterey St. (and area hotels) to the downtown business four days a week. The trolley costs 25 cents and runs every 15 to 20 minutes 3:30–9 PM on Thu.; noon–9 PM on Fri.–Sat.; and noon–5:30 PM on Sun.

San Luis Obispo Regional Transit Authority (805-781-4472; slorta.org) offers bus service connecting cities in San Luis Obispo County.

RTA–South County Area Transit (805-781-4472; scattransit.org) provides bus service in the county's southern beach communities, including Shell Beach, Pismo Beach, Grover Beach, Arroyo Grande, and Oceano.

✳ To See

HISTORIC BUILDINGS AND SITES Mission San Luis Obispo de Tolosa (church office 805-781-8220; museum and gift shop 805-543-6850; missionsan luisobispo.org), 751 Palm St., San Luis Obispo 93401. The mission museum and gift shop are open daily 9 AM–4 PM; till 5 PM in summer. Admission is free, with a suggested donation of $3. In 1769 Father Junipero Serra received orders from Spain to bring the Catholic faith to the natives of Alta California. Serra came to the Central Coast three years later, on September 1, 1772, and founded California's fifth landmark mission, which is named for Saint Louis, bishop of Toulouse, France. San Luis Obispo was the first mission with an extenstive tile roof—a practical design innovation that came in response to attacks by Indians who used flaming arrows to set the original thatched version on fire. After being renovated and replastered through the years, the mission church remains a picturesque Spanish-style sanctuary with broad, welcoming doors, a high wooden ceiling, and flowing flowery artwork adorning its walls and archways. The original padres' residence is now a museum where visitors can browse Chumash Indian artifacts and a rare collection of early California photographs chronicling the mission's history. Adjacent Mission Plaza hosts events throughout the year, including a free concert series on Friday evenings during summer. Two noteworthy attractions, the San Luis Obispo Art Center and San Louis Obispo Historical Museum, are just steps away.

San Luis Obispo County Historical Society Museum (805-543-0638; slochs .org), 696 Monterey St., San Luis Obispo 93401. Open Wed.–Sun. 10 AM–4 PM. Finished browsing the city's historic mission and interested in more local stories? Head across the street to the San Luis Obispo County Historical Society Museum, which is located in San Luis Obispo's original Carnegie Library, a granite-and-sandstone landmark built with a $10,000 grant from steel tycoon Andrew Carnegie. The museum has changing exhibits, historical archives, and a bookstore that features titles about the region's history, culture, and wine production. The nonprofit historical society also runs the Dallidet Adobe, an 1850s adobe home at 1185

Pacific St. with a Mediterranean garden that includes original trees and shrubs, two large redwood trees, and a memorial rose garden.

Ah Louis Store in Old Chinatown, 800 Palm St., San Luis Obispo 93401. In 1874 a Chinese immigrant named Ah Louis opened a small mercantile store in downtown San Louis Obispo to serve the growing community of Chinese workers building the local railroad. After World II, however, the city's Chinatown gradually vanished. Today most people pass through the city and never know that SLO's Chinatown ever existed. One of the few remnants: A plaque marks the Ah Louis Store, which stands in the heart of Old Chinatown at the corner of Palm and Chorro Sts. The property is designated a California State Historical Landmark and owned by Louis's descendants.

MUSEUMS AND GALLERIES San Luis Obispo Art Center (805-543-8562; sloartcenter.org), 1010 Broad St., San Luis Obispo 93401-3505. Open 11 AM–5 PM daily; closed Tue. Open seven days a week July 4–Labor Day. Free, though donations are welcome. At the west end of Mission Plaza, the San Luis Obispo Art Center showcases the legacy of Central California artists. It's also a community educational center that hosts art classes, workshops, and special events throughout the year.

✔ **San Luis Obispo Children's Museum** (805-545-5474; slocm.org), 1010 Nipomo St., San Luis Obispo 93401. Open 10 AM–3 PM Tue.–Fri., 10 AM–5 PM Sat., 1–5 PM Sun.; closed Mon. The museum's hours are subject to change, so it's a good idea to call or check the current schedule online before visiting. Admission $8; children under 2 are free. This three-story imagination center is a lively, hands-on, and just-plain-fun museum that's full of clever interactive exhibits and activities, rather than static displays. The museum underwent a major expansion in 2008 and now includes the first-floor Caves of Exploration—an indoor series of caves and science-based projects where kids can create their own movies of an erupting volcano using clay and play paleontologist as they dig up saber-toothed tiger bones and then reassemble the skeleton of a big cat. The second floor is a world of make-believe and try-on careers, home of a kid-sized city called Zoomtown and a pretend diner, fire station, doctor's office, bank, performance stage, and farmer's market. The third floor is aimed at the under-4 crowd. There's a train depot and full-sized Brio train for toddlers and preschoolers, along with a soft play area, messy-play table, and reading corner with board books.

✳ To Do

HIKING Bishop Peak (slocountyparks.com) is one of nine major peaks—the Nine Sisters—that extend from San Luis Obispo to Morro Bay. Bishop rises the highest, to an elevation of 1,559 feet above sea level. The main hiking trails to this peak can be accessed from Foothill Blvd. and from Highland Dr. in San Luis Obispo. For the Foothill entrance, park alongside the road (between Los Osos Valley Rd. and Santa Rosa St.). For the Highland entrance, take Highland Dr. to the end from Santa Rosa St. There are two main trails in the 350-acre Bishop Peak Reserve: the Bishop Peak Trail and Felsman Loop, both easy.

Carrizo Plain National Monument (blm.gov/ca), on Soda Lake Rd. off Hwy. 166. Known as California's Serengeti, this national monument is a huge, protected,

SLO WALKING TOURS

Local resident Steve Akers, a refugee from the Hollywood movie business and the founder of SLO Walking Tours, offers an enthusiastic narrative of the city's architecture, history, and legendary characters. He begins at the Mission San Luis Obispo de Tulsa, where the city got its start. His tours includes stops in Old Chinatown (where Akers shares photos and stories from the area's 1930s heyday); the Palm Theater ("America's First Solar Powered Movie Theater"); the downtown courthouse (where legendary SLO builder Alex Madonna got his start in the business by demolishing the city's original courthouse); and the former Anderson Hotel (where Charlie Chaplin and other celebs stayed en route to William Randolph Hearst's castle at San Simeon). Akers shares all these stories and many more, then takes visitors on a stroll down Bubblegum Alley. "I have a soft spot for Bubblegum Alley," he says. "It's a blend of disturbing and intriguing at the same time." The tours usually run about 1¼ hours. Akers is a knowledgeable guide, and he's even gracious when correcting out-of-towners who mispronounce the city's name. It's *San LEWIS Obispo*. Not San Lew-eeee.

INFO
SLO Walking Tours (805-215-3228; slowalkingtours.com; P.O. Box 15253, San Luis Obispo 93406-5253). Open daily. Cost: $10 for a one-hour-plus tour of downtown.

one-of-a-kind nature area of endangered species, unique habitats, and native grasslands spread across southeastern San Luis Obispo County. The San Andreas Fault, which cuts through the plain, is clearly visible here. The monument also contains a National Historic Site at Painted Rock, a 55-foot-tall rock formation spectacularly painted with prehistoric Chumash art. Hiking, biking, horseback riding, and nature tours are available. It's about a 65-mile drive from downtown San Luis Obispo. Check the Bureau of Lane Management website for detailed directions; rangers note that most online maps and GPS systems provide incorrect maps.

Lopez Lake Recreation Area (805-788-2381; slocountyparks.com), 6800 Lopez Dr., Arroyo Grande 93420, is a popular park that offers a variety of hiking trails for visitors. Other activities at Lopez Lake include water-skiing, windsurfing, biking, and boating.

BIKING San Luis Obispo prides itself on being one of California's most bike-friendly towns, offering an expanding network of paths and trails that meander through this bucolic college town and beyond. Visit **the San Luis Obispo County Bicycle Coalition** online (slobikelane.org) to check out cycling routes along coastal Hwys. 1 and 101, as well as quieter routes that wind through country back roads past the area's many vineyards. Another popular route is the Bob Jones Trail, which runs from inland to the shore at Avila Beach. Bike rentals are available at

Art's Cyclery (805-543-4416; artscyclery.com), 2140 Santa Barbara St., San Luis Obispo, which offers a wide selection of bikes for cruising various terrains.

GARDENS **San Luis Obispo Botanical Gardens** (805-541-1400), 3450 Dairy Creek Rd., San Luis Obispo 93405, is located inside El Chorro Regional Park, between San Luis Obispo and Morro Bay. The Preview Garden is open daily during daylight hours. Admission is free. Parking at El Chorro Regional Park is $2 in summer.

✴ Wineries

Baileyana Winery (805-269-8200; baileyana.com), 5828 Orcutt Rd., San Luis Obispo 93401. Tasting room: 10 AM–5 PM daily. Catharine Niven founded the Paragon vineyard here after she and husband Jack left the Kentucky horse world and settled in the Edna Valley in the early 1970s. Her boutique winery began with just 3½ acres of grapes in the front yard and has grown over the decades to become a respected producer of Chardonnay, Sauvignon Blanc, Syrah, and Pinot Noir. The winery's tasting room is housed in a little yellow schoolhouse originally built on the property in 1909. It's a pleasant spot to sip wine; you also can pick up cheese and snacks to enjoy in the Baileyana picnic area overlooking the vineyards.

Claiborne & Churchill Vintners (805-544-4066; claibornechurchill.com), 2649 Carpenter Canyon Rd. (Hwy. 227), San Luis Obispo 93401. Tasting room: 11 AM–5 PM daily. Owners Claiborne (Clay) Thompson and Fredericka Churchill, a pair of former academics, created their eco-friendly winery by crafting the building with 16-inch-thick walls made of rice straw bales, which maintains a constant cellar temperature without a heating or cooling system. Their modest Edna Valley winery offers German- and Alsace-inspired vintages on California's Central Coast. Claiborne & Churchill specializes in fruity but dry wines made from Riesling, Gewürztraminer, and Pinot Gris grapes. The winery also produces smaller lots of

SAN LUIS OBISPO'S GREEN ACRES

TASTINGS: SLO WINE SCENE

San Luis Obispo County is naturally divided by the San Lucia Mountain Range into two distinct wine regions. There's the Paso Robles area to the north and the SLO vineyards on the county's southern end, which thrive in the region's mild, maritime climate and long growing season.

The SLO scene includes three viticulture areas: the Edna Valley, where many vineyards cluster amid the rolling hills along state highway 227; the Arroyo Grande Valley, just south of Edna Valley; and the Avila Valley, which sprawls closest to the coast.

Wine growers here are known for their handcrafted production of Pinot Noir, Chardonnay, Syrah, Grenache, Viognier, and Zinfandel. Wineries tend to be small, family-owned operations, and many are located within 5 miles or so of downtown San Luis Obispo—just a short drive or a vigorous bicycle trek along the area's well-developed network of cycling trails.

If you're feeling energetic, the **San Luis Obispo County Bicycle Coalition** has created a series of do-it-yourself cycling tours for exploring wine

country. Maps and trip pointers are available online (slobikelane.org). The Tiffany Ranch Road Loop, for example, is a scenic 19.7-mile ride that begins at the San Luis Obispo Amtrak station, cruises past the local airport, and takes in several Edna Valley vineyards. The coalition helpfully includes a shorter route (13.4 miles) that offers a detour along Biddle Branch Rd., allowing you to bypass some hills at the south end of the valley—a suggestion that might come in handy on days when the afternoon winds kick up.

In downtown SLO the San Luis Obispo Vintners Association has set up a **Taste Center** at Osos and Monterey Sts. where visitors can sample a wide variety of selections and learn more about the nearby vineyards. Taste (805-269-8278; taste-slo.com), 1003 Osos St., features an Enomatic system, a high-tech pouring machine that dispenses 1-ounce servings at the push of a button. It works this way: Visitors purchase a wine card, load it with credit, and then help themselves a choice of about 70 wine selections from producers in the Edna Valley, Arroyo Grande, Avila Beach, and Nipomo areas. The center's staff also provide maps and other information to help plan excursions. Taste is open daily, but hours fluctuate throughout the seasons, so check online or call before you visit.

other wines, including a Dry Muscat, Chardonnay, Syrah, Cabernet Sauvignon, Sparkling Brut Rosé, and a port-style wine.

Chamisal Vineyards (805-541-9463; chamisalvineyards.com), 7525 Orcutt Rd., San Luis Obispo 93401. Tasting room: 10 AM–5 PM daily. Chamisal Vineyards (formerly the Domaine Alfred Winery) changed owners in 2008, but has been growing Chardonnay and Pinot Noir grapes on 80 acres in south San Luis Obispo since 1973. It was the first vineyard planted in the Edna Valley. The new owners have restored the winery to its original name, which comes from the fragrant chamise, a rugged white-flowered shrub that thrived on the property. A renovated red barn tasting room reopened in fall 2009 and is adorned with photographs celebrating the vineyard's history. "What's inside the bottle is the same delicious wine as it's always been, with winemaker Fintan du Fresne at the lead," says Brette Ann Womack, a hospitality manager at the winery. The winery doesn't serve food, but visitors are invited to bring their own picnics.

Edna Valley Vineyard (805-544-5855; ednavalley.com), 2585 Biddle Ranch Rd., San Luis Obispo 93401. Tasting room: 10 AM–5 PM daily. The Edna Valley Vineyard is known for Chardonnay and its modern 5,000-square-foot tasting room, which offers very nice views of the vineyards and nearby mountains. A partnership between the Niven family and Diageo Chateau & Estate Wines, the winery offers event throughout the year, including cooking classes, parties, and happy-hour gatherings with live music.

Kynsi Winery (805-544-8461; kynsi.com), 2212 Corbett Canyon Rd., Arroyo Grande 93420. Tasting room: 11 AM–5 PM; closed Tue.–Wed. This small family-run winery is housed in a renovated 1940s dairy on a backcountry road in the Edna Valley. Kynsi's offerings include Pinot Noir, Chardonnay, Pinot Blanc, Merrah (a Merlot/Syrah blend), and Syrah. The winery's label features a barn owl in honor of the resident owls that roost on the property.

Laetitia Vineyard and Winery (805-481-1772; laetitiawine.com), 453 Deutz Dr., Arroya Grande. Tasting room: 11 AM–5 PM daily. Located just off Hwy. 101, Laetitia focuses on producing Pinot Noir, Chardonnay, and méthode champenoise sparkling wines on 650 acres overlooking the Arroya Grand Valley. The winery has a hilltop visitors center, which can get busy on weekends. No food is served, but there are picnic tables and a bocce ball court.

Tolosa Winery (805-782-0500; tolosawinery.com), 4910 Edna Rd./Hwy. 277, San Luis Obispo 93401. Tasting room: 11 AM–5 PM daily. The solar-powered Tolosa Winery takes its name from San Luis Obispo's historic Mission San Luis Obispo de Tolosa, whose small vineyard was the first wine producer in the Edna Valley. Visitors will want to sample Tolosa's well-regarded Pinot Noir and Chardonnay, which make up 80 percent of the grower's wines. The tasting room here is a spacious, upscale center, a modern mix of glass, steel, and woodsy decor. The winery serves tapas on Friday nights and offers wine and artisan cheese pairings on Saturday afternoon. Guests also are welcome to bring their own food to picnic outside and savor the Edna Ranch, a picturesque spread spanning 750 acres of vineyards and hilly trails with sweeping views of the entire region (the winery periodically hosts hiking treks and other outdoor events).

Wolff Vineyards (805-781-0448; wolffvineyards.com), 6238 Orcutt Rd., San Luis Obispo 93401. Tasting room: 11 AM–5 PM daily. The vineyard includes 55 acres of

Chardonnay and 37 acres of Pinot Noir grapes, along with 12 acres planted in Syrah, Petite Syrah, Riesling, and Teroldego, a grape grown primarily in Italy. William A. Ausmus, author of *Wine & Wineries of California's Central Coast*, notes that winery owner Jean-Pierre Wolff, a Belgian-born research scientist, was one of the first growers to plant Petit Syrah after others insisted the grapes wouldn't thrive in the Edna Valley. "Now they are coming to him for grapes," Ausmus says. The owner practices sustainable agriculture, including use of falcons for pest management, and is working with various agencies to restore the steelhead trout population in the creek that runs through the property. Wolff Vineyards has a small tasting room and an area where visitors can bring their own food to picnic on the grounds.

Talley Vineyards (805-489-0446; talleyvineyards.com), 3031 Lopez Dr., Arroyo Grande 93420. Tasting room: Daily 10:30 AM–4:30 PM. Oliver Talley began growing vegetables in the Arroyo Grande Valley in 1948. His grandson Brian Talley now runs the family farm, which still produces bell peppers, lettuce, and avocados, as well as about 1,000 acres of grapes in this fertile valley. At Talley Vineyards, the house specialties are Pinot Noir and Chardonnay, which thrive in the valley's cool coastal climate. The winery also produces the Bishop Peak label, named for San Luis Obispo's landmark volcanic peak, and the Mano Tinta label, a fund-raising effort to aid farmworkers. The Talley tasting room is a spacious hacienda-style center surrounded by gardens and an outdoor courtyard. The winery has a picnic areas where visitors can sip wine and snack on cheese and olives while soaking up the surrounding countryside.

✳ Lodging

From cozy to kitschy, San Luis Obispo offers a selection of hometown-flavored inns and hotels, many of them just off the 101 freeway and close to downtown and the sprawling Cal Poly campus.

🐾 ⑂ **Apple Farm Inn** (805-544-2040, 800-255-2040; applefarm.com; info@applefarm.com), 2015 Monterey St. (just off US 101, close to downtown), San Luis Obispo 93401. Expensive. Credit cards are accepted. This venerable country inn brims with its trademark Victorian floral decor, canopy beds, wood-burning fireplaces, and flower gardens. Guests are welcomed with homemade hot cider. Some people find the place a bit fussy, while devoted Apple Farm fans savor their old-fashioned retreat, returning again and again to enjoy such niceties as fresh-baked cinnamon roll French toast for breakfast and afternoon tea

served under the sycamore trees. The most luxurious rooms are located in the main inn, while the adjacent Trellis Court has more modest motel-style offerings. The inn has its own bakery, and the Apple Farm restaurant is a local favorite for breakfast. Heated pool and spa.

🐾 ⑂ **Holiday Inn Express** (805-544-8600, 888-465-4329; hiexpress.com), 1800 Monterey St., San Luis Obispo 93401. Moderate. Credit cards are accepted. Located near Cal Poly, about a mile from downtown, this 100-room hotel is a good choice for a convenient, comfortable stopover in San Luis Obispo. The hotel completed a $2.5 million makeover in 2009, redecorating in tasteful Craftsman-style furnishings; after some back and forth following the renovation, the management decided to keep the welcome mat out for guests with pets, too. Rates include the hotel's breakfast bar. Four days a week the San Luis Obispo trolley stops out front and you can hop onboard to cruise downtown. Pool.

⚓ ♿ **The Madonna Inn** (800-543-9666; madonnainn.com; info@madonnainn.com), 100 Madonna Rd., San Luis Obispo 93405. Moderate–expensive. Credit cards are accepted. The Golfer's Room, Desert Sands, Rose Room, Vintage, and Mount Vernon are all wheelchair accessible. It's almost impossible not to like the Madonna Inn, the relentlessly pink, over-the-top landmark motor lodge, where 110 themed rooms boast irresistible names like Cloud Nine, Oriental Fantasy, Jungle Rock, and the Caveman, an all-rock suite that's a perennial favorite with honeymooners. The exterior of the hotel resembles a Swiss chalet. Inside, guests gape at the hotel's 8-foot waterfall urinal in the lobby men's room and the abundance

of ornate touches throughout the property, like the hand-carved marble balustrade and the 28-foot gold tree hovering above the oversized red leather booths in the inn's Gold Rush steak house. Robin Leach, Zsa Zsa Gabor, and Liberace would fit right in at the Madonna Inn dining room, and of course they'd adore the house's signature dessert—pink champagne cake. Alex Madonna, a builder who spent much of his working life on the road running construction projects, created the inn in 1958 as a place where "weary travelers could feel at home and enjoy a nice meal, in a comfortable atmosphere, and continue on their journey," his wife Phyllis writes in her memoir. Alex Madonna never wanted a swimming pool at his hotel, but after he passed away in 2004 family members finally built the one thing the Madonna Inn lacked: a spacious pool and spa area, done up in bright cotton-

THE POOL AREA AT THE MADONNA INN

THE GOLD RUSH STEAK HOUSE AND A
NEW ADDITION TO SLO'S LANDMARK
MADONNA INN: A POOL AREA

candy colors and perched along a hill-side. The pool opened in 2007 and it's a lovely, relaxing addition to the Madonna family's fantasyland, especially for weary travelers and kids after a long summer vacation drive on Highway 101.

&. **Petit Soleil** (800-676-1588, 805-549-0321; petitsoleilslo.com; reservations@petitsoleilslo.com), 473 Monterey St., San Luis Obispo 93401. Moderate–expensive. Credit cards are accepted. Nestled inside a cobblestone courtyard, the Petit Soleil B&B is a sweet slice of the French countryside in downtown San Luis Obispo. The inn's 15 guest rooms are nicely appointed with Provence-style furnishings and sunny fabrics; each room has a distinct personality and private bathroom. Nightly rates include a generous breakfast with freshly baked treats, such as scones, quiches, and lemon-

coconut pancakes, and owner Dianne Conner happily shares the recipes in her Petit Soleil cookbook. During the day guests can borrow the inn's bikes to explore the town. Each evening the complimentary happy-hour wine tasting features savory appetizers and selections from local and French wineries.

⁂ **Rinconada Dairy** (805-438-5667; rinconadadairy.com), 4680 W. Pozo Rd. (off Hwy. 58), Santa Margarita 93453. Moderate. No credit cards; cash and checks only. (Those with mobility issues should note that the farm has two ground-level rooms, but have small steps up; there's no specific wheelchair access.) Located 19 miles east of San Luis Obispo, this 52-acre sheep and goat ranch offers a rustic taste of farm life, most notably the owners' handcrafted cheeses. Guests staying on the farm have two choices for accommodations: The spacious Fiesta Room in the main house sleeps two, while the new Cottage in the Barn—a remodeled apartment added in 2010—sleeps four and includes a kitchen. Guests start the day with a bountiful breakfast featuring the farm's own eggs, bacon and sausage from the pigs, and homemade jams, granola, and baked goods. Then you can experience a typical day at Rinconada Dairy, including watching the cheesemaking during milking season or helping tend the flock of more than 200 sheep. "It seems to be the case that most people come here to go wine tasting," says owner Christine Maguire. "We have had a few people who actually wanted to help with the birthing, or feeding, or even milking! None of this is required. I can't have people help with cheese-making for health regulation reasons, but guests can observe. Gathering eggs is a popular and simple task." The dairy's flagship cheese, Pozo Tomme, is a pressed raw sheep's-milk cheese

A SLICE OF THE FRENCH COUNTRYSIDE IN DOWNTOWN SLO: PETIT SOLEIL'S FRONT COURTYARD

that's aged for a minimum of two months; it's sold at gourmet markets and restaurants (the dairy's website has a list of places where you can find Rinconada's cheese).

& **The Sanitarium** (805-544-4124; thesanitariumspa.com), 1715 Osos St., San Luis Obispo 93401. Expensive. Credit cards are accepted. This lovely Victorian white house was once, as the name suggests, a sanitarium in the 1880s. Suzi Kyle bought the place as an investment, and after it served stints as a fraternity and sorority house, she transformed the property into an airy seven-room B&B and art gallery. Located in a residential neighborhood just half a block from the Amtrak station, the Sanitarium is a free-spirited haven for travelers who are looking for a spot to unwind and don't require a host of hotel services. Visitors are invited to paint in the parlor studio (and often will find Kyle painting, too), relax in Moroccan soaking tubs, play the enormous black piano that once belonged to the owner's great-grandmother, or share their talents during impromptu creative sessions with other guests. "People are so full of talents," says Kyle. Vivid paintings and other artworks adorn nicely appointed guest rooms, most of which have fireplaces and balconies An overnight stay includes breakfast made with local organic fare in the house's spacious kitchen; then guests can expect to be on their own. Be sure to call for current rates—the B&B's website is rarely updated and the owner doesn't like e-mail or computers. One room is handicapped accessible.

& "♥" **San Luis Creek Lodge** (805-541-1122, 800-593-0333, ext. 210; sanluiscreeklodge.com; info@sanluiscreeklodge.com), 1941 Monterey St., San Luis Obispo 93401. Moderate–expensive. Credit cards are accepted. This 25-room lodge is one of San Luis Obispo's newer inns, a stylish B&B

amid the chain hotels on Monterrey Street. Built in 2003 and refurbished in 2008, the San Luis Creek Lodge is a cluster of three architecturally themed buildings—The Craftsman (Mission-style furnishings); The Plantation (Caribbean inspired); and The Londonderry (Tutor and topiaries)—connected by a small winding road designed to mimic San Francisco's Lombard Street. Owner Patty Oxford says there's no "standout" favorite among guests, but men tend to enjoy The Craftsman, honeymooners like The Plantation, and The Londonberry is especially popular in winter because rooms have fireplaces. All lodge rooms come with pleasing extras such as 220-channel satellite HD 40-inch Sony televisions and a free DVD library. Oxford opened in San Luis Obispo after a 30-year career working for some of the nation's top hotel companies. "So the inn represents my background, as my heritage is English (Londonderry building); Craftsman is inspired by my years in the Colorado mountains; and The Plantation is reminiscent of my years in Caribbean resorts," she says. The SLO trolley stops right outside four days a week. Full breakfast is included.

MORE HOTELS Downtown SLO is less than 10 miles from the coast, so you might want to consider lodging in nearby beach towns, too (see chapter 6).

✴ Where to Eat

San Luis Obispo is a good eating town that specializes in fresh and local.

✪ ✦ **Big Sky** (805-545-5401; bigsky cafe.com), 1121 Broad St., San Luis Obispo 93401. Open Mon.–Wed. 7 AM–9 PM, Thu.–Fri. 7 AM–10 PM, Sat. 8 AM–10 PM, Sun. 8 AM–9 PM. Moderate. Credit cards are accepted. This color-

ful downtown eatery is always bustling, and for good reason: Big Sky is a crowd-pleaser. The menu is a mix of locally grown fare infused with Asian and Moroccan flavors. You'll find a wonderful selection of homemade soups, sandwiches, and salads (the Thai Shrimp and glass noodle salad with mint and chiles is a treat). The offerings are tasty and simple, yet sophisticated enough to appeal to gourmets while affordable for families and the local college crowd. Big Sky is consistently mentioned on just about everyone's short list of best places in San Luis Obispo. Good selection of craft beers and Central Coast wines.

Ciopinot Seafood Grille (805-547-1111; ciopinotrestaurant.com), 1051 Nipomo St., San Luis Obispo 93403. Open daily, lunch at noon; dinner 5 PM–midnight. Expensive. Credit cards are accepted. Reservations suggested. Located in the Old Tortilla Flats Building downtown, this upscale seafood grill offers delectable tasting menus and an extensive wine list focused on red and white Pinots from around the world. There's an oyster bar and a savory tapas menu that includes Dungeness crabcakes topped with smoked tomato aioli, and stuffed Mexican prawns. The restaurant doesn't charge a corkage fee, so you can bring your own vino.

F. McLintocks (805-541-0686; mc lintocks.com), 868 Higuera St., San Luis Obispo 93401. Open daily 7 AM–9 PM (until 9:30 PM on Fri., Sat.). Moderate–expensive. Credit cards are accepted. F. McLintocks opened its first steak house in nearby Shell Beach more than three decades ago, and since then this boisterous restaurant/saloon has added three new locations, including this very popular outpost in downtown San Luis Obispo. This is the place for steak and ribs and

COCKTAILS AT THE POOL

ture jazz or folk performances, as well as the occasional poetry reading. On weekends breakfast is served until 2 PM.

Novo Restaurant and Lounge (805-543-3986; novorestaurant.com), 726 Higuera St., San Luis Obispo 93401. Open Mon.–Sat. 11 AM–dinner service (till midnight Thu.–Sat.); Sun. brunch starts at 10 AM. Moderate–expensive. Credit cards are accepted. Reservations suggested. Built in the 1890s as a cigar factory, Novo is one of San Luis Obispo's signature restaurants, a lovely oasis in the heart of downtown with an innovative menu and great atmosphere, too. The offerings are a fusion of bold flavors, with dishes like tandoori spiced prawns sautéed in saffron, and Malaysian chicken with toasted coconut. Enjoy dinner inside or step out to the multi-tiered wooden patio along San Luis Creek, where a giant oak grows through the middle of the deck and lights twinkle in the trees. Fans of Novo also will want to try the owner's new restaurant downtown, Chow, a California Asian bistro at 1009 Monterey St., next to the Fremont Theatre.

Splash Cafe (805-544-7567; splash bakery.com), 1491 Monterey St., San Luis Obispo 93401. Open Sun.–Thu. 7 AM–8:30 PM, Fri.–Sat. 7 AM–9:30 PM. Inexpensive. Credit cards are accepted. Pismo Beach's wildly popular chowder shack has opened an outpost in San Luis Obispo and serves up no-frills seafood at reasonable prices. The trademark clam chowder is creamy and rich, and you'll also enjoy other basic fare such as fish sandwiches, fried calamari, and curly fries. The SLO Splash Cafe offers a delectable extra—the Splash bakery, which sells fresh-baked baguettes and pastries, too. The restaurant is right next door to the cute Petit Soleil B&B.

other heaping entrées served with a country music soundtrack. The best deal of the week, however, is Thursday nights, when a giant outdoor mesquite barbecue pit is set up in front of the restaurant. There the cooks serve up mountains of mouthwatering grilled chicken, ribs, and just-picked artichokes to the hungry masses during the downtown farmer's market.

"♥" **Linnaea's Cafe** (805-541-5888; linnaeas.com), 1110 Garden St., San Luis Obispo 93401. Open daily 6:30 AM–11 PM (till 10 on Sun.). Inexpensive–moderate. Credit cards are accepted. A neighborhood hangout for more than two decades, Linnaea's is a downtown café beloved for its breakfast burritos, oversized waffles, and garden patio where patrons can linger over espresso drinks and chocolate cloud cake. The restaurant serves up a changing menu of veggie entrées at lunch and dinner (check out the weekly menu online). Evenings often fea-

✳ Entertainment

MOVIES Fremont Theatre (805-541-2141), 1025 Monterey St., San Luis Obispo 93406. Built in 1940, this is an old-fashioned art deco theater and a local landmark. In recent years three more screens have been added in an adjacent building, making this a fourplex showing first-run movies. The theater is also used for the San Luis Obispo International Film Festival.

NIGHTLIFE SLO is a college town, and you'll find a number of lively nightspots as you stroll downtown. The bar at **Korberl at Blue** (805-783-1135; epkoberl.com), 998 Monterey St., offers an impressive array of martinis. **Frog & Peach Pub** (805-595-3764), 28 Higuera St., caters to a younger downtown crowd with live music and Tuesday pint nights. **Downtown Brewing Co.** (805-541-0286; dtbrew.com), 1119 Garden St., features in-house brews on tap, including honey blonde ale, blueberry ale, and India pale ale, plus live music.

THEATER AND CONCERTS Performing Arts Center San Luis Obispo (805-756-2787, 888-233-ARTS; pacslo.org), 1 Grand Ave., San Luis Obispo 93407. The Performing Arts Center at Cal Poly hosts a wide range of cultural offerings, including top-name concert performers, traveling Broadway shows, the San Luis Obispo Symphony, and the annual Festival Mozaic (festivalmozaic.com), one of the West's most enduring classical music festivals, founded in 1971.

SLO Little Theatre (805-786-2440; slolittletheatre.org; boxoffice@slolittle theatre.org), 888 Morro St., San Luis Obispo 93401. Lovers of live theater will want to seek out the SLO Little Theatre, an ambitious downtown company and one of the oldest continuous-ly running community theaters in the nation. SLOLT began its theatrical journey in 1947 with *Blithe Spirit* and has staged nearly 400 productions since then.

✳ Selective Shopping

Downtown San Luis Obispo is an enjoyable place to stroll and shop. You'll find an assortment of small boutiques, vintage shops, and hometown retailers, like the **San Luis Surf Co.** (805-550-5210), 952 Higuera St., **Boo Boo Records** (805-541-0657), 978 Monterey St., and the irresistible **Tom's Toys** (805-541-2896), a well-stocked emporium at 682 Higuera St., as well as big-name retailers like Victoria's Secret, the Apple Store, Express, and Ross, all clustered on and around the 800 and 900 blocks of Higuera St.

THE NOVEL EXPERIENCE BOOKSTORE IN DOWNTOWN SLO

DOWNTOWN FARMER'S MARKET

Thursday night is San Luis Obispo's famous weekly farmer's market, a giant street fair that draws huge crowds of locals and visitors to downtown. By 5:30 PM five blocks of Higuera Street are closed to car traffic and the locals are lined up (and salivating) near the massive mobile barbecue pit smoking in front of F. McLintocks, always one of the most popular eateries at the weekly market.

The restaurant cooks pile giant slabs of ribs, chicken skewers, artichokes, and bushels of corn on the grill. At precisely 6 PM the F. McLintocks grill team belts out a chorus of "God Bless America" and opens for business. Offerings include BBQ chicken sandwiches, served on buttery soft hoagie rolls with a mound of onions and peppers, and grilled artichokes with chipotle aioli. Every bite is scrumptious.

Once you're done filling up, you'll be ready to stroll the market, which overflows for several blocks with booths crammed with fresh produce, nuts, and flowers from around the Central Coast. You'll find every imaginable vegetable, sweet peaches from See Canyon, olives from Paso Robles, fresh-baked pies from the Santa Ynez Valley, and fragrant lavender from several local farms.

San Luis Obispo's weekly market also features live bands rocking at every corner and a team of "bike valets" who watch the wheels of patrons who cycle to the market. It's a lively scene and a great taste of Central California's farms all in one place.

INFO

San Luis Obispo Downtown Farmer's Market (805-541-0286; downtown slo.com). Weekly produce market and street fair is 6–9 pm on Thu. Traffic closes along Higuera St. between Osos and Nipomo.

Novel Experience (805-544-0150), 779 Higuera St., San Luis Obispo. In the middle of downtown, the Novel Experience is an inviting indie bookstore with a good selection of titles and children's books, too. **Phoenix Books** (805 543-3591), 990 Monterey St., San Luis Obispo, is a good spot to find used titles.

✳ Special Events

Monthly: **Art after Dark** (sloarts council.org)—the first Friday of the month, galleries and other venues downtown open 6–9 PM.

March: **San Luis Obispo International Film Festival** (805-546-3456; slofilmfest.org).

April: **Wildflower Ride** (slobc.org)—100-mile bike rally.

May: **Roll Out the Barrels Wine Festival** (slowine.com).

June–September: **Concerts in the Plaza** (sanluisobispocounty.com)—Friday nights at Mission Plaza downtown.

July: **Festival Mozaic** (805-781-3000; festivalmozaic.com). **Central Coast Renaissance Festival** (805-927-0199; ccrenfaire.com).

September: **I Madonnari Chalk Art Festival** (aiacentralcoast.org).

September–October: **Plein Art Painting Festival** (sloartcenter.org).

October: **Central Coast Book & Author Festival** (805-546-1392; ccbookfestival.org), Mission Plaza.

October–November: **Cal Poly Homecoming** (calpoly.edu).

November: **Annual SLO Vintner's Harvest Celebration** (slowine.com).

November–December: **Santa's House** in Mission Plaza.

Paso Robles Area 5

PASO ROBLES AREA

"Paso Robles remains a work in progress, but I believe the region already shows some of the most striking potential in all of California."
—Renowned wine critic Robert M. Parker in a
2007 interview with *Food and Wine* magazine

What a difference a grape makes. Missionaries planted California's first vineyard near Paso Robles in 1797, and wine grapes have flourished ever since in this Central Coast community—more so now than ever before, as this old cow town has reinvented itself as a favorite haunt of foodies, locavores, and wine lovers lured by the region's growing reputation as a new hot spot for the California grape.

Just up the highway from San Luis Obispo, nearly midway between the poles of Los Angeles and San Francisco, Paso Robles is set amid an oak-studded expanse of ranchland dotted with fruit orchards, almond fields, grazing cattle, and mineral springs prized for generations by the native Salinan Indians for their healing powers. The name *Paso Robles* means "pass of the oaks," and the tree is the area's natural icon, its blue oaks, valley oaks, and other species not only visible on rural hillsides but also providing shade and beauty in the streets and green areas downtown. Even the main square features a clock tower that resembles a giant acorn, and the nearby Paso Robles Children's Museum has a giant, climbable oak display as a popular exhibit. Strict ordinances protect and preserve what remains of the oak forests that gave Paso Robles its name.

The native oaks may be the majestic symbol of the area, but wine grapes have become Paso's main attraction and economic lifeline. Commercial winemakers have long recognized the region's grape-friendly microclimates and the lengthy growing season of warm days and crisp cool evenings as ideally suited to vineyards and fine wine. Andrew York, an Indiana settler, established Ascension Winery (known today as York Mountain Winery) in 1882 in Paso Robles, and more vineyards and presses soon followed. But it wasn't until the early 1990s that the local growers started attracting national attention and winning awards, particularly for the Rhône varietals that have become a specialty in Paso, as residents call their town. Encouraged by land prices far more affordable than California's other big wine valleys, Napa and Sonoma, venerable winemakers and family-run operations

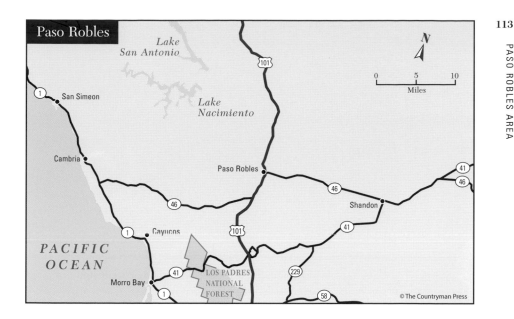

alike have transformed the sleepy hamlet few had heard about into the third largest wine-producing region in the state. Growers have systematically replanted old orchards with perfectly coiffed vineyards that now cover more than 29,000 acres along the rolling hillsides and country roads of northern San Luis Obispo County, with Paso as its epicenter.

The population grew with the expansion of the vineyards. Civic leaders spruced up downtown Paso Robles and its grassy main square, and Paso saw the arrival of a wave of upscale new establishments, from top-chef restaurants to elegant boutique hotels, adding a sophisticated layer to this town long dominated by the richly rustic traditions and culture of farming and ranching. Seasoned travelers and wine lovers have begun paying the area the highest of compliments: likening Paso's feel and offerings to the Napa of a quarter century ago.

PASO ROBLES VINEYARDS

Paso Robles's recent rapid growth inevitably slowed as the recession hit California businesses and tourism hard, but by then the region's place as a wine and tourism hub had become entrenched. The Paso Robles Wine Country Alliance says the region now has more than 180 wineries, a dramatic increase from a mere 50 in 2000.

Visitors will find the humble agricultural town of Paso's past juxtaposed with newer sensibilities—the luxury-minded inns, chain hotels, modern wineries, and wine bars that have sprung up in the past few years to fuel the town's appeal as a tourism destination. Paso offers vineyards and tasting rooms literally at every turn, including a trio of wine outposts that greets travelers arriving at the city's modern (and impressively immaculate) downtown transportation depot. (City planners elsewhere could learn a lot from the folks here.)

Some large and well-known growers have wineries in Paso Robles, but there still are many family-run farms and tasting rooms where owners personally welcome visitors and proudly pour their latest efforts. You'll meet vintners like Jeff Pipes, owner of the Pipestone Winery on the city's west side, a leader in the back-to-nature, biodynamic farming movement who runs his winery with solar power and tends his fields with a team of draft horses.

The region's bounty, of course, extends beyond the vines. Visitors also will find much to like at the area's olive oil tasting bars, cheese shops, and profusion of eateries and roadside farm stands that serve up fresh fare hyper-locally produced. Locally grown olives, mostly of the Tuscan variety, were planted by missionaries at the same time the first grapevines took root, and they, too, have achieved international praise. Paso Robles has been called the Sonoma of olives, nabbing awards for its olives and olive oils in competitions once dominated by Mediterranean producers. The state's largest olive festival is held every August in Paso's downtown City Park.

Downtown is an inviting place to stroll, sip, and snack, and the best place to start any visit to Paso. The City Park area is the hub of walkable Paso Robles. On Saturday mornings residents turn out at the grassy downtown square for the weekend farmer's market. It's a hometown scene, more modest than San Luis Obispo's Thursday-night market extravaganza, but there's an ample selection of seasonal

A VINEYARD SCENE IN PASO ROBLES

goodies, from heirloom tomatoes and berries to locally made artisanal jams and smoked fish caught by Central Coast fishermen. And, of course, local olives.

Located at Spring Street, between 11th and 12th Streets, City Park sits across from City Hall and the library, just a few steps from the historic Paso Robles Inn, the town's first hotel and hot springs purveyor. City Park also is walking distance to many of the centrally located restaurants, boutiques, and watering holes. Galleries call to passersby, among them the cheery Studios on the Park (at 1130 Park Street), an airy warehouse-like venue where adults and children can pop in to watch artists at work and join hands-on classes. On weekends during the tourist season a Belgian draft horse ferries guests in a carriage from the nearby Cheval Inn to restaurants around the park. On Friday and Saturday nights residents swarm the Park Cinemas (at 1100 Pine Street), downtown's nine-screen movie house. Many younger revelers also head across the street to Powell's Sweet Shoppe (at 840 11th Street), a dessert emporium franchise crammed with every treat imaginable.

After picking up pointers and maps of downtown (the Paso Robles Chamber of Commerce and Visitor's Center is at 1225 Park St., half a block from City Park), you'll be ready to hit the road. You'll want to visit some wineries, many of which offer tastings and behind-the-vines tours, but be sure to also visit the area's olive oil producers, organic markets, and perhaps a local brewery, too.

Along the way, collect ingredients for a picnic lunch: Many wineries have lovely outdoor picnic areas where you can relax under giant oak trees and savor cheese, fruit, veggies, and vino with spectacular views.

A string of excellent wineries are clustered on the city's hilly west side off Highway 46, among them the Summerwood Winery and Midnight Cellars. Highway 46 is a particularly scenic route that ambles west from Paso Robles for 20 miles of hilly countryside and sprawling vineyards before reaching the Pacific Ocean.

On the east side of town you'll find tasting rooms and tours of such well-known vintners as Eberle and Meridian. To veer a bit off the beaten path, cruise the winding pastoral route along Adelaida Road, home of the Tablas Creek Winery and the Mount Olive Organic Farm, a hillside spread with acres of fruit trees, produce, a market, and a barnyard zoo with llamas, goats, bunnies, and free-range chickens.

Paso's high season begins in May with the arrival of the annual Paso Robles Wine Festival and ends in October with the annual Harvest Wine Weekend, one of the largest outdoor wine events in California. In July the city hosts the popular California Mid-State Fair, a 12-day blowout that brings top entertainers to the Central Coast and includes a cattle drive through the streets of Paso Robles.

Looking to skip the crowds? Plan a visit during winter months. It's a peaceful time in Paso Robles and the Central Coast in general. There are few tourists and more than a few rainy days that transform the landscape into an endless expanse of glistening green acres. This isn't beach weather. But it is bargain time. In January and February wine-country innkeepers lower their rates and offer attractive extras, especially on weekdays. Best of all during the slow season: The farmers and knowledgeable pourers behind the wine bars (and olive-oil-tasting bars, too) have all the time in the world. They are happy to answer your questions and keep your glass full.

GUIDANCE Paso Robles Chamber of Commerce and Visitor's Center (805-238-0506; pasorobleschamber.com), 1225 Park St., Paso Robles 93446.

Paso Robles Wine Country Alliance (805-239-8463; pasowine.com). Good source of information about the wine country and upcoming events.

Paso Robles Downtown Main Street Association (805-238-4103; pasorobles downtown.org). Browse online to check out upcoming events and downtown news.

San Luis Obispo County Visitors & Conference Bureau (805-541-8000; 800-634-1414; sanluisobispocounty.com), 811 El Capitan Way, Suite 200, San Luis Obispo 93401. A good resource for information and events throughout San Luis Obispo County.

The *Paso Robles Press* (pasoroblespress.com). Local paper.

GETTING THERE Paso Robles sits inland in Central California at the northern end of San Luis Obispo County, about 20 miles from the coast at Cambria, or a slightly farther 38 miles from Hearst Castle.

Hwy. 101—which runs north to south—and Rt. 46—which starts at the coast and runs west to east—meet and briefly merge in Paso Robles. The local wine region includes the adjacent communities of Templeton and Atascadero. San Miguel, home of the landmark Mission San Miguel Arcangel, is about 9 miles to the north along 101.

By car:

From Los Angeles: Take Hwy. 101 north 216 miles through San Luis Obispo until you reach Paso Robles. The Paso Robles American Viticultural Area (AVA) begins at the top of the Cuesta Grade in Santa Margarita. Downtown Paso Robles is accessible via the Spring St. exit.

From San Francisco: Take Hwy. 101 south for 177 miles to Paso Robles area exits. The Paso Robles wine region begins as you enter San Luis Obispo County. Downtown Paso Robles is accessible by the 16th St. off-ramp.

From the coast: Take Hwy. 46 (Green Valley Rd.) east from the Cambria area (at US 1) until you reach Paso Robles. Hwy. 46 joins with Hwy. 101 just south of downtown Paso Robles. Hwy. 46 is a pastoral route that winds past numerous wineries in Paso Robles and Templeton. Caution: Take care when driving on the western end of 46 in poor weather; the coastal area sometimes is shrouded in thick fog that can limit visibility. Check road conditions before you go.

From the San Joaquin Valley: Take Hwy. 46 east to Paso Robles.

PASO ROBLES TRANSPORTION DEPOT: CLEAN AND CONVENIENTLY LOCATED

By bus: The one-stop **North County Transportation Center** (800 Pine St.) is a convenient hub that actually makes it easy to use public transportation. It's also not the sort of place you normally envision when you hear the phrase *bus depot*. The Paso Robles Depot is spacious and spotless with benches and a towering oak tree out front. It boasts three wine-tasting rooms (among them the Anglim Winery, a boutique vintner specializing in Rhône varietals, Pinot Noir, and Cabernet Sauvignon), along with an upscale consignment store (Twice as Nice) that's fun to browse while you're waiting for a bus or train.

Best of all, the depot is conveniently located. You step off the bus or train and land just a few blocks from the heart of downtown Paso Robles. The transportation center is staffed by a clerk who can answer questions about both buses and trains.

Here's the available bus service:

Amtrak Thruway Bus Service (800-872-7245; amtrak.com). Motor coach service connects with Amtrak train service throughout California. Passengers purchase train and Thruway motor coach tickets together from Amtrak.

Greyhound (805-238-1242; greyhound.com). The Greyhound depot is within the Transportation Center and open 8:30 AM–4:30 PM.

Paso Express (805-239-8747; pasoexpress.com). Bus line serving the city of Paso Robles.

San Luis Obispo Regional Transit Authority (805-541-2228; slorta.org). Rt. 9 stops in Paso Robles and also serves San Miguel, Templeton Park and Ride, Paloma Park in Atascadero, Santa Margarita, Cal Poly University, and San Luis Obispo.

By train: The **Amtrak depot** (800-872-7245; amtrak.com), 800 Pine St., Paso Robles, also is located within the Transportation Center. The double-decker Coast Starlight train runs between Los Angeles and Seattle. It makes two stops daily in Paso Robles—one going southbound at 1:36 PM and one northbound at 4:45 PM. There are no ticket sales on site, however, so riders have to buy tickets on the train, over the phone, or through Amtrak's website.

Check the Amtrak website for information about the Thruway bus service, which connects Paso Robles with train service in other California cities. For example, Amtrak's Surfliner train runs daily between San Diego and San Luis Obispo; passengers arriving in SLO can hop on a waiting Thruway bus that gets them to downtown Paso Robles within an hour. Trains and Thruway bus service can be booked together online.

By air: The **Paso Robles Municipal Airport** (805-237-3877), 4912 Wing Way, Paso Robles 93446, serves private planes, but there are no commercial carriers.

GETTING AROUND The Wine Line (805-610-8267; hoponthewine line.com) offers a "hop on, hop off" service that lets you cruise a choice of 60 wineries all day without the hassle of driving. The shuttle service began serving the west side of town and expanded during 2010 to include eastside wineries, too. Wine Line owner Jason Westfall says most riders visit

THE COAST STARLIGHT ARRIVES IN PASO ROBLES

SAN LUIS OBISPO COUNTY REGIONAL AIRPORT
(805-781-5205; sloairport.com), 903-5 Airport Dr., San Luis Obispo 93401, is 37 miles south of Paso Robles.

The San Luis Obispo airport has just two commercial carriers:
US Airways: 800-428-4322; usairways.com.
United Express: 800-241-6522; united.com.

Two car rental companies have Paso Robles offices (there are additional firms based at the SLO airport):
Budget: 805-226-9470; budget.com; 2631 Riverside Ave., Paso Robles 93446.
Enterprise: 805-239-0628; enterprise.com; 633 Spring St., Paso Robles 93446. Located downtown, this car rental office is convenient for visitors arriving by train or bus at the nearby transportation depot, which is several blocks away.

four to six wineries. The cost is $49.95 per person with pickup and return service within Paso Robles, Templeton, or Atascadero; locals and military qualify for a $10 discount. *Tip:* Check Yelp.com for occasional Wine Line discount deals.

✳ To See

MUSEUMS Mission San Miguel Arcangel (805-467-3256; missionsanmiguel .org; info@missionsanmiguel.com), 775 Mission St., San Miguel 93451. Open daily 10 am–4 pm. No charge, but donations welcome. Founded on July 25, 1797, the Mission San Miguel Arcangel became the 16th of California's famous 21 missions. It filled the gap between Mission San Antonio de Padua (at the remote Fort Hunter Liggett in Jolon) and Mission San Luis Obispo (to the south). Located 9 miles north of Paso Robles along the 101, Mission San Miguel Arcangel is less known than other missions, but it is renowned for having the best-preserved interior of any of the old outposts, reflecting the original mission life.

The unique, vividly colored murals inside the church stand in sharp contrast with the simple white stucco exterior of San Miguel. Barcelona-born artist Esteban Carlos Munras created the murals, but much of the work and designs, completed in 1821, was done by indigenous Salinan Indians. Tribal artists used local natural materials and motifs to make religious art unique among the missions, featuring sunbursts and a design of fruit and foliage that create a wallpaper effect. Other murals consist of faux columns and balustrades that offer the illusion of an elevated gallery.

In the 19th century the mission's colorful history included its secularization by the Mexican government, its brief conversion during the Gold Rush era into a saloon, dance hall, and way station for miners en route to San Francisco, and its return to the church just before the American Civil War. Rumors of buried gold treasure—accumulated payments extracted from passing miners during its saloon days—have circulated for 150 years.

The mission took a beating in the San Simeon Earthquake of December 22,

2003, a temblor that hit 6.5 on the Richter scale. It is still bouncing back; damage was so extensive that the Catholic Church considered closing the parish permanently. But the mission, still venerated by the Salinan tribe, remains a center of life in the small San Miguel community, and parishioners raised the $15 million needed for renovations. They finally returned in 2009 to celebrate their first Christmas Mass at the mission since the quake. The mission church, museum, and gift shop have reopened to the public as well, though repair work continues on the property.

✔ **Paso Robles Children's Museum** (805-238-7432; pasokids.org; questions @pasokids.org), 623 13th St., Paso Robles 93446. Open 10 AM–4 PM on Wed., Sat., and Sun.; 11 AM–4 PM on Thu. and Fri.; closed Mon. and Tue. $7 adults, $6 children, $5 seniors. Located at the Paso Robles Volunteer Firehouse, this hands-on center offers a number of distinctly Central Coast–centric exhibits, such as a giant ersatz oak tree children can climb, a grape stomp, and "El Mercado," a play market where children can shop and learn Spanish at the same time.

✳ To Do

FOR FAMILIES Charles Paddock Zoo (805-461-5080; charlespaddockzoo.org), 9100 Morro Rd., Atascadero 93422. The zoo was established in 1955 by Charles Paddock, a county park ranger who nursed wild animals back to health. Over the years the little zoo has grown to include more than100 animals on 5 park-like acres within Atascadero Lake Park. During 2010 the zoo staff began renovating and upgrading animal exhibits to create more naturalistic habitats. Open daily, 10 AM–5 PM Apr.–Oct.; the zoo closes at 4 PM the rest of the year. $5 adults, $4 children, $4.25 seniors; ages 2 and under are free.

Ravine Water Park (805-237-8500; ravinewaterpark.com), 2301 Airport Rd., Paso Robles 93446. On a hot Central Coast summer day, this is the place to race down 325-foot-long flume slides or drift along Kickback Kreek. The park also has a 9,000-square-foot Kiddie Cove.

GOLF Hunter Ranch Golf Course (866-271-6061; hunterranchgolf.com; 4041 Hwy. 46 East, Paso Robles 93446. A scenic 18-hole, par 72 course where the fairways are lined with century-old oak trees, lakes, and natural grasses. The golf shop is open 6:30 AM–dusk; course restaurant, 7 AM–7 PM.

SPA River Oak Hot Springs (805-238-4600; riveroakshotsprings.com), 800 Clubhouse Dr., Paso Robles 93446. Lounge indoors or outside in natural mineral springs heated by the earth, not by technology. Mineral springs have naturally occurring minerals and trace elements such as calcium, magnesium, potassium, sodium, iron, manganese, sulfur, iodine, and bromine. Private indoor soaks cost $12 per hour, while private outdoor soaks are $16 per hour. Additional spa services are available.

✳ Wineries

The Paso Robles region produces more than 40 wine grape varieties. The most common are Cabernet Sauvignon, Merlot, Syrah, Chardonnay, Zinfandel, Petit Syrah, and Sauvignon Blanc. You'll also find a wealth of Rhône varietals as you explore the wine-country scene at the northern end of San Luis Obispo County.

Despite the wine industry's dramatic growth here in recent years, many Paso Robles wineries still are family owned. The Paso Robles Wine Country Alliance estimates that about two-thirds of the wineries produce fewer than 5,000 cases annually. Wineries and tasting rooms can be found everywhere, from downtown Paso to the hills along scenic Highway 46 to the miles of two-lane roads that meander through the countryside.

Paso Robles vineyards are roughly divided equally between the west-side and east-side wineries, with downtown and Highway 101 providing the rough boundary line. Although all sorts of grapes and varieties of wine are produced on both sides of town, the climate on the hilly west side, with a moister ocean influence, is traditionally considered best for red wines, while the drier east side, with hotter days, cooler nights, and a sandier soil base, is said to be the best for white wine grapes. The division may be more a matter of convention than of geography or viniculture; when a group of west-side growers petitioned the federal Tax and Trade Bureau to create a separate west-side Paso Robles wine appellation, they were turned down because of vagaries about the boundaries and distinguishing characteristics of the two sides. The debate still rages among some growers in the region, however. The best solution: Taste both sides for yourself.

Planning tip: Before you go, request a free copy of the wine alliance's current tour guide (pasowine.com), a slim volume with maps that easily slips into a pocket. It's a good starting place for planning a trip.

Touring tip: The **Wine Line** (805-610-8267; hoponthewineline.com) is a "hop on, hop off" shuttle that lets you cruise your choice of 60 local wineries. The cost: $49.95 per person.

Here's a taste of what you'll find in the Paso Robles AVA:

Adelaida Cellars (805-239-8980, 800-676-1232; adelaida.com), 5805 Adelaida Rd., Paso Robles 93446. Open daily 10 AM–5 PM. It's a pretty drive to Adelaida Cellars, located on a hilltop ranch with elevations to 2,300 feet. Established in 1981 by the Van Steenwyk family, the winery specializes in estate-grown Pinot Noir, old-vine Zinfandel, and Cabernet Sauvignon. Visitors are welcome to picnic on the winery lawn.

Eberle Vineyards (805-238-9607; eberlewinery.com), 3810 Hwy. 46 East, Paso Robles 93446. Open 10 AM–5 PM, Oct.–Mar.; 10 AM–6 PM, Apr.–Sept. A pioneer of the Paso Robles wine scene, Gary Eberle planted the first commercial Syrah in California in the mid-1970s. His well-regarded winery is located on Paso's east side, where Eberle still produces Syrah as well as Cabernet Sauvignon, Zinfandel, Chardonnay, and Pinot Grigio. William A. Ausmus, author of *Wines & Wineries of California's Central Coast*, praises Eberle for "consistently excellent whites and outstanding reds," and suggests trying the winery's Muscat Canelli. A winery highlight: underground cave tours that go down 35 feet. The cost of the tour is $25, including a wine tasting and a session learning about the Paso Robles appellation.

Justin Winery (805-238-6032; justinwine.com), 11680 Chimney Rock Rd., Paso Robles 93446. Open daily, 10 AM–6 PM. This is one of Paso Robles's most acclaimed vineyards—the *Wine Spectator* has rated the winery's Isosceles as one of the top 10 wines in the world. Owner Justin Baldwin is a former investment banker and his wife, Deborah, worked in mortgage banking before they bought 165 acres on Paso's west side. Their property is one of the area's Far Out Wineries (faroutwineries.com)—an association of west-side vineyards that describe themselves as "off the beaten path but worth the drive." The focus of the winery is two Bordeaux-style blends—Isosceles, a blend of Cabernet Sauvignon, Cabernet Franc, and Merlot, and Justification, a blend of Cabernet Franc and Merlot. Additional wines include Cabernet Sauvignon, Syrah, Zinfandel, Chardonnay, and Sauvignon Blanc. Winery tours include tastings and cost $15 to $50, depending on whether you sign up for a beginning, intermediate, or advanced session. Reservations are suggested.

Meridian (805-237-6000; meridianvineyards.com), 7000 Hwy. 46, Paso Robles 93446. Open daily 10 AM–5 PM. Established in 1988, Meridian is one of the most widely distributed wines based in Paso Robles and is known for its Cabernet Sauvignon, Chardonnay, and Pinot Noir. A long driveway and gradual climb lead to Meridian's natural stone winery, which is surrounded by landscaped gardens and picnic grounds. The winery tasting room features Meridian's Limited Release wines. Snacking options include wine-and-cheese pairings ($10 for five wines and five selections from Vivant Fine Cheese); and wine-and-chocolate pairings ($10 for four reds and four artisan dark chocolates by Scharffen Berger).

Midnight Cellars (805-239-8904; midnightcellars.com), 2925 Anderson Rd., Paso Robles 93446. Open daily 10 AM–5 PM. Midnight Cellars started out as a barley farm. The Hartenberger family added insulation, built an addition to their horse barn, and converted the property into a winery. They ended up replacing the barley with 30 acres of vines. The winery focuses on handcrafted Zinfandel, Cabernet Sauvignon, and other red blends as well as Chardonnay. "This winery keeps getting better and better across the line," says William A. Ausmus, author of *Wine & Wineries of California's Central Coast*.

GAZEBO AT THE PEACHY CANYON WINERY

Peachy Canyon (866-335-1918; peachycanyon.com), 1480 N. Bethel Rd., Templeton 93465. Open 11–5 daily. A big fluffy brown cat named Peaches greets visitors to this tranquil hilltop winery, which offers eight different Zinfandels in the old-fashioned white schoolhouse that serves as Peachy Canyon's tasting room. Owners Doug and Nancy Beckett make other reds, too: Cabernet Sauvignon, Cabernet Franc, Malbec, and Petite Syrah. Just outside the tasting room a gazebo and picnic tables are scattered among the oak trees. Peachy Canyon is a sweet spot, especially when the afternoon breeze rustles the vineyards across the hilly landscape.

Pipestone Vineyards (805-227-6385; pipestonevineyards.com), 2040 Niderer Rd., Paso Robles 93446. Open Thu.–Mon. 11 AM–5 PM. Pipestone Vineyards is a small family winery with

WINE-COUNTRY Q&A WITH CHRISTOPHER TARANTO

Q. What is the current number of wineries in the Paso Robles AVA?
A. The correct statement is "more than 180 bonded wineries." There over 200 wineries in the area that are in different states of being and different versions of bond. For a wine consumer or traveler to the area, you really only have the opportunity to experience the wines of a little over 180 wineries.

Q. Do you see any major tourism trends in your area?
A. With travel trends seemingly staying close to home these days we see a resurgence in people wanting to travel for special events and festivals. We have two major ticketed events each year in Paso Robles Wine Country (Zinfandel Festival and the Paso Robles Wine Festival). Ticket sales are currently tracking ahead of last year (a down year) and hotels are reporting strong reservations during these event times. This makes us hopeful that we will see a rise in regional tourism.

Q. People generally are traveling less during the current economy, but they are still traveling and looking for good value. How has the Paso area responded?
A. With the growing trend of knowing the origin of your food and the back-to-agriculture movement that seems to be everywhere these days—wine and wine travel is well poised to take advantage of this. Actually, wine enthusiasts have long since been into knowing more about their wine and learning of its

a history of sustainable farming and producing handmade Rhône-style wines from Syrah, Grenache, Mourvèdre, Viognier, and Zinfandel. The winery sits in a secluded valley just west of Paso Robles, a mile or so off Hwy. 46 West. The Pipestone tasting room is surrounded by the vineyard and almonds, the farm's original crop. Free-range hens, dogs, cats, homing pigeons, and a goat named Lucy roam the property. Owner Jeff Pipes uses a team of draft horses to plow and till the soil. The property also is solar powered and is designed as a Wildlife Habitat by the National Wildlife Federation.

Summerwood Winery (805-227-1111; summerwoodwine.com), 2130 Arbor Rd., Paso Robles 93446. Open daily 10 AM–6 PM. As you reach Hwy. 46 West from Paso Robles, the Summerwood Winery is one of the first vineyards you'll see. The 46-acre property is a picturesque estate surrounded by a vast expanse of vineyards and white picket fencing. Inside, you'll find a spacious tasting room with a long marble tasting bar and oversized chairs. Summerwood produces Chardonnay, Viognier, Cabernet Sauvignon, Syrah, Sentio, Diosa, Diosa Blanc, and port. Winery tours are available; there's also a restaurant and B&B on the grounds.

Tablas Creek Vineyards (805-237-1231; tablascreek.com), 9339 Adelaida Rd., Paso Robles 93446. Open daily 10 AM–5 PM. In 1987 the owners of Tablas Creek

origins. That's part of the mystique since wine is all about a sense of place, right down to the labeling on the bottle. But what is great is that as more and more people are becoming foodies, we have a growing number of people traveling to wine country to discover more than just the wine. Many small farms and other added-value agricultural endeavors such as olive oil, nuts, and farm-to-table restaurants are plentiful here.

Q. Are you seeing more regional visitors?
A. Mostly Los Angeles. Some come from the inland areas of Fresno, Bakersfield, et cetera, and then a growing amount from the San Francisco Bay Area.

VINEYARDS IN PASO ROBLES

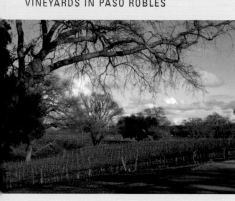

Q. Has the winery building boom stopped for now?
A. Yes. If new brands are popping up, they probably started their endeavor some years ago or are growers looking to diversify.

Christopher Taranto is the spokesman for the Paso Robles Wine Country Alliance (pasowine.com).

decided to plant vines imported from France on 120 acres west of Paso Robles. Robert Haas and the Perrin family figured the conditions were ideal for planting Rhône varietal grapes. They turned out to be right. Tablas Creek, one of the area's Far Out Wineries, produces estate-grown, internationally recognized Rhône varietals and blends that include Syrah, Mourvèdre, Viognier, and Roussanne. Daily tours showcase the on-site grapevine nursery, organic vineyard, winery, and tasting room. The tours are free, but appointments are requested. "The wine is like drinking France by way of California," writes author Janis Cooke Newman of the *Los Angeles Times*.

Paso Wine Centre (805-239-9156; pasowines.com), 1240 Park St., Paso Robles 93446. Open Mon.–Thu. 11 AM–8 PM, Fri.–Sat. 11 AM–9 PM, Sun. noon–7 PM. This downtown wine-tasting room and lounge opened in 2009 and features 48 Paso Robles region wines by the glass and many by the bottle, too. Enomatic machines dispense 1-ounce tastes, each costing $1–6. You'll find selections from many small wineries that don't have tasting rooms of their own. You'll also be helping a good cause. Owner Ryan Broersma says he donates all the profits from the Paso Wine Centre to providing clean drinking water in developing countries through the Wine for Wells project (wineforwells.org).

✳ Lodging

Before the recession slammed the brakes in California, the Paso Robles area saw a major hotel building boom that brought a slew of lodging chains to the area. The region also offers a mix of smaller country inns, motor lodges, and B&Bs. Depending on your budget, and whether you're seeking a taste of old or new Paso, you'll find lodging ranging from comfy rooms starting under $100 to deluxe suites that will set you back upward of $300 a night.

♿ **Adelaide Inn** (805-238-2770; adelaideinn.com; res@adelaideinn .com), 1215 Ysabel Ave. (intersection of Hwys. 101 and 46), Paso Robles 93446. Inexpensive. Credit cards are accepted. This old-fashioned motor court is an unexpected gem tucked amid a gulch of fast-food joints and chain motels clustered off the 101. In contrast with its slightly kitschy exterior, the Adelaide Inn's rooms are modern and freshly refurbished with comfortable beds, updated bathrooms, and pleasing earth-tone furnishings and recliners. Guests will like the free Internet and the muffins and fruit in the lobby each morning. The Adelaide Inn is a cozy good value, typically under a $100 a night. Your hosts are the Masia and Pacheco families. Pool, mini golf, refrigerators, microwaves.

🐾 ♿ **Hampton Inn & Suites** (805-226-9988; hamptoninn.com), 212 Alexa Court, Paso Robles 93446. Moderate. Credit cards are accepted. This new three-story Mediterranean-style property sits atop a hilly junction off Hwy. 46 West, overlooking an expanse of vineyards up the road. It's one of the new chain hotels that sprouted in the area (others include a Courtyard Marriott and Holiday Inn Express). Hampton is a comfortable and reasonably priced chain with offerings homier than many of its competitors, and better-than-average free food in the morning—something seasoned travelers and vacationing families alike can appreciate. Paso's Hampton Inn is convenient for exploring wineries on the town's west side. Budget-conscious travelers will be pleased to know that the Hampton Inn is a far more affordable alternative to the lavish LaBellasera Hotel (labellasera.com), another newcomer that sits just across the parking lot. Pet lovers will be happy that dogs are allowed to stay, though the hotel website doesn't call attention to the policy. Nightly rates include a breakfast bar in the lobby and Grab 'n Go bags (water, apple, cereal bar, and muffin) for guests in a hurry. Heated pool and whirlpool.

🍴 **Hollyhock Farms** (805-239-4713, 805-712-1880; hollyhock-farm.com, hollyhock@tcsn.net), 200 Hollyhock Lane, Templeton 93465. Moderate–expensive. Credit cards are accepted; two night minimum on weekends. Dick Rogers, a retired Los Angeles detective, and his wife Kim, a refugee from the corporate world, moved to the Central Coast in the mid-1990s to grow heirloom tomatoes, melons, peaches, pluots, squash, peppers, and French plums on 30 lush acres in Templeton. They opened a roadside produce stand and welcomed overnight guests at their Hollyhock Farms B&B, a homey rural oasis with a U-pick flower field. The farm has a cottage with a wood-burning fireplace that sleeps two, and a two-bedroom bungalow that accommodates up to four people. Guests are treated to a country breakfast featuring such goodies as oatmeal pancakes (the farm's most requested recipe), chicken-apple sausage, the farm's own organic eggs made to order, fresh-squeezed orange juice, and bowls of in-season fruits. "We farmed for 15 years and I decided last year to end the commercial farming, but to plant a large garden for ourselves, family, and guests of the B&B," says Dick Rogers. "That's what we are doing now . . . it's a slice!"

🦋 ♿ ⁗1⁗ **Hotel Cheval** (866-522-6999; hotelcheval.com; info@hotelcheval.com), 1021 Pine St. (down the street from City Park), Paso Robles 93446. Expensive. Credit cards are accepted. The 16-room Hotel Cheval is an elegant boutique inn with a warm, woodsy vibe and tasteful touches throughout the property. As the hotel name suggests, the owners—Sherry and Robert Gilson—are equestrians, and their passion is on display throughout the Cheval, from the horseshoe-shaped Pony Club wine bar to the hotel's mascot—a retired farm horse named Chester who squires guests around town in a carriage. (He takes a break from his duties during rainy winter months.) Guest rooms are both cozy and luxurious with high ceilings, 400-thread-count cotton sheets, and flat-screen TV; some have fireplace, too. The Cheval opened its doors in 2007, and it's a sweet spot for a splurge or special occasion getaway. Nightly rates include breakfast, which from Monday to Friday is a continental breakfast delivered to your room; on weekends, guests are treated to a breakfast buffet in the Pony Club.

♿ **Just Inn** (805-238-6932, 800-238-6932; justinwine.com; innkeeper@justinwine.com), 11680 Chimney Rock Rd. (on the grounds of Justin Winery), Paso Robles 93446. Expensive. Credit cards are accepted. Set amid a working (and much-acclaimed) winery on 160 acres of oak-lined hills, the Just Inn is a romantic spot to escape the everyday world. By day, you can roam the English gardens, please your palate, and expand your wine education with behind-the-scenes winery tours; in the evening you can curl up in one four European-style suites with fireplaces, feather beds, and marble baths. (The suites, though, are pricey—starting at $375 a night.) Another highlight: the inn's cozy bistro style restaurant, Deborah's Room, where the menu changes with the season. Justin and Deborah Baldwin are your innkeepers. Heated pool, spa.

♿ **Paso Robles Inn** (805-238-2660, 800-676-1713; pasoroblesinn.com; info@pasoroblesinn.com), 1103 Spring St. (downtown, just off Hwy. 101), Paso Robles 93446. Moderate. Credit cards are accepted. The Paso Robles Inn is a sprawling brick landmark originally built in 1889, the same year the city incorporated. The inn's hot springs and inviting gardens are two reasons guests keep coming back. Another reason: the prime location. Sited downtown, this hisoric inn is steps from City Park, so you can easily stroll to restaurants, shops, wine-tasting bars, and the local movie house. In 1999 the hotel's owners redrilled the property's legendary mineral springs and added 30 new spa rooms with hot mineral waters. With its old-fashioned coffee shop and restored grand ballroom, the inn remains a slice of old Paso. Pool, spa, steak house. Your hosts are the Martin family.

♿ **Summerwood Inn** (805-227-1111; summerwoodwine.com), 2130 Arbor Rd., Paso Robles 93446. Expensive. Credit cards are accepted. One of the first wineries you'll find as you head west on Hwy. 46 is the lush Summerwood vineyards, an expansive property with the look and feel of a genteel southern plantation. Visitors who want more than just an afternoon sampling the Syrah can revel in a wine-country immersion experience by staying overnight on the 46-acre estate. The winery's inn is designed with pampering in mind: Nine deluxe guest rooms are nicely appointed with fresh-cut flowers, fireplace, and satellite TV, and the winery's chefs whip up gourmet farm breakfasts each morning. Perks include 24-hour room service, behind-the-scenes winery tours, and afternoon wine tasting and hors d'oeuvres for guests.

✴ Where to Eat

Artisan (805-237-8084; artisanpaso robles.com), 1401 Park St., Paso Robles 93446. Open for lunch Mon.–Sat. 11 AM–2:30 PM; Sun. brunch 10 AM–2:30 PM; dinner Sun.–Thu. 5–9 PM, Fri.–Sat. 5–10 PM; bar menu served daily 2:30–5 PM. Expensive. Credit cards are accepted. Locals, foodies, and even cranky out-of-town critics regularly mention Artisan as one of the town's premier restaurants. Chef Chris Kobayashi has created a contemporary American bistro in the heart of Old Paso. Chef Koby, as he is known, uses ingredients that mirror the seasons of California's Central Coast and adds his own signature to dishes, such as Artisan's wild mushroom lasagna with spring artichokes, stinging nettles, and parsley pesto. Ask for a booth facing the restaurant's open kitchen.

Basil (805-238-9945), 828 11th St., Paso Robles 93446. Open Mon.–Thu. 11 AM–3 PM and 5–9:30 PM; Fri. 11 AM–3 PM and 5–10 PM; Sat. noon–10 PM; Sun. noon–9:30 PM. Moderate. Credit cards are accepted. This popular little Thai restaurant, right across from City Park, offers a pleasing mix of ambience and affordability. There's an ample selection of curries, wok-fried dishes, and spicy seafood specialties, along with cocktails and wine by the glass served at the dining room's wide aqua-splashed bar. Basil offers a particularly good deal for lunch. Order a $10 dish and your waiter soon appears with a beautiful (and generous) platter of food that comes with salad, rice, pineapple, and soup, too. Try the Tom Kha Kai, a light and flavorful coconut milk soup with tofu (or substitute chicken), baby corns, cabbage, and green onions.

Cowgirl Café (805-238-6403; cowgirl cafe.net), 1316 Pine St., Paso Robles. Open Daily 6 AM–2 PM. Inexpensive–moderate. Credit cards are accepted. A reader at Yelp.com offers this advice: "WARNING!! This is not the place to go if you are watching your diet." True enough. The Cowgirl Café is a guilty pleasure, a friendly western-themed diner known for no-fuss fare and heaping portions. The locals often wait for a half an hour or more on weekends to dive into blueberry pancakes and biscuits and gravy, a house favorite. For a real diet buster, try the cinnamon rolls, which are served warm and oozing with cream cheese frosting.

❂ **Farmstand 46** (805-239-3661; farmstand46.com), 3750 Hwy. 46 West, Templeton 93465. Open daily 7 AM–7 PM. Moderate. Credit cards are accepted. This roadside deli is a slice of country heaven: delicious, healthy, local. What's good? Well, everything. And the ingredients are grown just steps away from the restaurant.

Farmstand 46 is a joint venture between the Four Vines winery next door and chef Tom Fundaro of downtown's Villa Creek Restaurant. Their new effort is "Farm to Table" express: Hungry diners stop by and select gourmet healthy food that's created while they wait from the herbs and vegetables grown outside the restaurant in raised beds. There's a mouthwatering menu of sandwiches that you can pick up to go or take outside to savor while sitting in the sunshine on silver patio chairs. Farmstand 46 also serves wood-fired pizzas, pasta salads, espresso, and a daily selection of fresh soups. One winter menu included apple parsnip soup; chili verde; and white bean pancetta and escarole soup. The blackboard menu changes, but the owners make it easy to keep up—via Twitter: twitter.com/farmstand46.

F. McLintocks Saloon & Dining House (805-238-2233; mclintocks .com), 1234 Park St., Paso Robles 93446. Open Sun.–Thu. 11:30 AM–9 PM, Fri.–Sat. 11:30 AM–10 PM; breakfast is served Sat.–Sun. starting at 7 AM. Moderate–expensive. Credit cards are accepted, as are rservations. This country-music-blaring, cowboy-pleasing steak and rib joint is a Central Coast favorite; its Paso outpost sits in the middle of the action downtown. Come here to chow on tri-tip and BBQ pork ribs, as well as a bevy of rib-sticking appetizers. We're talking onion rings with "Famous Cowboy Salsa," Bronco Wings doused with spicy hot sauce, and a McClintocks, ahem, specialty called Deep-Fried Turkey Nuts. You're on your own with that one. The restaurant opens for breakfast on weekends. Chicken-fried steak, anyone?

Panolivo (805-239-3366; panolivo .com), 1344 Park St., Paso Robles 93466. Open Mon.–Thu. 7 AM–3 PM, Fri. 7 AM–3:30 PM and 5–9 PM, Sat. 8 AM–3:30 PM and 5–9 PM, Sun. 8 AM–3:30 PM. Moderate–expensive. Credit cards are accepted. This sunny café, popular for its fresh-baked pastries, croissants, and crusty breads, brings a taste of Provence to Paso Robles. Panolivo is a pleasing spot for breakfast; the French toast made with brioche is delicious. The restaurant also serves lunch (salads, sandwiches, panini, French-inspired entrées) and only opens for dinner two nights a week, so you'll have to wait for Friday or Saturday to try the wine tapas nights.

FARMSTAND 46 IS A NEW DELI/FARMSTAND/COFFEE BAR ON HWY. 46 WEST IN TEMPLETON

Thomas Hill Organics (805-226-5888; thomashillorganics.com), 1305 Park St., Paso Robles 92446. Open Sun., Mon., Wed., 11 AM–8 PM; Thu.–Sat. 11 AM–9 PM; closed Tue. Moderate–expensive. Credit cards are accepted. Joe and Debbie Thomas grow their own vegetables and fruit (they have 800 fruit trees) on a 10-acre farm. Their just-picked ingredients form the centerpiece of the dishes served at this stylish little bistro and wine bar. The restaurant is a sweet spot, though the place is easy to miss— it's tucked away in a downtown alley near Park and 13th St. So follow the signs (and the heavenly aromas) and enjoy the restaurant's constantly changing menu. Thomas Hill is an especially good choice for lunch, offering a creative selection of salads such as a cauliflower panna cotta with wild arugula and diver scallop seviche with ponzu, carrot-ginger mousse, and Asian greens. Diners also can take home a T-Hill basket, a selection of produce from the Thomases' farm that's determined by the week's harvest and includes their recipes. Local wines by the glass or bottle.

Villa Creek (805-238-3000; villacreek .com), 1144 Pine St., Paso Robles 93446. Open Tue.–Sun. 5:30–10 PM for dinner; bar opens at 4 PM; closed Mon. Moderate–expensive. Credit cards are accepted. Reservations recommended. Villa Creek is a sophisticated, dimly lit haven downtown. Come here for a sit-down gourmet feast or happy-hour grazing from the restaurant's excellent bar menu. Chef Tom Fundaro grew up on the Central Coast and specializes in simple, rustic dishes centered on the cuisine of early California. His menu ranges from grass-fed steaks to butternut squash enchiladas, with a strong emphasis on ingredients that are sustainably farmed and raised. Dinner at Villa Creek can get pricey (entrées start at $20 and climb from there), but

the restaurant offers midweek specials such as Taco Tuesdays, when you can you can enjoy *carnitas*, fish, and chicken tacos for $2.50 in the bar. Good selection of wine by the glass.

FOOD PURVEYORS ¶ Amsterdam Coffee House (805-239-7779), 725 13th St., Paso Robles 93446. This downtown java spot serves up strong Joe and free WiFi. What more do you need in the morning?

Firestone-Walker Brewing Co. & Tasting Room (805-238-2556; fire stonebeer.com), 1400 Ramada Dr., Paso Robles 93446. When you've had enough wine, come to Firestone-Walker to try the Double Barrel Ale, produced with a traditional oak-barrel fermentation process at this craft brewery. Complimentary guided tours of the brew house and cellar are on Sat. and Sun. at 1:30 PM and 3:30 PM.

Vivant (805-226-5530; vivantfine cheese.com), 840 11th St., Paso Robles 93446. Danika Bowler, a purveyor of local and rare cheeses, supplies cheeses to local businesses and runs a small cheese shop downtown.

We Olive (805-239-7667; weolive .com), 1311 Park St., Paso Robles 93446. Take a break from wine tasting and belly up to We Olive's excellent tasting bar, where you can sample various olive oils grown in the area— typically a selection of at least 20. The store also sells fresh olives, tapenades, and other items.

✳ Selective Shopping

FARMS Central Coast Lavender Farm (805-467-3500; centralcoast lavender.com), 6630 Northstar Lane, Paso Robles 93446. Visit Lila Avery-Fuson's Lavender Farm Stand to learn more about the fragrant herb's aromatherapy and culinary uses. There's a seasonal lavender U-pick, too.

☙ **Happy Acres Family Farm** (805-434-7580; happyacresfamilyfarm.net), 1955 Templeton Rd., Templeton 93465. This is a family-friendly goat and dairy farm on 56 acres where visitors can make goat cheese, milk the goats and buy organic products such as goat's milk lotion, soap and ice cream.

☙ **Mount Olive Organic Farm** (805-237-0147; mtoliveco.com), 3445 Adelaida Rd., Paso Robles 93446. Sprawling across hundreds of hillside acres, Mount Olive has an olive orchard, fruit orchard, strawberry fields, chicken range, vegetable gardens—and a petting zoo, too. Visitors can tour the farm to learn about eco-friendly growing methods and sample homemade jams, salsas, breads, olive oils, and other products made from food grown here. (The farm closes Fri. and Sat.)

Pasolivo Olive Oil Tasting Room (805-227-0186; pasolivo.com), 8530 Vineyard Dr., Paso Robles 93446. Drive out to the Willow Creek Olive Ranch, home of the Pasolivo tasting room. The ranch is a leading producer of estate-developed extra-virgin olive oil. You'll enjoy sampling the varietals grown on the property, learning how olive oil is made and touring the state-of-the-art press. This is another choice spot to pick up goodies to bring home.(The tasting room closes on Tue. and Wed.)

FARMER'S MARKETS (northcounty farmersmarkets.com). When you visit Central California, it's easy to stumble upon open-air farm markets most days of the week. Growers set out baskets of fresh produce, fruit, and flowers. Many other farmers and artisans bring a wide range of organic, homegrown goods such as locally pressed olive oil, olives, jams, honey, almonds, and lavender products of all descriptions. Browse the markets for goodies to take home or to savor on the spot. Here's quick rundown:

Paso Robles: Sat. (8 AM–noon) and Tue. (3–6 PM) at City Park downtown.

Templeton: Sat. (9 AM–12:30 PM) at 6th and Crocker Sts.

Atascadero: Wed. (3–6 PM) at Sunken Gardens, El Camino Real and East Mall.

Cambria: Fri. (2:30–5 PM) on Main St. next to Veterans Memorial Hall.

San Luis Obispo: Thu. (6–9 PM) on Higuera St. downtown.

✴ **Special Events**

March: **Zinfandel Festival** (pasowine.com).

May: **Paso Robles Wine Festival** (pasowine.com). **Great Western Bicycle Rally** (greatwesternbicycle rally.com).

Summer: **Friday Night Concerts in the Park** (pasoroblesdowntown.org).

July–August: **California Mid-State Fair** (805-239-0655; midstatefair.com), at the Paso Robles Event Center, draws 300,000 visitors to a carnival, concerts, and livestock auctions. **Central Coast Shakespeare Festival** (centralcoastshakespeare.org).

August: **Paso Robles Olive Festival** (805-238-4108; pasoroblesolivefestival .com).

October: **Harvest Wine Weekend** (pasowine.com).

November: **Wine Vine Run** (wine vinerun.com).

December: **Annual Vine Street Victorian Showcase** (pasorobles downtown.org).

Coastal SLO 6

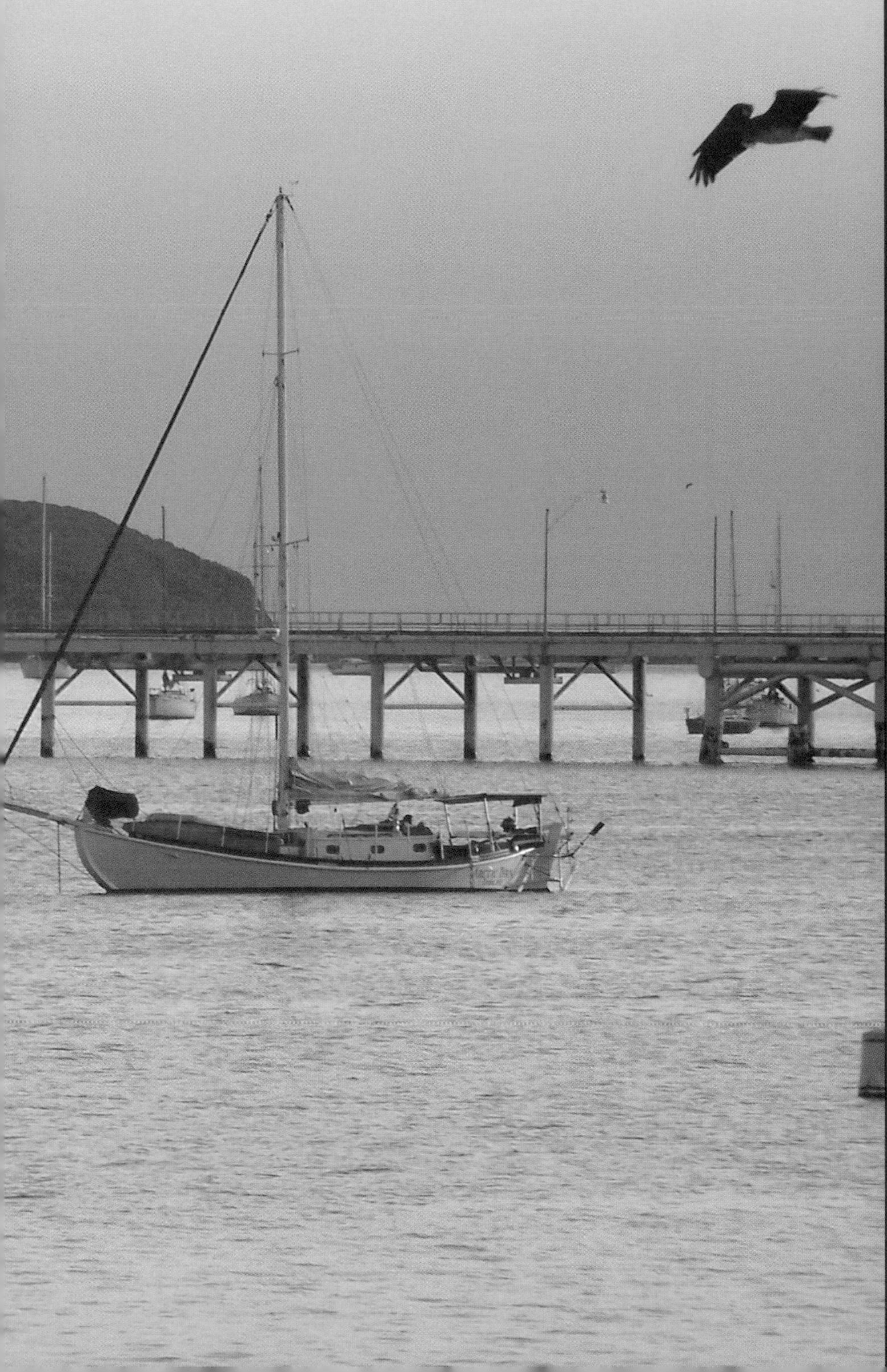

COASTAL SLO

"San Simeon was the place God would have built—if he had the money."

—George Bernard Shaw on the Hearst Castle

The California Dream is on opulent display 362 days a year at Hearst Castle, Central California's signature landmark. The hilltop mansion has been a state park since 1958 and offers the rest of us a rare glimpse inside the glittering world and staggering wealth of newspaper mogul and art collector William Randolph Hearst. You'll find Hearst's "Enchanted Hill" perched high atop Highway 1 along the San Luis Obispo County coastline, a zigzagging stretch of small towns, surf beaches, and an impressive collection of state parks splayed out one after another along the Pacific's rugged edge.

Sixty miles south of Hearst's well-preserved crown jewel of the California park system you'll find a vastly different kind of state park at Oceano Dunes. This freewheeling zone near Pismo Beach at San Luis Obispo County's southern edge is the only beach in California where you can legally drive a car onto the sand. Oceano has 3,600 acres, including an off-roading area where daredevils in all-terrain vehicles blast their way through the dunes with abandon.

THE SLO COAST

In between you can explore a string of vast and beautiful coastal wilderness parks, preserves, and beaches, among them Morro Bay State Park, site of a great blue heron rookery, and Montaña de Oro, or "mountain of gold," an 8,000-acre state park named for the brilliant display of golden wildflowers that bloom there each spring.

If you take the time to detour off Highway 101 in favor of the slower,

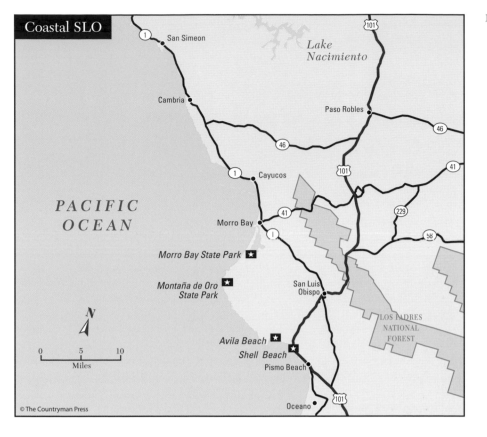

Coastal SLO

San Simeon

Lake Nacimiento

Cambria

Paso Robles

46

46

Cayucos

101

41

PACIFIC OCEAN

41

229

Morro Bay

58

Morro Bay State Park ★

Montaña de Oro State Park ★

San Luis Obispo

N

LOS PADRES NATIONAL FOREST

0   5   10
Miles

Avila Beach ★
Shell Beach ★
Pismo Beach

© The Countryman Press

Oceano

101

coastal Highway 1, you'll be pleasantly surprised by the offerings up and down the SLO coast.

This is a particularly choice region for sea kayaking, and you'll find great spots for surfing, swimming, and fishing, too. The area also is heaven for bird-watchers and nature lovers in general. The National Audubon Society routinely ranks Morro Bay among National Audubon's top 10 for the huge number of species spotted during the annual Christmas bird count. You'll spy otters in the waters here, and gray whales cruising along the coast during their annual migration. Each winter thousands of vivid orange butterflies converge on Pismo Beach's Monarch Butterfly Grove, the largest in California.

The beach towns here are an eclectic mix, and you'll find much to like about the SLO coast's down-to-earth, no-airs style. The best part: You can go

SURFING BY THE PISMO BEACH PIER

DOWNTOWN PISMO BEACH

to sleep at a beachfront inn or rustic campground listening to waves crashing onto the shore and still be just a short drive away from the wine-country delights of Paso Robles and the city of San Luis Obispo.

Each cluster of beach towns has its own distinct feel and offerings. On the county's southern end, you'll find a string of beach communities just a few miles from downtown San Luis Obispo and the Cal Poly campus. Farthest south is Oceano, which has a popular campground right on the sand near Pismo Beach and vendors ready to rent you ATVs for some off-roading action. Nearby Pismo, the "Clam Capital of the World," is a rough-and-tumble town of about 8,000 residents. The downside: Pismo has a gritty side with a downtown pier area rife with tattoo parlors and tacky souvenir shops. The upside: 23 miles of sandy white beaches and a lively surf scene. It's fun to walk out on the Pismo Pier to watch the expert surfers working the swell and the local fishermen hauling in dinner.

At the northern edge of Pismo Beach, you'll want to savor Shell Beach, a compact beach neighborhood with several very inviting bluff-top hotels and a peaceful, beautiful public beach. Shell Beach is a good choice for an idyllic escape whether you're visiting the San Luis Obispo area for work or play.

ON THE PISMO PIER

Next comes Avila Beach, a seaside town that was forced to bulldoze and rebuild its quaint downtown in the late 1990s after one of California's worst coastal oil leaks slowly contaminated the entire area. Much of Avila Beach was out of commission for several years, but the town is back to welcoming visitors. The funky pink 1960s-era Inn at Avila Beach still overlooks the shore, but downtown has been largely rebuilt with sherbet-colored shops, cafés, and hotels along the beach. This clean and perky new Avila feels a bit like Downtown Disney, but with a beach. Two miles up the road, the nat-

STROLLING AROUND AVILA BEACH

ural hot springs at Sycamore Mineral Springs Resort have been a Central Coast sanctuary since the 1800s.

Along the northern end of SLO County, you'll find another cluster of beach communities. About 20 miles up the coast from Avila Beach, Morro Bay is a working fishing village with a touristy but highly likable Embarcadero area of waterfront shops, restaurants, and other attractions. The towering bulk of Morro Rock rises just offshore, the town's dominant and almost always visible landmark. Morro Bay is one of California's lushest bird sanctuaries. You can rent a kayak on the Embarcadero (or at one of two nearby state parks) and paddle out to an estuary abounding with cormorants, herons, pelicans, seagulls, and many other species. Right in the middle of the bay, there's a barge where dozens of sea lions like to lounge in a noisy, jostling heap sunning themselves, barely glancing up as kayakers and sailors glide past their playground and snap photos.

Past Morro Bay on Highway 1, you'll reach Cayucos, a beach hamlet with a 900-foot-long wooden pier. *Men's Journal* lauds tiny Cayucos as one of its 25 favorite "hideouts and secret spots." Indeed, this is a sweet spot to pull over and stroll the pier. Come here to fish or to just watch the gaggle of young surfers in the water waiting for the next set.

AVILA BEACH

Q & A
WITH CENTRAL COAST SURFER
AND AUTHOR ERIC SODERQUIST

Q: While working on *The California Surf Project*, you roamed beaches from the Oregon border to Baja Mexico. How do the Central Coast beaches stack up in terms of surf spots?

ES: The Central Coast is unique and beautiful. There are plenty of surf spots, but it's the whole experience that makes me love our little gem.

Q: What's your favorite local beach?

ES: Old Shell Beach is my favorite. My aunt owned the Shell Beach Café for over 20 years and the whole family grew up working there. It's now **Zorro's Café** (805-773-9676; 927 Shell Beach Rd.). I live down the street and wander down on my bike to surf. There's a great community, especially the old guys at the dog park. My favorite spots are just north of my home. Get as close to the beach as you can and glance around at the reefs, find a nook and enjoy.

Courtesy of Chronicle Books

Q: What's the best spot for kayaking?

ES: Kayaking is fabulous around **Dinosaur Park** (an 11-acre oceanfront park along Shell Beach Road in Pismo Beach; pismobeach.org), just south of my house. The caves, cliffscapes, and wildlife are very inspiring.

SAN SIMEON

photo by Chris Burkard, courtesy of Chronicle Books

Q: What are your favorite breakfast places?

ES: My favorite spot is **Zorro's**. Also, **Seaside Cafe** (805-773-4360; 1327 Shell Beach Rd.) is where I start my day with a great cup of illy coffee; they have epic pastries too, and you have to try the eggs Benedict.

Q: Is there a must-visit spot for first-time travelers to the SLO Coast?

ES: Wander the San Luis Creek (in downtown San Luis Obispo) on **Farmer's** Market Thursday from 7–9 P.M. Stroll through the **Mission San Luis Obispo de Tolosa** and have a glass of wine at **Novo** (See San Luis Obispo chapter).

Shell Beach resident Eric Soderquist is co-author with Chris Burkard of The California Surf Project, *a beautifully illustrated diary of two surfers who quit their jobs, packed up their boards, and surfed their way down the coast.*

More info: thebookprojectca.com.

Fifteen miles farther up the road, Cambria is a quirky, art-centric town that proclaims itself "free of chain stores and brimming with charm." True on both counts. Cambria is a community of about 6,000 residents, including a good number of artists, musicians, and poets. The town boasts two particularly notable natural attributes: the stands of towering Monterey pine trees that encircle the city and tranquil Moonstone Beach, so named for the lovely white, translucent stones found there. You'll find a wealth of small shops and galleries as you meander around town.

MORRO ROCK

Many visitors come to Cambria en route to the Big Sur coast or as part of a pilgrimage to Hearst Castle, which is about 6 miles away at San Simeon. Northward from the castle along this scenic and sometimes foggy stretch of US Highway 1 lie the Piedras Blancas elephant seal rookery, the Monterey County line, and the winding wilds of the Big Sur Coast.

Many visitors choose Cambria as a base camp while visiting the castle. It's also a straight shot along scenic Highway 46 from the coast to the Paso Robles wine country.

But almost any spot on the SLO Coast makes a good base of operations for an extended stay, because everything is so relatively close. Between Oceano to the south and San Simeon to the north, a mere hour's drive, you have access to a wide range of camping, hiking, eating, and pampering pleasures, both urban and rural, from goggling at the gold-leafed domain of America's true royalty at Hearst Castle to hunkering over a paper plate on a weathered outdoor patio at Morro Bay, where ice-cold beers and sublime Dungeness crab quesadillas are served up to hungry kayakers. From a traveler's point of view, it's hard to imagine another 60-mile stretch of highway that offers a more varied array of vistas, experiences, and opportunities to learn, relax, and play.

GUIDANCE Avila Beach Business Association (visitavilabeach.com). Information about Avila attractions and events.

Cambria Chamber of Commerce (805-927-3624; cambriachamber.org) is at 767 Main St., Cambria 93428.

Morro Bay Chamber of Commerce and Visitors Center (805-772-4467; morrobay.org), 845 Embarcadero Rd., Suite D, Morro Bay 93442.

Pelican Network (pelicannetwork.net). A nature directory of the Central Coast.

Pismo Beach Conference & Visitors Bureau (805-773-7034; classiccalifornia .com), 581 Dolliver St., Pismo Beach 93449. The **Pismo Beach Chamber of Commerce** (805-773-4382; http://pismochamber.com) is at the same address.

San Luis Obispo County Visitors and Conference Bureau (805-541-8000; sanluisobispocounty.com/visitors/ca-central-coast-towns/pismo-beach), 811 El Capitan Way, #200, San Luis Obispo 93401. Check online for information about SLO beach towns.

Surfline (surfline.com). Check surf conditions along the coast.

GETTING THERE San Luis Obispo County is about 200 miles north of Los Angeles and 220 miles south of San Francisco.

By car:

From Southern California: Head north on US Hwy. 101 until you reach the San Luis Obispo area and you'll see signs for each of the beach cities. You also can reach coastal SLO from the south via US Hwy. 1, which passes Oceano, Pismo Beach (and its Shell Beach area), Avila Beach, Morro Bay, Cambria, and San Simeon.

From San Francisco: Head south on the 101, the most direct route. Travelers also can opt for the scenic coastal route along Hwy. 1, by way of Big Sur.

From the east, including Fresno and Bakersfield: Take Hwy. 46 west. To reach San Luis Obispo County's northern beach cities, you'll stay on Hwy. 46, through Paso Robles, until you reach Hwy. 1 and the town of Cambria on the coast. If you're heading to the southern end of SLO, take Hwy. 46 to Paso Robles, then head south on Hwy. 101.

By air: **San Luis Obispo County Regional Airport** (805-781-5205; sloairport .com), 903-5 Airport Dr., San Luis Obispo 93401, is located just south of the city of San Luis Obispo off Hwy. 101. The terminal has free WiFi. (See the San Luis Obispo chapter for information about airlines and rental cars.)

Ride-On Transportation (805-541-8747; ride-on.org)—a nonprofit, community-based cooperative—provides shuttle service from the airport and Amtrak station.

DOWNTOWN MORRO BAY

The airport website (sloairport.com) also lists taxis and limousine operators currently serving the airport.

By train: **Amtrak** (local station 805-541-0505; nationwide reservations 800-872-724; amtrak.com), 1011 Railroad Ave., San Luis Obispo 93401, runs its Pacific Surfliner service daily between San Diego and San Luis Obispo. Amtrak's Coast Starlight service runs from Los Angeles to Seattle, with stops in San Luis Obispo. Amtrak also serves Grover Beach.

By bus: **Santa Barbara Airbus** (800-423-1618; santabarbaraairbus.com) offers coach service from Los Angeles International Airport to the Central Coast, with stops in San Luis Obispo and Pismo Beach.

Greyhound bus terminal (800-231-2222; greyhound.com) is now located at the San Luis Obispo Amtrak station.

GETTING AROUND **San Luis Obispo Regional Transit Authority** (805-781-4472; slorta.org) offers bus service connecting cities in San Luis Obispo County.

RTA-South County Area Transit (805-781-4472; scattransit.org) provides bus service in the county's southern beach communities, including Shell Beach, Pismo Beach, Grover Beach, Arroyo Grande, and Oceano. The county's regional transit service also operates the trolleys in three local beach communities.

Avila Beach Trolley (805-781-4472; avilatrolley.org) runs from downtown Avila Beach to Spyglass Dr. in Shell Beach on weekends. Free.

Cambria Village Trolley (cambriachamber.org) runs along Main St., past the village shops, galleries, and eateries, and goes to Moonstone Beach, too. Free.

VIEWS OF SCENIC SHELL BEACH

Morro Bay Trolley (morro-bay.ca.us) runs from Memorial Day weekend through the first weekend in October. There are three different routes through town, including service from the Morro Strand campground to the Embarcadero. $1 adults, 50 cents children.

✳ To See

HISTORIC SITES The SLO coast has two landmark lighthouses. **The Point San Luis Lighthouse** (805-546-4904; sanluislighthouse.org) was built in 1890 near Avila Beach. A West Coast listening station during World War II, the lighthouse was updated in 1969 when its Fresnel lens was replaced by an automated electric light. The lighthouse's grounds offer dramatic vistas stretching from Avila to the Vandenberg Air Force Base to the south, and you can often see whales, sea lions, and otters along the coast here. Public tours are offered on Sunday. Docent-led hikes on the Pecho Coast Trail also are available. **Piedras Blancas Lighthouse** (805-927-2968; blm.gov), located just north of San Simeon, is named for a white rock outcropping located off the end of the point. In 1866 this location was chosen to fill the gap between the lighthouses at Point Conception and Point Sur. Tours of the light station are offered Tue., Thu., and Sat.

Nit Wit Ridge (805-927-2690), 881 Hillcrest Dr., Cambria, is a historic landmark of a different type: Garbage collector Arthur Harold Bea built this house entirely of junk—rocks, wood, beer cans, tile, car parts, and abalone shells—during the course of 51 years. He called it his Hearst Castle. Nit Wit Ridge may be an offbeat roadside attraction, but it's also considered folk art architecture and designated as a California State Historic Landmark. The current owners, Michael and Stacey O'Malley, offer tours; $10 donations are suggested.

SEA LIONS BATTLING FOR SPACE ON A BARGE IN THE HARBOR

THE HEARST CASTLE

On a hilltop overlooking coastal Hwy. 1, with glorious views of pastures and Pacific waves, tycoon William Randolph Hearst's palatial mansion stands in all its Gilded Age splendor—now a museum, state park, historic landmark, and working cattle ranch (the grass-fed, humanely raised beef it produces is justly prized). La Cuesta Encantada, the Enchanted Hill, otherwise known as Hearst Castle, ranks among California's most enduring and popular attractions.

Located 40 miles north of San Luis Obispo, Hearst Castle (800-444-4445; hearstcastle.org; 750 Hearst Castle Rd., San Simeon 93452) is adjacent to a beautiful San Simeon State Park, which features hiking, camping, and other activities. With more than a million visitors a year, the castle lags behind only the big theme parks to the south in popularity as a tourist destination. If you plan on touring the castle, book reservations ahead of time online.

The property began as a coastal cattle ranch founded in 1865 by George Hearst, a miner who struck it rich during the California Gold Rush. His son, newspaper magnate William Randolph Hearst, decided to build a modest bungalow with a great view of the ranch he had loved as a boy. But the project, designed by architect Julia Morgan and built in 1919, soon expanded to a Moorish castle that incorporated architectural styles, sculptures, and art that Hearst had admired from all over Europe, from mausoleums to coliseums. The finished mansion ended up at 90,000 square feet, with 56 bedrooms, 61 bathrooms, 19 sitting rooms, ornate pools inside and out, a theater, an airfield, a private zoo, and 127 acres of gardens. Presidents and starlets, celebrities and kingmakers flocked to the rich man's playground by the sea: Franklin Roosevelt, Winston Churchill, Charles Lindbergh, Charlie Chaplin, the Marx Brothers, Cary Grant, Clark Gable, Greta Garbo, Mary Pickford, and Howard Hughes all stayed and played at the castle, just to name a few from Hearst's A-list.

There is so much to see and do at the castle that you can visit it many times and have a different experience each time.

✳ To Do

BEACHES The SLO coast spans more than 60 miles. Cruise Hwy. 1 and pull over when you see someplace you like. At the county's northern end, **Morro Strand State Beach** (805-772-2560; parks.ca.gov), 2 miles south of Cayucos off Hwy. 1, **Montaña de Oro State Park** (805-528-0513; parks.ca.gov), 6 miles south of Morro Bay, and **San Simeon State Park** (805-927-202; parks.ca.gov), close to Hearst Castle, are all choice spots for swimming, hiking, beachcombing, and picnicking. The parks are open for day use as well as overnight camping.

CASTLE TOURS

There are five guided tours at the castle. Tour 1: The Experience Tour is a 1¾-hour overview of the castle and grounds recommended for first-time visitors, who get to ogle the outdoor Neptune Pool that took 12 years to build and the indoor Roman Pool with its blue tiles and flecks of real gold shimmering throughout. It starts at the visitors center near the estate entrance and includes a bus ride up the hill. Other tours are more focused: one limits itself just to the upper floors of the main house; another devotes 1¾ hours to the North Wing; there's an outdoor garden tour; and the Evening Tour lets visitors experience the castle at night, just like the glitterati who flocked here in the Roaring Twenties. There is also a new "Gardens and Vistas" self-guided tour, which is offered from March through Labor Day weekend and allows visitors to stroll the castle's gardens in late afternoon. Tours cost $24 adults, $12 ages 17 and under, with children under 6 admitted for free; the Evening Tour costs $30.

HEARST RANCH

The surrounding lands are used to graze cattle and are still owned by the Hearst Corporation. The grass-fed beef can be purchased at Hearst Castle store or online, or eaten at local restaurants. Sebastian's General Store and Cafe (805-927-3307; 442 Slo San Simeon Rd., San Simeon) is known for its French dip and barbecue using the hormone-free, grass-fed beef from the ranch.

THE VISITORS CENTER

features a museum store, a gift shop, and a theater that shows *Hearst Castle: Building the Dream* every 45 minutes on a five-story-tall screen.

W. R. HEARST MEMORIAL STATE BEACH AND SAN SIMEON STATE PARK

The beautiful sandy beach has picnic sites, barbecue grills, restrooms, and easy beach access; kayaks and boogie bards can be rented, and there is fishing from San Simeon Pier. San Simeon State Park's coastal bluffs offer unobstructed ocean views, archaeological sites, hiking, fishing, and whale-watching. The park also offers a Junior Ranger Program for children.

The pier at **Cayucos** is a popular local surf spot, though Surfline.com notes that surfers usually will find consistently better waves farther south along the coast near Pismo Beach. **Moonstone Beach** in Cambria (sanluisobispocounty.com) is a gorgeous area with a boardwalk that shadows the coast. You'll often spot birds, seals, and other wildlife along the shore.

At the county's southern end, **Oceano Dunes State Recreational Area** (805-473-7220; parks.ca.gov) offers off-roading in the dunes; **Pismo State Beach** (805-489-1869; parks.ca.gov) has hiking, swimming, and surf fishing. You also can swim

PARASAILING OVER SHELL BEACH

and stroll the sand near the **Pismo Pier**, get lost on the secluded beach at **Shell Beach** (there's a public access location near the Cliffs Resort), and play along the waterfront in downtown **Avila Beach**.

G O L F Avila Beach Golf Resort (805-595-4000; avilabeachresort.com), 6450 Ana Bay Rd., Avila Beach 93424. This seaside resort includes a par 71, 6,500-yard championship course. The front nine holes are situated within oak-lined valleys. The back nine transverse a tidal estuary. It's a challenging course in a lovely setting.

Morro Bay Golf Course (805-782-8060; slocountyparks.com), 201 State Park Rd., Morro Bay 93442. This 18-hole course offers exercise in a bucolic natural setting in the heart of Morro Bay State Park. There's a pro shop and driving range; rental clubs and lessons also are available.

SEA KAYAKING along the coast here is a blast, and no prior experience is needed. Morro Bay, Avila Beach, and Montaña de Oro State Park are all choice spots, and you can find rentals anywhere you go (sanluisobispocounty.com). One favorite nature zone: Rent kayaks on the Embarcadero and within minutes you'll be paddling toward the towering hulk of Morro Rock in the distance. The bay here teems with herons, gulls, pelicans, and dozens of other species, and the calm waters have an abundance of sea grass and kelp, excellent environments for sea life and the

THE GOLF COURSE AT MORRO BAY STATE PARK

ELEPHANT SEAL COLONY AT PIEDRAS BLANCAS

No trip up Highway 1 in the Central Coast is complete without a stop at Piedras Blancas, home to one of California's largest elephant seal rookeries, where you can see the giant seals barking, bellowing, battling for mating rights, and basking in the sun.

About 15,000 animals call this stretch of sand and rocky waters home. The 70-pound newborn pups are adorable, but the bulls are seriously intimidating. They can reach 16 feet and 3 tons, three times the weight of the average female.

The vista point at Piedras Blancas (elephantseal.org) is 4.4 miles north of Hearst Castle on Highway 1—look for the parking lot on the ocean side of the highway, where you'll find great viewing spots overlooking the mammoth sea mammals. Docents are on hand to answer questions.

ELEPHANT SEALS AT PIEDRAS BLANCAS ON HWY. 1

There is no charge and no reservations needed; the viewing area is open 8 AM–sunset year round. Pregnant females arrive in December to give birth at Piedras Blancas, then wean the frisky pups through March while the males, with their elephantine probosci, roar like, well, elephants.

critters that feed on it. You'll cruise past sea lions swimming beside you in the bay and, if you're lucky, you'll spot a few otters, too. **Rock Kayak** (805-772-2906; rock kayak.com; 845 Embarcadero St., Morro Bay) is an experienced outfitter located right on the Embarcadero. Staff members will give you some quick training and safety tips before you set out.

✳ Wineries

Harmony Cellars (805-927-1625; harmonycellars.com), 255 Harmony Valley Rd., Harmony 93435. Open daily 10 AM–5 PM. The town of Harmony (population 18) is little more than a small cluster of small businesses a few miles south of Cambria. You could easily zip past on Hwy. 1 (as most people do) and miss this charming hilltop winery. Founded in 1989 by Chuck and Kim Mulligan, Harmony Cellars has grown from a 2,000-case micro winery to a 5,500-case boutique production facility. The Mulligans produce a variety of wines, including Pinot Noir, Chardonnay, Syrah, Zinfandel, Merlot, and Harmonie, a white table wine that's a blend of

PEACOCKS ROAM KELSEY SEE CANYON VINEYARDS

Chardonnay, Chenin Blanc, and White Riesling. The winery has a spacious tasting room with a long bar for unhurried tasting sessions, as well as a pretty outdoor garden with sweeping views that's ideal for an off-the-beaten-path picnic. But be careful that you don't overindulge: The narrow road back down the hillside could be tricky to navigate after one too many glasses of wine.

Kelsey See Canyon Vineyards (805-595-9700; kelseywine.com), 1947 See Canyon Rd., San Luis Obispo 93405. Open daily 11 AM–5 PM. Hidden away between Avila Beach and San Luis Obispo, the Kelsey Winery is a likable family farm with a tasting room attached to a big white barn. A flock of outspoken peacocks roams the front vineyard and stare dolefully at visitors from the farmhouse roof. What began as a retirement project in 1999 blossomed into a full-time labor of love for winery owners Dick and Dolores Kelsey. The apples used in their Apple Chardonnay and Apple Merlot are harvested from decades-old orchards on the family ranch in See Canyon, where the winery's Chardonnay grapes also are grown.

✳ Lodging

From oceanfront campgrounds to deluxe beach inns, the SLO coast offers a range of accommodations and a tradition of hospitable service. Many properties welcome pets. Prices peak during summer, though many hotels still are less expensive than their counterparts in Big Sur and Santa Barbara. In winter months you can find real bargains on hotel rooms.

&. ⁽'ı⁾ **Avila La Fonda Hotel** (805-595-700; avilalafondahotel.com; info@avilalafondahotel.com), 101 San Miguel St., Avila Beach 93424. Expensive–very expensive. Credit cards are accepted. Avila La Fonda borrows its name from Santa Fe's La Fonda Hotel, a landmark just steps from the New Mexico city's central plaza. Owner Micheal Kidd wanted to create his own Mission-style retreat at the center of Avila Beach. He built his La Fonda from the ground up with attention to every detail: The facade, for example, is a modern version of traditional Mexican casa architecture. The Spanish Mission-style lobby is the same width as the San Miguel and Lompoc missions. Thirty-five of the hotel's stained-glass windows depict early Avila Beach, and a mural outside portrays the beach town before the first settlers arrived. The hotel offers 30 suites with cushy extras, such as Jacuzzi tubs for two, and 12-cup coffeemakers and grinders with fresh coffee beans. There's also a snack pantry with inexpensive sodas and treats. Avila La Fonda is a block from the beach and walking distance to restaurants and shops in the compact downtown area. Kidd also owns the nearby Inn at Avila Beach, a funky pink outpost (at 256 Front St.; avilabeachca.com) with a great rooftop deck overlooking the beach.

🐾 ♿ "🍴" **Avila Village Inn** (800-454-0840; avilavillageinn.com), 6655 Bay Laurel Dr., Avila Beach 93424. Moderate–expensive. Credit cards are accepted. Located a mile from the beach, this pretty Craftsman-style inn opened

its doors in 2005 and is an especially good choice for pet lovers (dogs are welcome) and golfers (the Avila Beach Resort Golf Course is right next door). The inn's 30 rooms are decorated with Mission-style furniture and have fireplaces, wet bars, and flat-screen TVs; there's a separate building with a fitness center. The inn has rental bicycles, and guests can pedal from the nearby Bob Jones Bike Path to the beach.

🐾 ♿ **Blue Dolphin Inn** (800-222-0159; cambriainns.com; bluedolphininn@cambriainns.com), 647 Moonstone Beach Dr., Cambria 93428. Expensive. Credit cards are accepted. Located on Moonstone Beach, the Blue Dolphin is an upscale property that caters to adults looking for a quiet getaway. (The hotel's owner also owns the nearby Sand Pebbles Inn, which welcomes children.) The inn's contemporary rooms are freshly remodeled and very comfortable, with pillow-top mattresses and 32-inch flat-screen TV. Six specialty oceanfront rooms are

AVILA LA FONDA HOTEL IN AVILA BEACH

VIEWS OF SCENIC SHELL BEACH

named (and designed) for bodies of water around the world where dolphins are found. Guests have a choice of staying, for example, in Key Biscayne (with white wooden beach-style furnishings and wicker porch chairs that evoke the Florida Keys) or Saldanha Bay (with a four-poster dark wood bed and African prints and accents that feel like the savanna). Nice touch: Rates include a complimentary breakfast delivered to your room at the time of your choosing. So you can start your day by sipping java and freshly made waffles while gazing out to the sea. Free Internet, and pets are welcome.

🐾 ♿ ¶ **Cliffs Resort** (800-826-7827, 805-773-5000; cliffsresort.com), 757 Shell Beach Rd. (just off the 101, in the Shell Beach section of Pismo Beach), Shell Beach 93449. Moderate–expensive. Credit cards are accepted. Located 10 miles from downtown San Luis Obispo, the Cliffs is an airy beachfront hotel that renovated all 160 guest rooms in 2009 with modern, sand-colored furnishings and floor-to-ceiling plantation shutters. Many rooms are less than $200 a night, even in summer, though prices go up for

ocean views. Popular with both families and business travelers, the Cliffs is convenient to everything in the SLO area but not in the middle of anything, except an incredible natural setting. As its name suggests, the hotel sits atop a cliff and overlooks a pristine sweep of beach below. A path at the edge of the property meanders down to a secluded cove, where you can swim or explore a rocky peninsula with dozens of tide

CLIFFS RESORT IN SHELL BEACH

pools. The hotel also has a restaurant, plus an inviting pool area with a fire pit and great views.

☗ ☖ "♉" **Dolphin Bay Resort & Spa** (805-773-4300; thedolphinbay.com; sdamery@thedolphinbay.com), 2727 Shell Beach Rd., Shell Beach 93449. Expensive–very expensive. Credit cards are accepted. This is a luxury-minded resort with very spacious, fully equipped one- and two-bedroom villas originally designed as condo units. All 63 villas have kitchens with granite countertops and a full complement of appliances, though you might want to forgo cooking to enjoy the sophisticated California cuisine served in the hotel's Lido restaurant. Executive chef Evan Treadwell specializes in creative fare using local ingredients; he also offers monthly cooking classes at the hotel. Dolphin Bay is a Mediterranean-style resort that sits atop an oceanfront bluff. It's a scenic spot and just a short stroll along a beach path to Shell Beach's secluded cove. (The hotel is next door to the Cliffs Resort.) The property is a particularly good choice for an extended-stay getaway. Heated pool.

☖ "♉" **Embarcadero Inn** (805-772-2700; embarcaderoinn.com; info @embarcaderoinn.com), 456 Embarcadero, Morro Bay, in the heart of Morro Bay. Moderate. Credit cards are accepted. Located within walking distance of many Embarcadero restaurants and shops, this is a pleasant and affordable small hotel with prime views of Morro Bay. The inn's 33 rooms are spacious and equipped with refrigerator, microwave, and coffeemaker; many have fireplace. All stays include a complimentary continental breakfast.

✪ ∞ ☖ **Inn at Morro Bay** (800-321-9566, 805-772-5651; innatmorrobay .com; info@innatmorrobay.com), 60 State Park Rd. (just inside the state park, across from the golf course), Morro Bay 93442. Moderate–expensive. Credit cards are accepted.

AT THE EMBARCADERO IN MORRO BAY

Nature lovers will adore this picture-perfect white inn perched in the middle of a vast heron sanctuary. Nestled on 4,000 acres, the 98-room hotel sits inside Morro Bay State Park and has a soothing ambience. Rooms are decorated in a simple French country style; the most popular are bay-view rooms, which boast private hot tubs on outdoor patios overlooking the bay—an unexpected luxury in the middle of a nature preserve. "You can see a lot of wildlife out there," says Diana Hanauer, the inn's general manager. (Budget note: During the winter off-season, rooms rate drop as low as $59 a night.) The Inn at Morro Bay celebrated its 50th birthday in 2009 and has been undergoing renovation work throughout the property. The decor includes some new personal touches including a series of park wildlife photographs taken by Hanauer and other hotel staffers. (Budget note: During the winter off-season, rooms rate drop as low as $59 a night.) The inn's waterfront restaurant, Orchid, is a lovely setting with bay views and very good food, including a killer chocolate lava cake. This unpretentious retreat offers a welcome respite from the bustling scene at Morro Bay's Embarcadero.

Pool, golf, kayaking, bird-watching, hiking.

& **Kon Tiki Inn** (805-773-4833; kontikiinn.com; kontiki@charter internet.com), 1621 Price St., Pismo Beach 93449. Moderate. Credit cards are accepted. This is a big, clean, no-frills hotel with a tropical motif and a friendly office staff decked out in Hawaiian shirts. Rooms are basic and a bit dated, but the big selling point of the Kon Tiki—and the reason families return year after year—is that every single room has a balcony and a great ocean view. There's a pool and hot tub area, and you can walk down to the beach. A continental breakfast is included. Steamers is the on-site restaurant.

& **Olallieberry Inn** (805-927-3222, 888-927-3222; olallieberry.com; info@olallieberry.com), 2476 Main St., Cambria 93428. Moderate–expensive. This cute little B&B was built in 1873 and is one of the oldest buildings in Cambria. There are nine guest rooms—six in the main house and three in the innkeeper's cottage. Rooms have fireplace and private bath and are furnished with antiques. Days here start with a bountiful breakfast with such favorites as olallieberry-

THE SLO COAST

stuffed French toast, ricotta cheese pancakes, or olallieberry yogurt with fresh fruit and granola. At 5 PM guests enjoy wine and hors d'oeuvres, including signature dishes like baked Brie with—you guessed it—olallieberries. Owners Marjorie Ott and Marilyn and Larry Draper also offer cooking classes. The Olallieberry Inn is surrounded by a lush garden and attracts a faithful following of guests who return year after year. It's a short walk to the village.

🐾 ♿ **Pickford House** (805-927-8619, 888-270-8470; thepickfordhouse.com; innkeeper@thepickfordhouse.com), 2555 MacLeod Way, Cambria 93428. Daily, weekly, and monthly rates. Credit cards are accepted. This Cambria mansion opened in the 1980s as an upscale B&B dedicated to the film stars of the 1920s (such as Mary Pickford, Rudolph Valentino, John Barrymore, Clara Bow, and Lillian Gish) who cavorted at William Randolph Hearst's nearby castle. The Pickford House has switched gears and now offers lodging for group stays only, so you have to rent the house. Located away from town, the inn has nine spacious, themed rooms adorned with antiques and claw-foot tubs; there's a dining room and 1860s-era bar with a saloon-like atmosphere. Innkeeper Patricia Moore welcomes "well-behaved pets and children."

♿ **Sand Pebbles Inn** (800-222-9970; cambriainns.com; guestservices@sandpebblesinn.com), 6252 Moonstone Beach Dr., Cambria 93428. Moderate–expensive. Credit cards are accepted. This inviting sand-colored inn is a family-friendly property that's steps from the boardwalk on Cambria's scenic Moonstone Beach. Rooms are comfy (beds have pillow-top mattresses); some have fireplaces and patios with ocean views. Nightly rates include

a continental breakfast. Check the hotel website for specials. DVD library, Internet access.

♿ **Sycamore Mineral Springs Resort** (805-595-7302; sycamore springs.com; info@smsr.com), 215 Avila Beach Dr. (just up the road from Avila Beach), San Luis Obispo 93405. Moderate–expensive. Credit cards are accepted. This lush sanctuary has been a destination spa since 1886 and remains a timeless oasis surrounded by more than 100 acres of forest, hills, and meadows. The resort rests atop hot mineral springs. All rooms have private balcony tubs fed with sulfur mineral springs water, so you can sit and soak outside under a canopy of oak trees. The accommodations range from modest rooms to deluxe suites with four-poster beds and gas fireplaces. This isn't a sleek modern spa, but rather a well-tended older property that offers a tranquil getaway in a beautiful setting. Guests can stroll the grounds (or cruise in golf carts) to a wide range of spa treatments and daily tai chi, yoga, and Pilates classes in the yoga dome. The resort also has a meditation garden (including a labyrinth walking path), and miles of hiking and biking trails that wind through towering oaks and sycamore trees. The Gardens of Avila restaurant offers a menu of California cuisine infused with Asian flavors and a daily happy hour, too. The resort's redwood mineral tubs, classes, spa services, and restaurants also are open to day visitors.

CAMPING Popular campgrounds, especially near the coast, fill up fast during summer, so you'll want to book ahead. Some areas close down or limit offerings during off-season winter months. Be sure to call ahead or check online for the most current information.

ⁱ1ⁱ **Morro Bay State Park** (805-772-7434, reservations 800-444-7275; parks.ca.gov), Morro Bay State Park Rd. (a mile from Hwy. 1), Morro Bay 93442. This is one of California's most civilized state parks and even features an 18-hole golf course and a marina where you can rent kayaks. The campground here is very popular, so you'll want to make reservations as far in advance as possible. The park offers a wide range of activities for campers and day visitors. Come here to hike, sail, fish, and savor bird-watching amid an amazing heron rookery, where you'll be treated to the sight of such unusual birds as white pelicans. Take a break from roughing it to enjoy dinner at Orchid, the bay-front restaurant at the Inn at Morro Bay, also located inside the 4,000-acre park. Overnight campers will find showers, restrooms, fire rings, and picnic tables; RV hookups are available, with a maximum camper length of 35 feet. There's also a small, and somewhat static, Natural History Museum on site that's not

MORRO BAY AND ITS FAMOUS MORRO ROCK LANDMARK

nearly as interesting as the real-life natural setting right outside.

Morro Strand State Beach (805-772-2560, reservations 800-444-7275; parks.ca.gov) 2 miles south of Cayucos on Hwy. 1, Morro Bay 93442. Park kiosk open only in summer; reservations suggested. A 3-mile stretch of beach connects the southern and northern entrances to this scenic park. Fishing, windsurfing, jogging, and kite flying are popular activities at Morro Strand, which is available for day use as well as overnight camping. Morro Strand has picnic tables, restrooms, and a comfort station, but no showers. The maximum RV length is 24 feet. Reservations are required Memorial Day–Labor Day weekends. The Morro Bay Trolley stops in the park during summer, so you can hop on and ride to Morro Bay's nearby Embarcadero area.

Montaña de Oro State Park (805-528-0513, reservations 800-444-7275; parks.ca.gov; slostateparks.com), 3550 Pecho Valley Rd. (6 miles south of Morro Bay), Los Osos 93402. Summer reservations needed. Montaña de Oro is one of California's largest and most glorious state parks. This vast coastal wonderland spans 8,000 acres of rugged cliffs, sandy beaches, canyons, and hills, including 1,347-foot Valencia Peak. It's open to the public for day use and also has campsites for tent camping and campers (the maximum length is 27 feet), as well as more rustic equestrian and environmental sites. Campsite reservations are required Memorial Day weekend–Labor Day; the rest of the year the campground is available on a first-come, first-served basis. Visitors will find restrooms and picnic areas. Docents at the park information center, open weekends throughout the year and daily during summer months, can answer questions

about park history and wildlife.

Oceano Dunes State Recreational Area (805-473-7220, reservations 800-444-7275; parks.ca.gov), 928 Pacific Blvd. (off Hwy. 1), Oceano 93445. Reservations highly recommended. Oceano is a playground for off-highway enthusiasts from throughout the United States, and it has the most extensive coastal dunes remaining in California. It's a noisy, raucous scene, so if you're looking for a quiet camping experience, go elsewhere. This is the only California beach that allows motorists to drive on the sand. Other activities here include swimming, surfing, surf fishing, and hiking. Camping is allowed on the beach and in the open dune area. Rangers recommend beach camping for visitors with four-wheel-drive vehicles only. Vault toilets and chemical toilets are provided. Campsites are available by reservation year-round; you can rent ATVs nearby. Try **BJ's ATV Rentals** (805-481-5411; bjsatvrentals.com). Owner John Aitkens and Evelyn Valentino have been in business here since 1982, and their guides put a premium on safety. Plan rides for the morning before the wind kicks up; the winter scene here is calmer than the craziness of summer. Nearby, you'll also find **Pismo State Beach** (805-489-1869, 805-473-7220), 555 Pier Ave., Oceano 93445, which offers hiking, swimming, surf fishing, and overnight camping. Campsites at Pismo State Beach have showers, restrooms, and fire rings.

Port San Luis (805-903-3395; portsanluis.com; camphost@portsanluis.com), Babe Lane, Avila Beach. RV camping is allowed in the Port San Luis area, and spaces are available on a first-come, first-served basis. No tent camping is allowed. Ten full-hookup sites are available off Babe Lane. In addition, camping is permitted in a

PISMO BEACH

portion of the Coastal Gateway trailer boat parking area. Campfires are prohibited, and all pets must be kept on leash. Call to make arrangements.

San Simeon State Park (805-927-2020; reservations 800-444-7275; parks.ca.gov), Van Gordon Creek Rd. at San Simeon Creek Rd., Cambria 93428. Reservations needed during summer months. San Simeon State Park is a beautiful public beach and campground 5 miles south of Hearst Castle. Come here to visit the castle, of course, but also to picnic, hike, fish, surf, beachcomb, and watch the birds and whales along the coast. Campground reservations can be made Mar. 15–Sept. 30; the rest of the year the campground is open on a first-come, first-served basis. The park's San Simeon Creek campground offers 115 campsites for tent camping or recreational vehicles. The creek runs through the campground, and it's a scenic spot. Each campsite has a fire ring and picnic table; there also are restrooms with flush toilets and coin-operated showers. The maximum length for an RV is 35 feet.

✳ Where to Eat

Cracked Crab (805-773-2722; crackedcrab.com), 751 Price St., Pismo Beach 93449. Open Sun.–Thu. 11 AM–9 PM, Fri.–Sat. 11 AM–10 PM. Moderate–expensive. Credit cards are accepted, but not reservations. Located between Main and Pomeroy Sts. in Pismo, the Cracked Crab serves heaping buckets of shellfish. Patrons get to mix and match their choice of several types of crab, shrimp, and slipper lobster, which are served with sides of corn on the cob, red potatoes, and spicy Cajun sausage. The house special, the Big Bucket For Two, is pricey ($68), but it's a treat for diners who love seafood and don't mind wielding a wooden mallet to crack down on a messy meal. The menu includes other seafood entrées, along with token steak and chicken dishes; beer and wine are served. The Cracked Crab is a lively spot, and you might have to wait in line on weekends.

Custom House Restaurant (805-595-7555; oldcustomhouse.com), 404 Front St., Avila Beach 93424. Open Sun.–Thu. 8 AM–9 PM, Fri.–Sat. 8 AM–10 PM. Moderate–expensive. Credit cards are accepted. The Custom House's history in Avila Beach dates back to the early 1900s when nearby San Luis Bay was designated an official US Port of Entry and a local builder put up the Old Custom House as the port's headquarters on the waterfront. In 1999 the historic building was razed, along with nearly everything else downtown, in the wake of a massive oil leak under the town. Then in 2002 the Custom House had a rebirth in a newly constructed restaurant on the same choice spot overlooking the beach and Avila's piers. It's an airy, upscale, crowd-pleasing outpost that serves seafood, steaks, sandwiches, and salads, along with a breakfast menu. There's a full bar inside. But the highlight of the Custom House is dining outside on the restaurant's inviting patio, where patrons (and their dogs) enjoy dining alfresco with views of the beach.

DePalo and Sons (805-773-1589), 2665-L Shell Beach Rd., Shell Beach. Open 7 AM–10 PM daily. Moderate. Credit cards are accepted. This neigh-borhood deli and market has a few tables outside for dining, but mostly it's a bustling take-out eatery where you can grab a gourmet sandwich or ready-made meal to go. DePalo and Sons is close to the shore in Shell Beach; it's a handy spot to stop for picnic provisions before you hit the beach for the day.

F. McLintocks (805-773-1892; mclintocks.com), 750 Mattie Rd., Shell Beach 93449. Open Mon.–Thu. 4:30–9 PM, Fri. 4–9:30 PM, Sat. 4–10 PM, Sun. 4–9 PM. Expensive. Credit cards are accepted, as are reservations. McLintocks is an oak-pit place with a boisterous cowboy personality and a country music soundtrack. This is the original F. McLintocks restaurant that debuted on the Central Coast more than three decades ago, and it has attracted a loyal following ever since. (The other outposts are in Arroyo Grande, Paso Robles, and San Luis Obispo.) There's a good (if pricey) selection of steaks on the menu, along with burgers and a selection of rib-sticking appetizers. The offerings are tasty and filling. What more could you want?

THE CUSTOM HOUSE OFFERS ALFRESCO DINING WITH VIEWS OF THE BEACH

THE SPLASH CAFE IN PISMO BEACH

Giuseppe's Cucina Italiana (805-773-2870; giuseppesrestaurant.com), 891 Price St., Pismo Beach 93449. Open Mon.–Fri. 11:30 AM–3 PM, Sun.–Thu. 4:30–10 PM, Fri.–Sat. 4:30–11 PM; Giuseppe's Express opens daily at 11 AM. Moderate–expensive. Credit cards are accepted, but not reservations. For 20 years Giuseppe Difronzo has been serving up fresh southern Italian fare, just-baked bread, and an extensive wine list in Pismo Beach. The restaurant's homemade pastas are good, and include a flavorful roasted butternut squash ravioli. There's also an ample pizza menu, from a simple Margherita (fresh toma- toes, basil, and buffalo mozzarella) to the more adventurous Diavolo pizza (organic spicy Tuscan salami, Gaeta olives, house marinated hot peppers, and creamy mozzarella). Giuseppe's has opened a satellite deli across the street, Giuseppe's Express (at 800

Price St.), so you can grab an Italian cheese steak sandwich on the run if you aren't up for a sit-down meal.

Splash Cafe (805-773-4653; splash cafe.com), 197 Pomeroy Ave., Pismo Beach 93449. Open Sun.–Thu. 8 AM–8:30 PM, Fri.–Sat. 8 AM–9 PM. Inex- pensive. Credit cards are accepted. Don't let the line snaking out the door scare you away. It moves fast. And Splash Cafe definitely is worth the wait. Located in downtown Pismo, just a short stroll from the pier, this bright blue fish shack with white plastic tables and chairs is renowned for its creamy clam chowder ($4.50 a bowl). The chowder lives up to its advance billing. The menu also includes other seafood fare, such as calamari and curly fries ($5.75) and a seafood salad ($6.50), along with burgers, hot dogs, and breakfast sandwiches. The food is inexpensive, and it's a crowd-pleaser. This little eatery is a favorite on

Yelp.com, where dozens of enthusiastic yelpers keep spreading the word.

Frankie and Lola's (805-771-9306; frankieandlolas.com), 1154 Front St., Morro Bay 93442. Open daily, 6:30 AM–2:30 PM. Inexpensive–moderate. Credit cards are accepted. Located at the intersection of Front St. and the Embarcadero, this hip little diner puts a tasty spin on breakfast. The menu includes "French Toast: Brule, Soufflé, Flambé." Translation, the toast is soaked in cinnamon crème brûlée, baked in the oven (soufflé), and then finished with a caramelized pecan praline topping (flambé). Yum. There's also a fried green tomato Benedict on grits. Lunch gets interesting, too: Try the chèvre and baguette (warmed goat cheese with tapenade and oven-dried tomatoes) or the Frankie Burger, served with avocado, an over-medium egg, and an onion ring.

✪ **Giovanni's** (805-772-2123; giovann isfishmarket.com), 1001 Front St., Morro Bay 93442. Open daily 9 AM–6

ORDERING AT GIOVANNI'S FISH MARKET AND RESTAURANT

PM. Inexpensive. Credit cards are accepted. This humble fish market /restaurant on the Embarcadero has been a favorite local haunt for 25 years. Giovanni's is the place to enjoy fresh fish and a Bloody Mary on the outdoor patio overlooking the Morro

GIOVANNI'S FISH MARKET AND RESTAURANT ON THE WATER IN MORRO BAY

Bay fishing fleet. The Dungeness crab quesadillas alone are worth the trip. Even better: Nothing on Giovanni's menu costs more than $10.

Indigo Moon (805-927-2911; indigo mooncafe.com), 1940 Main St., Cambria 93428. Open for lunch daily 10 AM–4 PM; dinner Wed.–Sun. 5–9 PM. Moderate–expensive. Credit cards are accepted. Located in Cambria's east village, Indigo Moon is a casual, relaxing spot to nosh. You'll enjoy cheese plates, flavorful soups, salads, and sandwiches, as well as a good selection of wine by the glass, inside the restaurant or on the pleasant outdoor patio. Save room for desserts. They're homemade and include morsels like a cherry and pear crisp served with a drizzle of cream.

Orchid/The Bay Club (805-772-5651; innatmorrobay.com), 60 State Park Rd., Morro Bay 93442. Open for breakfast 7–10 AM; Bay Club noon–9 PM; dinner at Orchid served Wed.–Sun., starting at 5 PM. Moderate–expensive. Credit cards are accepted. Location. Location. Location. That's the best reason to stop for a meal at the tranquil Inn at Morro Bay, where the dining room has a wall of glass windows overlooking the bay and Morro Rock. Executive chef Anthony Reeves's menu in the main dining room, Orchid, features sustainable seafood, Hearst Ranch grass-fed beef, and produce from local growers; there's a three-course nightly tasting menu with wine pairings. At breakfast and lunch the adjacent Bay Club offers simpler fare, such as sandwiches, tapas, and salads. And while you're dining in the middle of a nature sanctuary you'll savor the nonstop show of birds and sea lions in the bay just outside.

Wild Ginger (805-927-1001; wild gingercambria.com), 2380 Main St., Cambria 93428. Open for lunch 11 AM–2:30 PM, dinner 5–9 PM; closed Thu. Moderate–expensive. Credit cards are accepted, but not reservations. The chef-owner of Wild Ginger, Singapore transplant Deborah Mok, has brought her native country's Asian fusion cooking to Cambria, where the menu and daily specials draw on the cuisines of Vietnam, Korea, Hunan, Szechuan, India, and, most of all, Thailand. The small restaurant looks especially inviting at night with twin neon palm trees flanking the entrance. Homemade desserts—tarts, cobblers, cheesecakes, and fruit sorbets—are a specialty.

Windows on the Water (805-772-0677; windowsonthewater.net), 699 Embarcadero, Morro Bay 93442. Open Fri., Sat., Sun, 11:30 AM–2:30 PM (summer only); dinner daily 5 PM. Expensive. Credit cards are accepted. Reservations suggested. Windows on the Bay is an airy, romantic restaurant right on the water in Morro Bay. This hot spot serves sophisticated fare sure to delight foodies and wine lovers. The menu is modern California cuisine prepared in an open kitchen, and the menu mirrors the produce and fresh catches of the season. Each night there are new offerings on the seafood bar, such as prawn martinis and oysters on the half shell, and the restaurant's chefs create Brie and caramelized onion flatbread and a changing menu of pizzas in a wood-burning oven. Sun.–Thu. Windows on the Water features a three-course chef's prix fixe menu for $30 per person.

FOOD PURVEYORS Avila Valley Barn (805-595-2810, 805-595-2816; avilavalleybarn.com), 550 Avila Beach Dr., San Luis Obispo 93405. Stop by for fresh vegetables, fruits, pies, and an assortment of baked goods to go.

Joe Momma's (805-627-1500; joe mommasbeachstay.com), 310 Front St., Avila Beach 93424. A coffee shop right across from the shore in Avila Beach.

Linn's (805-927-0371; linnsofcambria .com), 2277 Main St., Cambria 93428. Linn's is a local favorite for olallieberry pie à la mode and other baked goods.

Tea Cozy (805-927-876; teacozy.com), 4286 Bridge St., Cambria 93428. This small house off Cambria's main drag serves high tea and scones.

Two Dogs' Coffee Co. (805-772-2633; 2dofscoffee.com), 1612 Main St., Morro Bay 93442. Get your java fix and check your e-mail here.

✳ Selective Shopping

Bargain hunters will like the factory outlet center in Pismo Beach. **Prime Outlets** (805-773-4661; primeoutlets.com), 333 Five Cities Dr., Pismo Beach, offers Polo Ralph, Lauren, Nike Factory, Calvin Klein, Aeropostale, and other outlet stores. You'll see the center right off Hwy. 101.

The beach towns offer more interesting handcrafted shopping options. In Cambria you want to browse in the artsy town's many galleries, among them the **Seekers Art Glass Gallery** (805-927-4352; seekersglass.com), 4090 Burton Dr., which stocks the work of glass artists; and **Moonstones American Craft Gallery** (805-927-

AT THE SHELL SHOP IN MORRO BAY

3447; moonstones.com), 4070 Burton Dr., which sells jewelry, intricate hardwood jewelry boxes, sculpture, peaceful fountains, and colorful kaleidoscopes. There are numerous antiques emporiums, including **Antiques on Main** (805-927-4292), 2338 Main St.; **Birds of a Feather** (805-927-2391), 2020 Main St.; and the **Cambria Antique Center** (805-927-2353), 2110 Main St. Cambria also has some specialty shops, such as **Exotic Nature** (805-927-8423; exotic-nature.com), 83 Main St., which is crammed with botanical lotions, potions, and aromatherapy products.

In Morro Bay you'll find some gems among the touristy offerings near the Embarcadero. **The Garden Gallery** (805-772-4044; thegarden-gallery.org), 680 Embarcadero, is an eclectic original, a beautiful shop brimming with exotic outdoor sculptures, pottery, and plants. Nearby, kids and adults alike will love browsing the quirky offerings of the **Shell Shop** (805-772-8014), 590 Embarcadero, which stocks sea treasures from around the world.

FARMER'S MARKETS The SLO beach towns host weekly open-air markets (northcountyfarmersmarkets .com); some include seafood right off the boats.

Avila Beach: Fri. 4–8 PM on the Promenade on Front St., Apr.–Sept. (805-602-8266).

Baywood/Los Osos: Mon. 2–4:30 PM, at 2nd and Santa Maria Sts. by the bay.

Cambria: Fri. 2:30–5 PM on Main St. next to Veterans Memorial Hall.

Cayucos: Fri. 9:30 AM–noon during summer outside the Vet's Hall, 10 Cayucos Dr.

Morro Bay: Sat. 3–6 PM. Fishermen and farmer's market at Main St. and Morro Bay Blvd.

Shell Beach: Sat. 9 AM–1 PM. Farmer's market with produce, flowers, jams, and other items at Dinosaur Caves Park (at Cliff St. and Shell Beach Rd.).

✴ Special Events

January: **Morro Bay Winter Bird Festival** (morrobaybirdfestival.org)—four-day celebration of birds and bird-watching. **Cambria Art and Wine Festival** (805-927-3624; cambriaart wine.org).

January–February: **Monarch Butterfly Grove tours** (monarchbutterfly .org) in Pismo Beach, site of the annual migration.

February: **Big, Bad & Ugly Surf Contest** (surfline.com) at Morro Rock.

March: **Central Coast Orchid Show and Sale** (805-929-5749; fcos.org), 800 Branch St., Arroyo Grande.

April: **Cambria's Annual Chili Cook-Off and Car Show** (cambria chamber.org/events.php).

May: **Avila Beach Blues Festival** (otterproductionsinc.com) at the Avila Beach Resort.

June: **Morro Bay Music Festival** (mbmusicfest.com)—a free waterfront event at the Embarcadero. **Pismo Beach June Car Show** (866-450-7469; thepismobeachclassic), featuring more than 800 classic cars and street rods.

July: **Rock to Pier Run** (805-772-6278; morro-bay.net). Six miles on the sand from Morro Rock to Cayucos Pier.

October: **City To The Sea Half-Marathon & 5K** (805-546-3100, ext. 2507)—from downtown San Luis Obispo to Shell Beach Rd. to Pismo Beach's Dinosaur Caves Park. **Annual Clam Festival** (pismochamber.org) in Pismo Beach—carnival, clam dig, music, and Famous Clam Chowder Cook-Off. **Morro Bay Harbor Festival** (morro-bay.net)—a wine and seafood fair with live music.

The Big Sur Coast

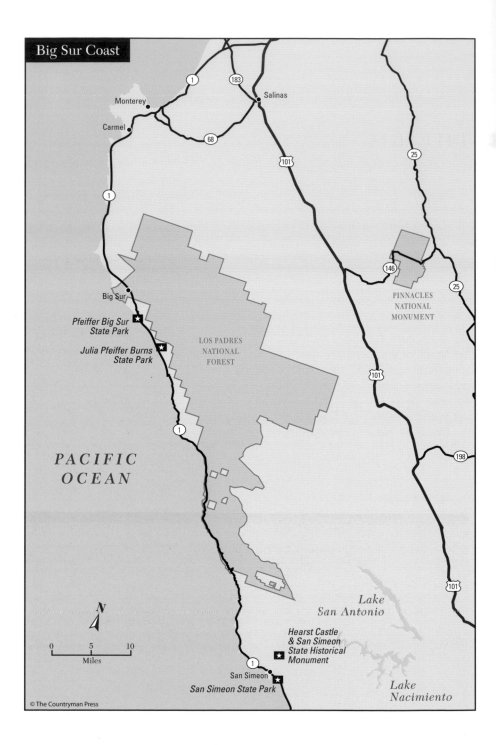

Big Sur Coast

Monterey

Carmel

1

183

Salinas

68

101

25

Big Sur

Pfeiffer Big Sur
State Park

Julia Pfeiffer Burns
State Park

1

146

25

PINNACLES
NATIONAL
MONUMENT

LOS PADRES
NATIONAL
FOREST

101

PACIFIC
OCEAN

198

101

N

0   5   10
Miles

Lake
San Antonio

Hearst Castle
& San Simeon
State Historical
Monument

San Simeon

San Simeon State Park

Lake
Nacimiento

© The Countryman Press

THE BIG SUR COAST

"It was here in Big Sur I first learned to say Amen!"

—Henry Miller, *Big Sur and the Oranges
of Hieronymus Bosch*

Big Sur is California at its most extreme, an untamed and fiercely beautiful landscape of soaring redwoods, misty coves, craggy mountains, and spectacular rock formations rising out of the Pacific Ocean. Life here can be as adventurous and fast as the pounding surf of Pfeiffer Beach, or unhurried and startlingly quiet, still enough for the early-morning chatter of Big Sur's brilliant Steller's jays to echo between the cabins and live oaks at Pfeiffer Big Sur State Park.

This is the place to come to experience natural California—to hike, swim, camp, fish, and plunge into cool, crystalline seas—while also having the option to

CRUISING THE BIG SUR COAST

SECLUDED PFEIFFER BEACH

enjoy gourmet dining and deluxe resorts hidden away in one of the state's most unique and quirky historical settings. Rough and genteel, rustic and refined, Big Sur offers a complete range.

Big Sur's name is derived from the original Spanish term for the area, *El Sur Grande*—the big south. The name became easy shorthand for the vast unexplored and unmapped wilderness south of Monterey, where a traveler could disappear by accident or by choice, and where ships periodically crashed along the rocky coastline.

Change has never come easily along this rugged 90-mile stretch between Carmel to the north and San Simeon to the south. It took 18 years of bulldozing, blasting, and backbiting before California's legendary Highway 1 opened here in 1937. The route connected Big Sur's farmers and ranchers to the outside world and paved the way for visitors to discover the region's natural wonders. More than seven decades later the two-lane Highway 1 remains Big Sur's only major byway, offering a twisting and, at times, white-knuckle ride with spectacular vistas of the Santa Lucia Mountains on one side, and the rocky shores of the Pacific splayed out along the other.

Electricity came to Big Sur in the early 1950s, though some pockets along the coast and in the backcountry are still off the grid more than half a century later. For many locals, isolation is a perk, not a hardship. Artists, artisans, writers, nature lovers, beatniks, hermits, hikers, eccentrics with a lot of money, and free spirits with no money at all have long sought refugee here. In 1957 novelist Henry Miller wrote about coming to Big Sur to escape "the air conditioned nightmare" of modern life. A few years later an aspiring 22-year-old writer named Hunter Thompson took a job as a security guard at the Big Sur Hot Springs, where he holed up in a cabin writing by day and prowled the grounds packing a pistol by night. The owner eventually fired Thompson after he wrote a magazine piece describing the people of Big Sur as "expatriates, ranchers, out-in-out bastards and general deviates," according to *Esalen: America and the Religion of No Religion* by Jeffrey J. Kripal. Not too long afterward the property was transformed into the Esalen Institute, ground zero of the "Human Potential Movement." In 1965 Elizabeth Taylor and Richard Burton arrived to film *The Sandpiper* at another Big Sur landmark, Nepenthe restaurant, which remains a favorite destination for visitors who eagerly queue up for $14 hamburgers served with stunning views of the Big Sur coastline.

Despite an influx in recent years of big-money investors from the Bay Area and Southern California buying second-home hideaways, Big Sur remains a sparsely populated oasis dotted with rustic encampments, sprawling wilderness parks, and a smattering of lodges, retreats, and restaurants scattered along Highway 1. Billboards are taboo here. Most development is outlawed, too, due to the some of California's most stringent land-use laws and the efforts of environmental groups such as the Big Sur Land Trust, which has bought up 30,000 acres of shoreline, wildlife habitat, streams, forests, grasslands, rangelands, and riparian corridors for preservation since 1978.

Only about 1,000 people live along the Big Sur Coast year-round. The main industry is nature tourism. Nearly 3 million people visit this remote corner of Monterey County each year. They come to hike, camp, kayak, horseback ride, bird-watch, beachcomb, soak up spa treatments, or just soak up the ambience of a natural world where condors and eagles still soar overhead, and humpback, gray, and blue whales cruise the coast on their journeys north and south.

For retired California park ranger Dave Garcia, the lure of Big Sur is the abundance of species and unusual plant life, such as albino redwood trees and pinecones the size of pineapples found atop Cone Peak, one of California's highest mountains. Each year Garcia leads a volunteer vacation trek to Big Sur for the Sierra Club, and he particularly enjoys sharing the camping experience with newcomers to the Central Coast.

REDWOODS IN BIG SUR

Summertime is the high season in Big Sur. The weather is often mild to warm, and sunshine breaks through the Central Coast's foggy blanket most days. Lodging options run the gamut and include tent camping in the region's string of wilderness parks, rustic cabins, roadside motels, spiritual retreats, and two world-class resorts, where you can expect to pay upward of $500 a night.

Most visitors arrive by car because public transportation is extremely limited. Bus service from Monterey extends only as far south at Nepenthe

A BEAUTIFUL VIEW ALONG THE BIG SUR COAST

restaurant along Highway 1, and only runs on weekends during winter months. Be sure to check road and weather conditions along California's Central Coast before setting out; roads sometimes wash out during heavy winter rains. You'll want to schedule your trip to arrive in Big Sur during daylight hours to savor the exceptionally beautiful drive along Highway 1, which is designated a National Scenic Byway. There's also a practical reason to set out early: Traffic sometimes moves slowly on Highway 1, and the coastal route's winding stretches and hairpin turns can be tricky to navigate in the dark.

FIRE AND MUDSLIDES OFTEN LEAD TO ROAD AND TRAIL CLOSINGS IN BIG SUR

GUIDANCE Big Sur Chamber of Commerce (831-667-2100; bigsur california.org), P.O. Box 87, Big Sur 93920. The office is open 9 AM–1 PM Mon., Wed., and Fri.

Monterey County Convention and Visitors Bureau (888-221-1010; seemonterey.com), P.O. Box 1770, Monterey 93942.

GETTING THERE The heart of the Big Sur Valley, about 150 miles south of San Francisco and 300 miles north

of Los Angeles, is surrounded by the Ventana Wilderness Area and the Los Padres National Forest. The primary access route is Hwy. 1, which hugs the coast and runs the length of Big Sur, a sprawling unincorporated area that spans about 90 twisting and turning miles along the coast. There's no official town, but the hub of Big Sur is located near the Big Sur Post Office on Hwy. 1. You'll also find restaurants, motels, the local library, and Pfeiffer Big Sur State Park along this mile or so stretch of highway, which is sometimes called the Big Sur village. Other Big Sur destinations are scattered up and down the coast in more remote areas.

By car: Gas stations are few and far between along the Big Sur Coast, and gas prices typically are higher than elsewhere in California. Fill up the tank in Monterey or Carmel to the north or in San Luis Obispo County to the south before heading to Big Sur—and don't let the needle dip too low.

Be sure to check maps carefully and get directions before setting out. Many Big Sur lodgings, campsites, and attractions are marked by small signs that blend in with the natural setting and can be easy to miss.

From San Francisco: Take Hwy. 101 South to Hwy. 156 West. Connect to Hwy. 1 South. Continue through Monterey and Carmel to Big Sur.

From Los Angeles: Take Hwy. 101 North to San Luis Obispo. Connect to Hwy. 1 North and follow this all the way to Big Sur.

By bus: The **Monterey-Salinas Transit System** (888-688-2881; mst.org) offers daily bus service between Monterey and the Big Sur Valley from Memorial Day through Labor Day. During winter months, bus service is only available on weekends. The Rt. 22 bus stops at Point Lobos State Reserve; Andrew Molera State

JULIA PFEIFFER BURNS STATE PARK

Park; Pfeiffer Big Sur State Park and Big Sur Lodge; the River Inn; and Nepenthe restaurant, the end of the line. The bus is wheelchair accessible and has bike racks. Service is sometimes suspended during severe weather or high winds, so you'll want to call ahead for the current schedule

By air: **Monterey Peninsula Airport** (montereyairport.com) is the closest airport, about 30 miles from Big Sur. The major airlines are American/American Eagle, Allegiant, United/Sky West, and US Airways. Ground transportation options include rental cars from Alamo, Avis, Budget, Hertz, Enterprise, and National. Various companies provide taxi service from the airport, but be prepared to pay a premium. The **Central Coast Cab Co.** (831-646-8294), for example, charges about $85–100 for a Big Sur run. **Monterey-Salinas Transit** (888-688-2881; mst.org) also serves the airport.

San Francisco International Airport (sfoairport.com) is 150 miles from Big Sur, and many airlines offers commuter flights to Monterey.

By train: **Amtrak** (800-872-7245; amtrak.com) offers trains from Seattle or Los Angeles to Salinas in Monterey County. Salinas is the closest Amtrak station, located 49 miles from the heart of Big Sur.

✳ To See

POINTS OF INTEREST Henry Miller Library (831-667-2574; henrymiller .org), Hwy. 1, Big Sur 93920. Step onto the library's grassy grounds and you're instantly planted in 1969 or thereabouts at this funky little slice of retro hippiedom. Inside you'll find a bookstore stocked with novels by Henry Miller (the

THE HENRY MILLER LIBRARY IS A QUIRKY STOP ALONG HWY. 1

THE HENRY MILLER LIBRARY

library's namesake, who once lived up the road), as well as books by Gary Snyder, Jack Kerouac, John Steinbeck, and other California writers who passed through Big Sur. There's a wide-open lawn for lounging, an outdoor sculpture garden, and a skinny wood patio where visitors can grab a free cup of java or catch an impromptu jam session by musicians who stop by to play in the shadow of the library's redwood grove. Open daily, except Tue., 11 AM–6 PM. Free.

Big Sur Spirit Garden (831-667-1300; bigsurspiritgarden.com), 54570 Hwy. 1, Big Sur 93920. The Big Sur Spirit Garden overflows with sculptures, statues, peacock feathers, and handmade treasures in an open courtyard area. Located steps from the Big Sur Bakery, the garden also is an educational center and performance space that hosts artists, performers, and musicians from Big Sur and across the world.

Point Sur Lighthouse (831-625-4419; pointsur.org). Built in the 1880s, Point Sur is a turn-of-the-20th-century light station that's open to the public and is listed on the National Register of Historic Places. From 1889 until 1974 keepers worked atop Point Sur to guide sailors along the rocky coast. The unique stone lighthouse still guides ships with its light, though it is now totally automated. The lighthouse is a state park, and volunteers lead three-hour walking tours and moonlight treks through the property. Admission is $10; moonlight tours are $15.

A HIKING PATH IN BIG SUR

✳ To Do

WILDERNESS AREAS The region's sprawling parks and rugged beaches are scattered along the Big Sur coast and offer activities such as hiking, bird-watching, whale-watching, swimming, fishing, and horseback riding in pristine settings. Some wild spaces still may be closed due to damage from fire and mudslides; for current information on parks and hiking trails, contact the Big Sur Rangers Station (831-667-2315). The station has a recorded information line that is updated regularly; staffers also can answer questions.

LITERARY CENTRAL COAST

"Cannery row in Monterey in California is a poem, a stink a grating noise, a quality of light, a tone, a habit, a nostalgia, a dream."

—John Steinbeck, *Cannery Row*

The Central Coast is John Steinbeck country. He was a Nobelist, a journalist, a larger-than-life figure whose books were both banned and celebrated—California's greatest writer. And there are few better places to learn about the man, his work, and those he wrote about than the **National Steinbeck Center** in his hometown of Salinas.

Interactive displays explore and explain Steinbeck's life and work, themed theaters showcase classic films based on his books—*East of Eden* (set in Salinas), *Cannery Row, Of Mice and Men*, and others—while the Valley of the World exhibit tells the "field to feast" story of the Salinas Valley's farms and farmworkers. The center is about 50 miles northeast of Big Sur in Monterey County and also houses the Steinbeck archives.

Also in Salinas just two blocks from the center is the restored **Steinbeck House** (steinbeckhouse.com) at 132 Central Ave. The old Victorian is now a memorabilia-filled restaurant serving lunch and afternoon tea. There also are Sunday tours of the house offered Memorial Day–Labor Day, 1–3 PM.

Coastal Monterey is home to the Steinbeck title location of *Cannery Row*. Cannery Row is no longer a smelly, clanging, bustling street of fish-processing plants, but a colorful tourist attraction of cool shops, restaurants, galleries, preserved buildings from the Steinbeck era, and the exquisite **Monterey Bay Aquarium** (831-648-4800; montereybayaquarium .org), 886 Cannery Row, Monterey.

INFO

The National Steinbeck Center (831-796-3833, steinbeck.org) is at 1 Main St. in Salinas, off Hwy. 101. Hours: 10 am–5 pm daily. $10.95 adults, $7.95 ages 13–17, $5.95 ages 6–12; those 5 and under get in free.

Andrew Molera State Park (831-667-2315; parks.ca.gov). This 4,800-acre nature wonderland and campground is the largest state park along the Big Sur coast. Andrew Molera sits on the northern end of Big Sur, about 20 miles south of Carmel. Nature lovers can hike along more than 20 miles of trails that climb through golden meadows and oak woodland, meander across the Big Sur River, and overlook 3 miles of beach. Another option: Explore this beautiful terrain on horseback (831-625-5486; rides cost $40–70). Monarch butterflies return to Big Sur in October, and Andrew Molera is one of the best places to see them. In 2009

the Ventana Wildlife Society opened a new Discovery Center (ventanaws.org /discovery_center; 9 AM–4 PM, Fri.–Sun.; free), where naturalists explain the group's work with the endangered California condor and offer tours of their songbird-banding lab.

⊗ **Julia Pfeiffer Burns State Park** (831-667-2315; parks.ca.gov). As you cruise Hwy. 1, be sure to make a detour at Julia Pfeiffer Burns State Park to take in the McWay Falls Overlook Trail. This is a magical spot, where 80-foot waterfalls cascade onto a turquoise cove and sandy shores below. Just 0.64 mile long, the trail is more of a walk than a hike along a scenic coastal path. Come here to stroll, picnic, and snap photographs against a beautiful natural backdrop. In December and January watch the gray whales that migrate south for winter. In March and April the whales reappear just offshore as they return to their North Pacific feeding grounds. Located 37 miles south of Carmel, the park

ABOVE: THE WATERFALL AT JULIA PFEIFFER BURNS STATE PARK. BELOW LEFT: THE COASTAL VIEW FROM THE PARK. BELOW RIGHT: ALONG THE MCWAY FALLS OVERLOOK TRAIL.

TRAILS INSIDE PFEIFFER BIG SUR STATE PARK

also offers hikers the more rigorous Ewoldsen Trail, a 4.6-mile trek with an old-growth redwood forest, sweeping canyon and ocean views, and a climb to an elevation of 1,600 feet. (Be sure that you don't confuse this park with the similarly named Pfeiffer Big Sur State Park, which is 12 miles to the north.)

⁰ᴵ⁰ **Pfeiffer Big Sur State Park** (831-667-2315; parks.ca.gov). This popular park is a 1,006-acre wilderness expanse of redwoods, conifers, oaks, sycamores, and open meadows in the heart of Big Sur, about 26 miles from Carmel on Hwy. 1. Hiking options include the Pfeiffer Falls and Valley View Trails, a 2.4-mile uphill trek that is a challenging and fun outing for active families. At the top of the Valley View Trail you'll be rewarded with a well-placed bench, where you can sit back and savor sweeping views of the entire Big Sur Valley. The park welcomes day visitors and overnight guests (campsites and comfortable cottages are available). There's a small shop, a nature center, a restaurant where you can pick up sandwiches, and WiFi at the lodge.

✳ Lodging

During summer months, Big Sur accommodations in all price ranges fill up quickly, so you'll want to make reservations as far in advance as possible. Some property owners keep a waiting list in case of cancellations, but others won't be bothered. As one motel manager told me, "You can leave your name, but I won't call."

✐ ♿ ⁰ᴵ⁰ **Big Sur Lodge** (831-667-3100, 800-424-4787; bigsurlodge.com; info@bigsurlodge.com), 47225 Hwy. 1 (inside Pfeiffer Big Sur State Park), Big Sur 93920-9542. Expensive. Credit cards are accepted. Nestled amid giant redwoods and live oaks inside a state park, the Big Sur Lodge's 60 cottages are boxy brown and apartment-like on the outside, but nicely appointed and surprisingly cozy inside. The units have Mission-style furnishings, skylights, modern bathrooms, kitchenettes, and inviting wooden decks out back that are perfect for curling up with a good book. Guests staying in larger cottages also are treated to wood-burning fireplaces. Nature lovers will relish having hiking trails just steps away in the lush 1,000-acre park. The lodge is centrally located in Big Sur, just a short drive to some of the area's best restaurants—and that's good news because the lodge's dining room serves mediocre buffet-style fare at dinnertime. A good choice for families with children, the Big Sur Lodge offers a relaxing natural setting that adult couples enjoy, too. A heated pool is open Mar.–Oct.; WiFi is available near the park store.

Deetjens Big Sur Inn (831-667-2377; deetjens.com), 48865 Hwy. 1 (30 miles south of Carmel), Big Sur 93920. Moderate–expensive. Credit cards are accepted. Long before the advent of Trip Advisor and Yelp online, guests visiting this rustic Big Sur landmark—listed on the National Register of Historic Places—shared on-the-spot reviews in well-used diaries in each of Deetjen's 20 rooms and cabins. "I am grateful for this little room," writes a visitor named Christine. "Just room enough for your soul." Another man shares his history of escaping to the woods here: "The first time I came here in '59 I knew I was coming back. In the '60s I chopped wood for a room and a meal. My third trip in the '90s, good old Deetjens . . . Thin walls, big fires, friendly people. If heaven isn't like this, I want to be sent back." Helmuth and Helen Deetjen, aka Grandpa and Grandma, founded this funky lodge on the river in the 1930s and filled each room with antiques and furnishings crafted by Grandpa himself. When the Norwegian immigrant died in 1972, he turned over his beloved inn to the Deetjens Big Sur Inn Preservation Foundation so that travelers could continue to enjoy the peace and beauty

he had discovered amid the redwood forest. Deetjens' cabins remain an authentic slice of old Big Sur. There still are no TVs or phones for distractions. The management is dedicated to preserving a quiet environment and offers this less-than-encouraging note to families considering a visit there: "To insure a peaceful stay for all our guests, we can accommodate children under 12 only if you reserve both rooms of a two-room building." One room is handicapped accessible; there's an on-site restaurant open seven days a week, serving breakfast and dinner.

 ♧ ☺ **Glen Oaks Big Sur** (831-667-2105; glenoaksbigsur.com; frontdesk @glenoaksbigsur.com), Hwy. 1, Big Sur 93920. Expensive. Credit cards are accepted. This friendly and stylish adobe motor lodge offers simple, modern rooms in the Big Sur village along Hwy. 1. The renovated guest rooms are compact but airy and lovely, with king- and queen-sized beds and a

CABINS AT BIG SUR LODGE INSIDE PFEIFFER BIG SUR STATE PARK

PFEIFFER BEACH: A BURIED TREASURE

The Big Sur coast has an abundance of stunning beaches and incredible views, many of them within sight of Highway 1, with this unforgettable exception: the windswept arc of sand, ocean, and time-carved stone known as Pfeiffer Beach.

The beach is off the beaten track, the turnoff unsigned and easily missed if you don't know where to find the 2.5-mile twisting, single-lane road that gets you there from the coast highway. Pfeiffer Beach is well worth the effort. It's a serene, secluded inlet set beneath cliffs and dominated by inviting and climbable rocky outcroppings. At the north end a jagged cliff has been hollowed into a spectacular archway. You can enter the arch during low tide—there are tide pools on the other side—but the crashing waves eventually send climbers scrambling for higher rocks or dry land.

PFEIFFER BEACH, WHERE ROCKS FORM CAVES

The ocean here is cold, with large rocks meeting the waves close to shore and sending up blasts of foamy spray, so it's more a place for gazing, sunbathing, and activities on the sand rather than a long soak and swim. The wind blowing in off the water is frequently strong enough to pick up the sand and send it flying at beachgoers at times. But the view is unparalleled, and sunsets are gorgeous.

There are restrooms but no lifeguards or other services at Pfeiffer Beach; the parking lot fills up quickly on weekends. Bring a picnic lunch and come here to relax in an unspoiled bit of Big Sur nature.

GETTING THERE

The one-lane road that takes you west from Hwy. 1 to Pfeiffer Beach is Sycamore Canyon Rd., but it is not signed. Look for the only ungated, paved road going west of the highway between Pfeiffer Big Sur State Park and the Big Sur Post Office. It's a sharp turn, and the narrow, twisting one-lane road requires slow, careful driving; going in and down to the beach, drivers should pull over as needed and yield to traffic coming up and out. The road ends at the beach parking lot, and a well-marked walking path takes you the rest of the way.

OFF THE BEATEN PATH: PFEIFFER BEACH

ON THE ROCKS AT PFEIFFER BEACH

AT THE GLEN OAKS MOTEL IN BIG SUR ON HWY. 1

decor that incorporates stone, Peroba wood, and bamboo and is nicely complemented by organic cotton bedding and feather duvets. More spacious cabins and one cottage also are available. Glen Oaks is walking distance to restaurants and the Big Sur Library.

& **Post Ranch Inn** (831-667-2200; postranchinn.com; reservations@post ranchinn.com), Hwy. 1, P.O. Box 219, Big Sur 93920. Very expensive ($550–2,800 a night). Credit cards are accepted. Post Ranch has won just about every imaginable travel industry honor: best luxury resort, best spa, most romantic getaway, one of the world's foremost green hotels, sexiest place to stay anywhere. The list goes on and you wonder: Can any place really be that special? And then you drive past the guard shack at the entrance to this majestic slice of Central Coast heaven and catch a glimpse of the wide-open golden acres inside,

then the simple cottages and tree houses perfectly perched alongside the Pacific Ocean, all in gentle harmony with the stunning beauty of natural surroundings. You can't help but drink deeply from the Post Ranch Kool-Aid and immediately begin plotting to extend your stay here. The resort's eco-friendly practices—its use of sustainably harvested and renewable building materials, recycling programs, and organic food—have been in place since 1992. That's when Bill Post began transforming his sprawling ranch into a nature hideaway where guests would be soothed and pampered, while even the endangered California red-legged frog species and Smith's blue butterfly would be protected. "This is the face of high-end green luxury," declares the *Los Angeles Times*. And the best part is that each luxurious detail, from the complimentary organic mini bars to the extensive list of biodynamic wines, has a green story all its own. All rooms have king-sized bed, wood-burning fireplace, satellite music system, and breakfast included. On-site restaurant; spa.

&. **Treebones Resort** (877-424-4787; treebonesresort.com; treeboneslodge @yahoo.com), 71895 Hwy. 1, Big Sur 93920. Moderate. Credit cards are accepted. Treebones is a remote tent village perched high atop a hill over-looking the Pacific Ocean on the remote southern end of the Big Sur coast. It boasts 16 yurts, a guest house, and five campsites for guests who enjoy staying in the middle of nowhere

away from civilization. The yurts are the big attraction here, and these are no run-of-the-mill tents. The Tree-bones yurts are circular fabric struc-tures with wooden frames, and they come fully loaded with amenities such as polished pine floors, queen beds with buttery soft linens, skylights, and French doors that open out to a red-wood decking. One über yurt has a Ping-Pong table inside. Nature lovers come here to rough it in style, and despite its out-of-the-way location some 45 minutes south of Big Sur " village, the place is usually booked solid during summer months. The main hardship: The yurt encampment doesn't have bathrooms; guests have to walk over to the nearby lodge. Owners John and Corinne Handy pride them-selves on the serenity of the environ-ment and ask that guests only bring children 6 and older. Visitors are advised to bring flashlights, a cooler with lunch snacks, sturdy walking shoes, binoculars, and surfboards. On site are a heated pool with Pacific views, hot tub, restaurant, and organic garden.

TREEBONES RESORT FEATURES LUXURY YURTS AND GREAT VIEWS

&. "¶" **Ventana Inn and Spa** (831-667-2331; ventanainn.com; ventana reservationve@ventanainn.com), 48123 Hwy. 1 (across the highway from Post Ranch Inn), Big Sur 93920. Very expensive. Credit cards are accepted. Secluded and elegant, Ventana is a favorite haunt of well-to-do vacationers and celebrities who relish their privacy and don't blink at spending a small ransom for spacious villas with wood-burning fireplaces, in-room aromatherapy treatments, and moonlit soaks under the stars in private hot tubs. The resort sits on 242 acres that rise 1,200 feet above the Pacific Ocean. The main order of business here: pampering, relaxing, and feasting. Ventana's popular restaurant, Cielo, was destroyed by fire in summer 2008, and a new main dining room reopened in late 2009 with a menu focused on seasonal ingredients from the Central Coast.

RETREATS

Esalen Institute (831-667-3000; esalen.org; info@esalen.org), 55000 Hwy. 1, Big Sur 93920. Moderate–expensive; work exchange scholarships are available for students who help in the kitchen or cabins. Credit cards are accepted. Founded on the cliffs above the Pacific amid the social and political tumult of the 1960s, Big Sur's pioneering educational institute was founded on grounds sacred to the Esalen Indians, from whom the center takes it name. Esalen is a mecca for visitors and students seeking personal and spiritual transformation or simply relaxation. Guests enroll here for weekend and five-day programs offered year-round. Meals are served family-style and feature fresh organic fare from Esalen's kitchen. (*The Esalen Cookbook* by former chef Charlie Cascio is a beautiful volume loaded with stories and recipes from visiting students and cooks who create 750 meals a day here.) Another Esalen highlight: The institute's mineral hot springs are available to guests around the clock. The baths are open to general public, and welcome night owls 1–3 AM daily only. The cost is $20 and reservations are required.

New Camaldoli Hermitage (831-667-2456; contemplation.com/Hermitage/home.html; monks@contemplation.com), Hwy. 1, Big Sur. Inexpensive. Since 1958 Camaldolese monks have savored a picturesque hilltop sanctuary that revolves around a daily rhythm of solitude, prayer, work, and study. Located on 899 acres at an elevation of 1,300 feet, the Hermitage overlooks the Pacific Ocean and is surrounded by California chaparral, redwood, madrone, bay laurel, and an oak forest. The monastery offers retreats and provides no-frills, single-room accommodations with half-baths and personal gardens. Guests are encouraged to be silent during their stays. Meals (mostly vegetarian) are eaten alone, but visitors are welcome to join daily services. Reservations are accepted six months in advance.

CAMPING Big Sur offers a string of exceptional state parks and other campgrounds scattered along the coast. Some wilderness areas, particularly those east of Hwy. 1, remained closed in 2010 in the wake of the wildfires and mudslides. Be sure to call ahead for current information on campsite availability and weather conditions. The **Big Sur Rangers Station** (831-667-2315) has a recorded info line, and rangers also are available to answer questions.

Andrew Molera State Park (831-667-2315; parks.ca.gov), Big Sur Station #1 (on US 1, along the northern end of Big Sur), Big Sur 93920. The 4,800-acre park and campground has 24 hike-in campsites and scenic trails that wind through 20 miles of meadows, beaches, and hilltops. Campsites, located about 0.3 mile from the main parking area, are available on a first-come, first-served basis. No reservations are accepted. Dogs are not allowed. Activities include hiking, birdwatching, horseback riding, fishing, and swimming. The campground has restrooms and picnic facilities. Discovery Center on site.

Limekiln State Park (831-667-2403; parks.ca.gov), Hwy. 1, Big Sur 93920. At the southern end of Big Sur, Limekiln spans 716 acres and has 28 campsites near the beach. As retired park ranger Dave Garcia notes, "It's one of the few parks where you can camp right next to the beach. You walk 200 yards to the redwoods, you'll find steelhead, and you can kayak right off the beach out to the ocean. There's almost nowhere you can do that." The park reopened for hiking and camping in July 2010 after being closed for nearly two years after a massive wildfire. The Falls Trail remained closed at press time, but the Limekiln Trail and

Hare Trail were open. Limekiln is located along Hwy. 1 on the southern end of Big Sur, 2 miles south of Lucia and 56 miles south of Carmel. It has showers, restrooms, and picnic areas; campsites are available on a first-come, first-served basis. Peak season is May 15–Sept. 15.

Plaskett Creek Campground (805-434-1996; recreation.gov), P.O. Box 1018 (off Hwy. 1, near Gorda), Templeton 93465. Located on the east side of Hwy. 1, on the southernmost end of Big Sur, this campground sprawls across a grassy meadow under a canopy of pine and cypress trees. Plaskett Creek offers 44 sites with parking pads, picnic tables, fire rings, and barbecues. Restrooms were renovated in late 2009. The campground is run by the US Forest Service, and campsites are available on a first-come, first-served basis. Sites can be used for tent or RV camping. The campground is short walk to Sand Dollar Beach, a large sandy beach. Hiking trails snake along the bluffs overlooking the beach and coves below.

ⓣ Pfeiffer Big Sur State Park (831-667-2315, reservations 800-444-7275 May–Oct.; parks.ca.gov, reserve

CABINS AT PFEIFFER BIG SUR STATE PARK THROUGH THE TREES

america.com), Big Sur Station #1 (26 miles south of Carmel on Hwy. 1), Big Sur 93920. Reservations suggested. Conveniently located near the heart of Big Sur village, Pfeiffer Big Sur State Park has more than 200 campsites. This popular park offers a majestic natural setting teeming with black-tailed deer, gray squirrels, raccoons, and unusual birds like water ouzels and belted kingfishers. Campers will enjoy the scenic hiking trails and the joy of tromping amid redwoods the size of skyscrapers. The park's amenities include a small store, WiFi service, and a café at the lodge inside the park. There are flush toilets, showers, and picnic areas. Reservations are accepted during the high season May–Oct.; campsites are available on a first-come, first-served basis during the rest of the year.

Ventana Campground (831-667-2712; ventanawildernesscamp ground.com), Hwy. 1 (30 miles south of Carmel, just off Hwy. 1), Big Sur 93920. This lovely campground is set in a 40-acre redwood-lined canyon, where 92 campsites are scattered amid the contours of Post Canyon and a small stream that runs through the grounds. Ventana Campground offers rustic camping with a sprinkling of conveniences, such as three bathhouses with hot showers. The campsites are private; each comes with a picnic table and fire ring. There are showers, flush toilets, and running water nearby; a small camp store is on site. The property is open May–Oct. and is managed by the deluxe Ventana Inn and Spa, which is just up the hill on Hwy. 1.

✳ Where to Eat

Food tends to be expensive in Big Sur due to the area's remote location and limited number of establishments. The recent recession, however, did bring sporadic dinner specials as some of the more down-to-earth eateries reduced prices and portions.

Big Sur Bakery (831-667-0520; big surbakery.com), Hwy. 1, Big Sur 93920. Open daily at 8 AM; closed Mon. for dinner. Moderate–expensive. Credit cards are accepted, and reservations are available for dinner. Don't miss this delectable Big Sur outpost, which is located in an old ranch house and steps away from Big Sur's Spirit Garden. The bread is baked fresh daily in a wood-fired oven, and there's often a line for the $5.50 lattes and delectable take-out sandwiches and other snacks. The bakery also is a sit-down restaurant, with an always tempting menu that features gourmet burgers and entrées such as rockfish scampi and grilled prime rib steak with red wine sauce. In 2009 the restaurant's owners published *The Big Sur Bakery Cookbook: A Year in the Life of a Restaurant*, which is as much a local history as a gourmet cookbook.

Big Sur River Inn and Restaurant (831-667-2700, 800-548-3610; bigsur riverinn.com), Hwy. 1 at Pheneger Creek, Big Sur 93920. Open daily. Expensive. Credit cards are accepted. Reservations recommended in summer. This woodsy inn and restaurant is a lively gathering place alongside the Big Sur River, a choice spot for dragging bent-willow deck chairs into the shallow water out back and soaking your feet in the crisp, clear currents that run through the property. The restaurant is a brightly decorated and inviting wooden cabin, where the food is nicely prepared and the River Inn's special Bloody Marys go down smoothly. The eclectic-organic menu features local produce, free-range chicken, and sustainably harvested seafood. Many dinner entrées cost $20 or more, though in 2010 the restaurant offered dinner spe-

VOLUNTEER VACATIONS

Each year the Sierra Club (sierraclub.org) hosts a weeklong service camping trip to Big Sur where participants work with a ranger on projects to restore public lands and wilderness areas. The 2009 "Secrets of the Big Sur" trip, for example, cost $445 and included lodging at the Piedras Blancas Light Station, which is off-limits to the general public. Volunteers work hard, but also enjoy guided hikes in the Cone Peak area and the opportunity to view sea otters, condors, peregrine falcons, and other wildlife. "We usually have time in the afternoon to do some exploring or some hiking or swimming," says tour leader Dave Garcia.

cials and a lighter stimulus menu. There's often live music. Located 25 miles south of Carmel, the inn also has a general store and gas station. Full bar, spacious outdoor deck for dining.

Nepenthe (831-667-2345; nepenthe bigsur.com), 48510 Hwy. 1, Big Sur 93920. Open 365 days a year. Expensive. Credit cards are accepted. Reservations recommended. Rita Hayworth and Orson Welles came to Big Sur in the 1940s, fell in love with a sweet log cabin on a hill overlooking the south coast, and bought the place on the spot—with a $167 down payment. They never returned. In 1947 the Hollywood stars sold the property to a local couple, Lolly and Bill Fassett, and Nepenthe was born. Big Sur's famed restaurant offers indoor and outdoor dining in a spectacular clifftop setting 800 feet above the Pacific. Sandwiches, burgers, and salads are featured at lunch; the dinner menu includes beef, fish, and chicken entrées. The house Ambrosia Burgers are tasty, and you'll find an impressive selection of California wines. Coming to Nepenthe, of course, isn't about the meal. The menu is rather basic. People come here year after year to linger and sip and soak up a quintessential Big Sur experience.

Ripplewood Restaurant (831-667-2242; ripplewoodresort.com), Hwy. 1, Big Sur 93920. Open daily 8 AM–2 PM. Moderate. Credit cards are accepted. This homey little breakfast spot along Hwy. 1 is close to what passes for downtown Big Sur. The menu includes omelets and cinnamon French toast with homemade applesauce for breakfast; sandwiches and tacos for lunch. You'll find simple fare and friendly service at the restaurant, which is next to the rustic Ripplewood resort. Outdoor garden dining.

Sierra Mar (831-667-2800; postranch inn.com/dining.shtml), Hwy. 1, P.O. Box 219, Big Sur 93920. Expensive–very expensive. Credit cards are accepted. Reservations required. Lunch for two at the Post Ranch Inn's acclaimed ocean-view dining room can easily set you back $120. But that's a fraction of what you'd spend if you stayed the night at Big Sur's deluxe eco-lodge, and the restaurant is a choice spot for a special-occasion meal. Idyllic and innovative, Sierra Mar is routinely mentioned as one of California's finest restaurants. The four-course prix fixe menu changes daily; much of the menu is locally grown.

MONTEREY COUNTY: DON'T-MISS EXPERIENCES

Two hours south of San Francisco, Monterey County is blessed with 99 miles of prime Pacific coastline, highlighted by Big Sur, Carmel, and the city of Monterey. One of California's biggest agricultural regions, Monterey County has been dubbed the "Salad Bowl of the World" due to the wide variety of fruits and vegetables grown here.

As you cruise north on Highway 1, leaving Big Sur and heading back toward civilization, you'll reach the picturesque coastal communities of Carmel, Monterey, and Pebble Beach after about 30 miles. Inland is the farm community of Salinas.

Here are four experiences you won't want to miss while visiting the Monterey region:

1. Cannery Row. This stretch of Depression-era factories and warehouses once served as the hub of the Central Coast's sardine canning industry (nearly 250,000 tons of sardines were processed here in 1945, the year John Steinbeck published his famous novel *Cannery Row*). In recent decades, the old buildings have been transformed into a likeable jumble of shops, restaurants, and waterfront attractions perched along Monterey Bay. Sidewalk hustlers peddle trinkets and tours, and restaurants dole out tasty cups of clam chowder to entice hungry diners to step inside. There's a lot of history here, and it's practically hallowed ground for Steinbeck fans, but there are definitely tourist-trap elements, too, with food and drink that can be on the pricey side and parking that's difficult at best. Yet the circus-style atmosphere can be surprisingly fun, and the Monterey chowder really is superb (the free samples are definitely worth stopping for). Seafood at popular places like the **Fish Hopper** (831-372-8543; www.fishhopper .com; 700 Cannery Row, Monterey) is just-off-the-boat fresh and served up with great views. You'll find plenty of curiosities and Steinbeck-era memorabilia to browse (just follow the signs); comfy hotels like the **Spindrift Inn** (800-841-1879; www.spindriftinn.com; 652 Cannery Row); and the new **Cannery Row IMAX Theatre** (831-372-462; 640 Wave St.) in the heart of the action. The **Monterey Bay Aquarium** is at the end of the row, built on the site of the old Hovden Cannery, next door to the lab of Steinbeck's old pal (and Cannery Row character) Ed "Doc" Ricketts. More info: canneryrow.com.

2. Monterey Bay Aquarium. This vast, world-class aquarium and research institute is a treasure that captivates visitors of all ages; it is perhaps the best reason of all to make a trek to Monterey. The aquarium celebrates and explores the depths of the Monterey Bay National Marine Sanctuary, which is right outside, and boasts an estimated 35,000 animals and plants representing more than 550 species of fishes, invertebrates, mammals, reptiles, birds, and plants. Highlights include the Outer Bay wing, which has a 1 million-gallon tank that approximates open ocean, with a giant kelp forest reaching three stories high. Exhibits here change regularly—2010 saw the arrival of ten young green sea turtles, several of which are now settled into a special exhibition called Hot Pink Flamingos: Stories of Hope in a Changing Sea. Adventurous kids will love Underwater Explorers, a unique program that allows visitors age 8 to 13 to suit up in scuba gear and get a fish's-eye view by submerging themselves in the bay outside the aquarium's giant picture windows. And don't miss the glass enclosure in the Ocean's Edge exhibit, where powerful waves crash around and over you with dramatic roars and foam—without getting anyone wet, of course. Info: Monterey Bay Aquarium (831-648-4800; montereybayaquarium.org), 886 Cannery Row, Monterey.

3. Grapevine Express. This innovative public transit line makes it easy to explore the region's agricultural wonders without the hassle of driving. The Grapevine Express runs between Monterey and the Carmel Valley and a day pass costs just $4.50—a steal compared to pricey wine country shuttles elsewhere in California. The bus stops near **Earthbound Farm** (831-625-6219; ebfarm.com; 7250 Carmel Valley Rd., Carmel) one of the nation's first and biggest organic farms. It offers cooking events, an organic café, farm stand, kids' garden, and a Cut-Your-Own Herb Garden. Other stops are close to such choice wineries as the **Bernardus Winery and Lodge** (831-659-1900; bernardus .com; 5 West Carmel Valley Rd.), a rolling 220-acre expanse of vineyards and live oaks in Carmel Valley Village, and **Chateau Julien** (831-624 2600; chateau-julien.com; 940 Carmel Valley Rd., Carmel), a French Country–style chateau that offers daily tours. Monterey-Salinas Transit (888-678-2871; mst.org/routes/list .htm) operates the Grapevine Express (Route No. 24) with stops at the Monterey Conference Center, Monterey Transit Plaza, the Barnyard Shopping Village, and Carmel Valley Village (carmelvalleycalifornia.com).

4. The 17-Mile Drive. This winding route is a dreamscape of big sky, crashing waves, and scenic pull-over spots along tony Pebble Beach, just off Highway 1. Pebble Beach sits on the tip of the Monterey Peninsula, between Pacific Grove and Carmel. The 17-Mile Drive is the only private toll road west of the Mississippi. You'll spy natural landmarks such as **Bird Rock**, **Cypress Rock**, and **The Restless Sea**, a rugged stretch of the Monterey Coast where many early sailors were shipwrecked. Other highlights include the picture-perfect fairways of the Links at Spanish Bay, Spyglass Hill, and the famed Pebble Beach Golf Links. (An

continued on next page

continued from previous page

interesting aside for golfers: In 1919, greens fees at Pebble Beach were $2 for gentlemen and $1.50 for ladies. Nowadays rates are $495 per person, plus cart fee, for an 18-hole round.) As you cruise Pebble Beach, stop for a picnic lunch among the shorebirds at Seal Rock (pick up provisions at the **Pebble Beach Market** next to **The Lodge at Pebble Beach**). Or, for a treat, plan on lunch or an overnight stay at **The Inn at Spanish Bay** (800-654-9300; pebblebeach.com), an oceanfront retreat popular with golfers and honeymooners. Five gates allow entry to the 17-Mile Drive; the price is $9 per car. Visit the Pebble Beach website (pebblebeach.com) for an interactive map.

A Few More Reasons to Visit: The **Monterey Jazz Festival**, held in September, attracts top performers and is the longest-running jazz festival in the world. The **AT&T Pebble Beach Pro-Am Golf Tournament** is held in February. The **California International Air Show** lands in Salinas each fall, featuring stunt pilots, wing walkers, and military precision flying teams. The **California Rodeo** in Salinas, held in July, is a major stop on the Pro Rodeo Cowboy Circuit. More information: seemonterey.com.

✳ Selective Shopping

The Phoenix (831-667-2347; phoenixshopbigsur.com/gafill.htm), 48510 Hwy. 1, Big Sur. Located downstairs from Nepenthe restaurant, this unique shop brims with treasures: handcrafted textiles, prints by local artists, jewelry, one-of-a kind patchwork quilts, hand-knit garments, and wall hangings. Great browsing!

Post Ranch Inn Mercantile (831-667-2795; postranchinn.com /mercantile.shtml). Hidden away on the grounds of the Post Ranch Inn, the hotel's compact boutique offers a good selection of books about Big Sur, including signed copies of *Down to a Soundless Sea*, Thomas Steinbeck's transporting collection of Big Sur–inspired short stories. Other offerings include the resort's fragrant signature lotions, potions, and sea kelp hair products, which make good souvenirs and gifts.

✳ Special Events

March: **Big Sur Mud Run** (bigsur mudrun.org). This popular competition is run in nearby Monterey and includes a course of hills, water, obstacles, drill sergeants, and, yes, plenty of mud.

April: **Big Sur International Marathon** (bsim.org). Attracting world-class athletes and local runners alike, the 26.2-mile marathon is stunning course from Big Sur's Pfeiffer State Park to downtown Carmel. Highway 1 is closed to traffic during the race, held the last Sunday in April and limited to 4,500 runners.

October: **Big Sur River Run** (bigsur riverrun.org). A tradition for three decades, the run starts at Pfeiffer Big Sur State Park.

November: **Big Sur Food and Wine Festival** (bigsurfoodandwine.org) is hosted by local restaurants and inns to benefit community nonprofit groups.

INDEX

187